SCIENCE AND TECHNOLOGY IN

COLONIAL AMERICA

The Greenwood Press "Daily Life Through History" Series

The Age of Charlemagne
John J. Butt

The Age of Sail
Dorothy Denneen Volo and James M. Volo

The American Revolution
Dorothy Denneen Volo and James M. Volo

The Ancient Egyptians
Bob Brier and Hoyt Hobbs

The Ancient Greeks
Robert Garland

Ancient Mesopotamia
Karen Rhea Nemet-Nejat

The Ancient Romans
David Matz

The Aztecs: People of the Sun and Earth
Davíd Carrasco with Scott Sessions

Chaucer's England
Jeffrey L. Singman and Will McLean

Civil War America
Dorothy Denneen Volo and James M. Volo

Colonial New England
Claudia Durst Johnson

Early Modern Japan
Louis G. Perez

The Early American Republic, 1790–1820:
Creating a New Nation
David S. Heidler and Jeanne T. Heidler

18th-Century England
Kirstin Olsen

Elizabethan England
Jeffrey L. Singman

The Holocaust
*Eve Nussbaum Soumerai and
Carol D. Schulz*

The Inca Empire
Michael A. Malpass

The Industrial United States, 1870–1900
Julie Husband and Jim O' Loughlin

Jews in the Middle Ages
Norman Roth

Maya Civilization
Robert J. Sharer

Medieval Europe
Jeffrey L. Singman

The Medieval Islamic World
James E. Lindsay

The Nineteenth Century American
Frontier
Mary Ellen Jones

The Nubians
Robert S. Bianchi

The Old Colonial Frontier
James M. Volo and Dorothy Denneen Volo

Renaissance Italy
Elizabeth S. Cohen and Thomas V. Cohen

The Roman City: Rome, Pompeii, and Ostia
Gregory S. Aldrete

Science and Technology in
Nineteenth-Century America
Todd Timmons

The Soviet Union
Katherine B. Eaton

The Spanish Inquisition
James M. Anderson

Traditional China: The Tang Dynasty
Charles Benn

The United States, 1920–1939: Decades of
Promise and Pain
David E. Kyvig

The United States, 1940–1959: Shifting
Worlds
Eugenia Kaledin

The United States, 1960–1990: Decades of
Discord
Myron A. Marty

Victorian England
Sally Mitchell

The Vikings
Kirsten Wolf

World War I
Neil M. Heyman

SCIENCE AND TECHNOLOGY IN

COLONIAL AMERICA

WILLIAM E. BURNS

The Greenwood Press "Daily Life Through History" Series

GREENWOOD PRESS
Westport, Connecticut • London

Library of Congress Cataloging-in-Publication Data

Burns, William E.
    Science and technology in colonial America / William E. Burns.
        p. cm. — (The Greenwood Press "Daily life through history" series, ISSN 1080–4749)
    Includes bibliographical references and index.
    ISBN 0–313–33160–X (alk. paper)
    1. Technology—United States—History—18th century. 2. Technology—United States—
History—17th century. 3. Science—United States—History—18th century. 4. Science—
United States—History—17th century. 5. United States—History—Colonial period,
ca. 1600–1775. I. Title. II. Series.
    T21.B85   2005
    509.73'09'033—dc22   2005020458

British Library Cataloging in Publication Data is available.

Library of Congress Catalog Card Number: 2005020458
ISBN: 0–313–33160–X
ISSN: 1080–4749

First published in 2005

Greenwood Press, 88 Post Road West, Westport, CT 06881
An imprint of Greenwood Publishing Group, Inc.
www.greenwood.com

Printed in the United States of America

The paper used in this book complies with the
Permanent Paper Standard issued by the National
Information Standards Organization (Z39.48–1984).

10 9 8 7 6 5 4 3 2 1

Every reasonable effort has been made to trace the owners of copyright materials in this book,
but in some instances this has proven impossible. The author and publisher will be glad to
receive information leading to more complete acknowledgments in subsequent printings of
the book and in the meantime extend their apologies for any omissions.

Dedicated to Paula Findlen, Margaret Jacob, and the memory of
Betty Jo Teeter Dobbs, mothers in learning

Contents

Acknowledgments   ix

Introduction   xi

Chronology   xix

1. Making a Living: Agriculture   1

2. Wood, Fruit Crops, and Other Tree Products   17

3. Making a Living: Manufacturing and Industry   27

4. The World of the Sea   41

5. Technology in Domestic Life   51

6. Architecture and Housing   65

7. Transportation   79

8. Reading and Seeing: The Technology of
    Words and Images   89

9. Science and Technology on the Land:
    Surveying and Cartography   97

10. Technology and War   107

11. Natural Knowledge in American Colonial Societies   121

12. The Scientific Revolution in Colonial America 133

13. The Age of Benjamin Franklin 145

Bibliography 165

Index 175

Acknowledgments

I thank the Folger Library, the Library of Congress, Founders Library of Howard University, and the Soper Library of Morgan State University for providing research materials. I also thank American Memory at the Library of Congress, the Schomburg Center for Electronic Texts and Images, and the Flowerdew Hundred Foundation for their generous permission to use their images for the illustrations. Finally, I thank my editors, particularly Kevin Downing at Greenwood, for their help.

Introduction

For more than 300 years, North America was shared and contested between Native Americans, settlers from different parts of Europe, and Africans brought as enslaved laborers. From the first invasions of America by the Spanish under Christopher Columbus, Hernan Cortez and the *conquistadors*, Europeans sought to control land and resources in the Americas. Among the tools for this task were the scientific and technical knowledge they brought with them. However, European science and technology had to change to suit the circumstances of the new land. Colonial explorers and settlers faced a new and unique situation, with unfamiliar challenges and advantages. The material conditions of North America were very different from those they had known at home. Some materials, most notably wood and land, were abundant in parts of America but scarce in Europe, while labor, abundant but poorly paid in Europe, was scarce and relatively expensive in America.

The colonial period was not technologically or scientifically stagnant, although colonial America, like all societies before the Industrial Revolution of the late eighteenth and nineteenth centuries, was not nearly as technologically dynamic as America—and the world—later became. People were born, grew old, and died in what seems to us to be an unchanging technological world. Science, although changing rapidly in the early modern period, had less effect on America than on Europe and was less relevant to people's everyday lives than it is now. The revolution that created modern science occurred during the same centuries that Europeans first conquered and settled America, but few traces of

America's future scientific leadership can be found in the colonial era. No seventeenth-century American approached the heights occupied by the Italian Galileo Galilei, the Frenchman René Descartes, or the Englishman Sir Isaac Newton. Not until Benjamin Franklin in the mid-eighteenth century was an American recognized as part of the scientific elite, and Franklin ascended not only because of the excellence of his science, but also because of the novelty value of a scientist from Philadelphia, at the edge of the civilized world.

But as slow as American progress may seem to us, to colonial Americans it was fast. In the colonial centuries American settlers went from small agricultural settlements where nearly everyone worked as part of a farm household to large cities with a varied economy and a variety of technological and scientific specialists. Over the same period, science developed from a body of knowledge based on the writings of the ancient Greeks to a highly experimental and mathematical discipline marked by the achievements of Newton.

SCIENCE AND TECHNOLOGY IN COLONIAL CULTURE

The terms *science* and *technology* did not have the same meanings in the American colonies that they have today. *Science* generally referred to all the different branches of knowledge, including theology and what we would now call the humanities, and *technologia* was a technical term, much used by the Puritan ministers of New England, for a description of how all of the different branches of human knowledge related to God's divine plan. The most common term for theoretical science in the early modern period was *natural philosophy*. The term *scientist* was not even coined until the nineteenth century, and a scientist like Franklin was called a "natural philosopher" or simply a "philosopher." Technology in the modern sense was called "the arts" or "the useful arts" and technological progress the "improvement of the arts."

Early modern natural philosophy did not have the cultural prestige that science now possesses. Most intellectuals in the colonies as well as in Europe, particularly before the eighteenth century, viewed theoretical knowledge of the natural world as less important to the fate of the soul than religious knowledge, less important in achieving social status than knowledge of the Greek and Latin classics, and less important in day-to-day life than knowledge of the law. Much of the scientific research that was done in the colonies was not done by professional scientists, of whom there were very few anywhere, but by physicians, ministers, and landowners who viewed science as a hobby rather than a livelihood.

Despite their amateur status, the scientists of colonial America found plenty to work on. From the earliest times of settlement, colonists examined, collected, and tried to classify the strange and unfamiliar plants and animals of their new world. Colonists studied natural philosophy at the many educational institutions founded in America, where it occupied a more prominent place in the curriculum as the decades went by. As people and ideas continued to cross the Atlantic, a subculture of popular science—scientific demonstrations, lectures, experiments, and books—formed in America as it had in Europe.

MULTICULTURAL ORIGINS OF COLONIAL TECHNOLOGY

Most colonial Americans, of course, were less concerned about the workings of the heavens than about the day-to-day problems of making a living and supporting a family. Theoretical science played a far smaller role in their lives than technology. The settlers of colonial America came from many parts of Europe and Africa, and American colonial technology mixed techniques and ideas from many cultures. Early modern European practices from many countries met and merged with African and indigenous American elements. Native American technology was particularly important. Despite the spectacular advantages European technology gave in some areas, early European settlers depended for day-to-day survival on technical procedures already developed by Native Americans. Many aspects of growing and preparing New World crops such as corn and tobacco were obviously dependent on Native American knowledge, although colonists often operated on a far more vast scale than did the indigenous inhabitants. Nor was it only the major crops for which settlers depended on Native techniques. Native Americans pioneered the tapping of maple trees and the other processes necessary to produce maple sugar, a practice unknown to Europeans. Colonists also coped with America's dense forests by borrowing a Native American tree-felling technique. Rather than chopping down trees, many colonists imitated Native Americans by "girdling," cutting or burning a circle through the bark around the tree and then leaving it to die and eventually fall.

Native American technology was also changed by contact with Europeans. Native Americans learned how to use colonial instruments ranging from guns to copper pots to iron fishhooks. In addition to appropriating European products through trade or warfare, Native Americans also valued European technical skills. After the Natchez massacre of the French who lived among them in the Louisiana territory in 1729, the only Frenchmen the Natives spared were a tailor and a carpenter "who were able to serve their wants" (Petit, "Letter from Father le Petit," 167).

Enslaved Africans also brought technical skills with them. The early cultivation of rice in South Carolina, where it became the staple commodity, relied on the knowledge and skills West Africans brought to grow, process, and irrigate the crop. In those areas where Africans and African-descended peoples, enslaved or free, had control over their physical environment, they replicated many aspects of West African life and technology in their new surroundings.

Immigrants and migrant workers from many parts of Europe, both countries that carried on colonization programs and those that did not, were attracted by the high pay and cheap land available in America. Often thrust into far closer proximity in America than they would ever find themselves back home, different groups of European colonists learned from each other. For example, when English colonists in the Chesapeake began to grow tobacco, they adopted techniques for growing and preparing the leaf commercially from the Spanish, the first European settlers to grow the plant. The log cabins built by the Scandinavian immigrants of New Sweden on the Delaware in the early seventeenth century spread among British- and German-descended colonists long after New Sweden itself had disappeared. Continental immigrants greatly enriched the technology of the English colonies. Pennsylvania Germans, coming from a culture where craftsmanship was very highly developed, led in developing some of the most famous colonial American inventions, including the Conestoga wagon and the long rifle.

MATERIAL CONDITIONS OF AMERICAN TECHNOLOGY

Although much colonial American technology and science was transplanted from Europe, it was transplanted into a very different ecology and economy. In heavily populated Europe, land was expensive and labor was cheap. In America, labor was more expensive, whether free or enslaved, but land was amazingly cheap. Water and wood were cheap in some places and expensive in others. The high cost of labor drove American settlers more than their European contemporaries to labor-saving technologies, such as mills that harnessed wind and water power to do work that would otherwise be done by muscle. Technologies for exploiting land to its maximum potential, on the other hand, were much less popular, as in many cases it was easier and cheaper just to move on when land was exhausted.

By the time colonization began at the end of the fifteenth century, Europeans had been cutting down their own forests for many centuries, and the great woods that at one time had covered much of the continent were long gone. To many early European explorers and settlers, eastern North America seemed to be a vast forest, whose trees both promised enormous wealth and presented a formidable obstacle to establishing fields for crops. Surprisingly, the history of Europeans and the American forest was even older than the first colonists knew. The earliest economic exploitation of America by people of European origin, although they did not settle, were the timber voyages made by Greenlanders to "Markland" (Nova Scotia) in the Middle Ages. In either case, they presented American settlers with challenges and rewards far different from those they had known in Europe. The Hispanic colonists of the Southwest, in contrast, had to make do without wood almost entirely.

America also had its own crops, different from the wheat, barley, and oats of the Old World. The most important by far for North American colonists was corn. Millennia of Native American cultivation and encouragement of the most useful strains had created a staple grain from wild grass. Already widely distributed among Native American peoples from South America far to the north, corn was also a staple crop in colonial communities everywhere from the Spanish colonies of the Southwest to New England, and eventually made its way to Europe and Africa. While corn kept colonists alive, other American crops made them rich. The Chesapeake colonies, Virginia and Maryland, had a tobacco-based economy throughout the colonial period. Tobacco turned many settlers into rich landowning, and slaveowning, gentlemen and ladies. Other, less glamorous, but useful New World crops included pumpkins and squashes.

TECHNOLOGY AND COLONIAL POWER

The Europeans who came to the Americas were not entering an empty land, regardless of the claims made by some of their propaganda. North America was a populated environment, and settlers, by fair means or foul (mostly foul) had to wrest control of the lands from their indigenous inhabitants. The establishment of European colonial control over territories inhabited by Native Americans was greatly facilitated by technological differences. Some technological assets served to overawe Native Americans, such as the vast ships in which the European settlers had crossed the oceans (Native Americans sometimes called European ships "moving islands"), or the powerful and noisy cannon that the newcomers used in both war and ceremony. Even a technology as seemingly unspectacular as writing impressed Native Americans in the earliest days of colonization. Some Natives in the early phases of contact interpreted the Europeans' technological devices as items of spiritual or magical power, unsurprising in people seeing and hearing the noise and effect of a gun for the first time. A more pragmatic but unsuccessful attempt to adopt European technology into Native American thinking was that of the Virginia chief Opechacanough, who after the great massacre of the English colonists in 1622, planted some of the captured gunpowder, hoping more would come up the next year. Of course, as Native Americans grew more familiar with European technology and even learned to use it themselves, it lost much of its glamour and mystery while retaining its devastating effects.

The most direct application of European technology to colonial power was war. Many of the most important European technological advantages over Natives from the first Spanish conquests to the great imperial wars of the eighteenth century were directly related to violence, such as crossbows, guns, iron weapons, and the techniques of fighting from horseback. Advances in European military technology were quickly applied to American struggles. The eighteenth century saw both the scale and the nature of colonial warfare transformed, as rivalries between colonial powers, culminating in the vast French–British struggle of the French and Indian War (itself only a theater of the global Seven Years War), became more important than conflicts between settler communities and Native Americans. Military technology evolved along with war itself, as European regulars rather than colonial militias came to dominate American warmaking.

Although the most direct, war was not the only way in which European technology helped colonists overcome Native Americans. European-made or settler-made goods and technologies penetrated Native communities, binding them ever more tightly into the global economy. Native Americans could learn the use of guns but were dependent on settlers to manufacture them. Less spectacular European technological goods, notably woven cloth and metal items such as knives, cooking kettles, and fishhooks were also greatly valued by Native American traders, as they did not have the sophisticated metallurgy of Native Mexicans and Peruvians. In some cases, the names Native peoples gave European settler groups reflected the impact their technology made on Native American consciousness. The Mohawks called the Dutch of upstate New York "the iron-workers," or "the cloth-makers."

Native Americans were not the only, and often not the most formidable, opponents colonists faced. North America was also a cockpit of rivalry between the European states of England, Spain, France, and the quickly eliminated seventeenth-century contenders, the Dutch Republic and Sweden. Technology and science were weapons, literally or metaphorically, for the powers to exclude European rivals from their claims in the Americas. The first invaders of the Americas, the Spanish, attempted to keep their new navigational knowledge secret from potential rivals, ultimately failing. The knowledge explorers and settlers gained of the plants, animals, economic resources, and geography of the New World served to establish the claims of the European powers. Maps not only served practical uses, but were also propaganda as colonial powers created and publicized maps that exaggerated their own claims and minimized those of rivals. Technological advances were quickly turned to military use.

SCIENCE, TECHNOLOGY, AND COLONIAL NATIONALISM

The technology and science that served European invaders in their wars and conflicts with the indigenous population and each other were eventually turned against the mother countries that claimed rule over the Americas by the colonists themselves, beginning with the American Revolution. As colonists acquired an increasing sense of themselves as members of a society separate from that of Europe, their attitudes toward science and technology changed also. Colonists, particularly in the developed cities of British America, resented their exclusion from the most advanced technology and turned this resentment against their governments. British-American manufacturers increasingly found themselves in competition with English businesses, who sometimes used the British Parliament to restrict competition from America. The rapid eighteenth-century growth of the iron industry was particularly strong evidence that America was becoming a technological power, one to which Parliament responded by attempting to limit American development of advanced iron technology including steelmaking. Colonists boasted (usually with exaggerated optimism) of the ability of America to do without imports and produce what it needed itself. Promoting independent technological development became a mark of the true patriot.

Science, while less directly related to war than technology, also helped foster a distinct national identity. It was no coincidence that colonial America's leading scientist, Benjamin Franklin, also became one of its leading patriots and statesmen. Most other leading colonial scientists, Benjamin Rush the physician and chemist, John Winthrop the astronomer, and David Rittenhouse the astronomer and polymath, supported the patriot cause. The exception was the young genius Benjamin Thompson, who fought for the British, left for Europe after the war, and became a famous physicist usually known by the title he acquired in Europe, Count Rumford. He never returned to America.

The Revolutionary War was, among other things, an awesome technical challenge. The colonists by themselves could not solve all the technical problems war presented. Fortunately, they had the aid of France, home of the most advanced engineering training in the world. French engineers ably assisted the American cause, and the colonists themselves pushed their technology to the limit. Independent America inherited a rich scientific and technological legacy from the colonial period.

Chronology

1492 Genoese mariner Cristoforo Colombo, in the employ of the Spanish government, encounters the islands of the Caribbean. Colombo's expeditions will be the first source of European knowledge of the Americas.

1497 An Italian sea captain in English service, John Cabot, discovers the cod fisheries off the coast of America. The news spreads rapidly in Europe.

1503 Spanish King Ferdinand of Aragon founds the Casa de Contratacion in Seville. Its purpose to control trade with the Americas, it includes a repository of navigational and cartographical knowledge. In addition to permitting the coordination of observations from different Spanish voyages, the Casa de Contratacion restricts knowledge from potential European rivals.

1520 Hernando Cortez, conqueror of Mexico, addresses the first of five letters to King Charles of Spain that add greatly to European knowledge of the North American mainland. The letters continue until 1526.

1526 The first Spanish book on New World natural history, Gonzalo Fernandes de Oviedo's (1478–1557) *Natural History of the Indies* is published at Seville.

1537 Papal Bull *Sublimi Deus* declares that the belief that Native Americans are human beings with souls is obligatory for Catholics.

1538   The first New World University is founded at Santo Domingo.

1540   This is the date of the earliest surviving printed sheet from the Americas, a *Manual for Adults* in Spanish from Mexico City.

Francisco Vázquez de Coronado sets out on an expedition north from Mexico that will last until 1542. It adds to Spain's knowledge of southwestern North America and the southern Great Plains, including early descriptions of the buffalo.

1550   The Dominican missionary Bartolomeo de las Casas (1474–1566) and the Spanish humanist Juan Gines de Sepulveda debate at Valladolid in Spain on whether the inhabitants of the New World are natural slaves in the Aristotelian sense. Gines de Sepulveda upholds the position that Native Americans are natural slaves and Las Casas opposes. The debate is inconclusive, but Las Casas's position eventually wins out intellectually.

1551   A university is founded in Mexico City, the first university on mainland North America.

1555   Richard Eden's *The Decades of the New Worlde or West Indies, Containing the Navigations of the Spaniards* is published in London. It includes a translation of a large part of Oviedo's work, as well as discussion of Spanish mining techniques.

1557   Andre Thevet, a Frenchman who had visited America, publishes in Paris *The Singularities of Arctic France*, one of the first works in French containing original knowledge of North America. Although Thevet claims to have visited Canada, his information for the regions was mostly based on other texts and interviews with sailors and other French people who had been to northern North America. Thevet is appointed Cosmographer Royal of France the same year.

1570   The reform of the Spanish council of the Indies leads to an effort to systematically gather natural and geographical information with questionnaires. The Antwerp mapseller and cartographer Abraham Ortelius (1427–1598) publishes *Theater of the World*, the earliest atlas, showing North America as a wide continent rather than as a narrow barrier between Europe and Asia, as it was often shown before by Swiss humanist and cartographer Martin Waldsemuller and others. The frontispiece adds a personification of America as a goddess to the traditional three of Asia, Europe, and Africa.

1571   The Spanish physician Francisco Hernandez (c. 1517–1587) arrives in Mexico with a royal commission to carry out a scientific exploration. He will leave Mexico and return to Spain in 1577. His great work on the natural history of Mexico will never be published in complete form.

1573 Spanish King Philip II issues the *Laws of the Indies*, which among other things sets forth how towns were to be planned and built in the Spanish possessions.

1575 Publication of Thevet's *Universal Cosmography*, with more information on America.

1585 The English scientist Thomas Harriot leaves England for Sir Walter Raleigh's Roanoke colony.

1588 Harriot's *A Briefe and True Report of the New Found Land of Virginia* is published. It includes discussion of the prospective colony's natural history, economic resources and geography, and enthusiastic claims about the economic potential of two American crops, corn and tobacco.

1589 The first edition of Richard Hakluyt's collection, *Principall Navigations, Voyages, and Discoveries of the English Nation* is published; it includes a number of accounts relating to America.

1590 Harriot's *A Briefe and True Report* is published in English, French, German, and Latin, including the first significant published map of the New World by an English cartographer, John White. The edition spreads knowledge of northeastern North America in Continental Europe.

1602 Publication of the first English account of coastal New England, John Brereton's *A Briefe and True Relation of the Discoverie of the North Part of Virginia*. Sebastian Vizcaino, in the service of the King of Spain, makes the first survey of the California coast.

1608 English colonists at the Virginia colony of Jamestown, founded the previous year, build the first glassworks in English America.

1610 The French explorer Samuel Champlain sets up an experimental garden in Quebec to investigate acclimating European crops in North America. He will also ship New World seeds and plants back to Paris.

1612 Captain John Smith, leader of the Jamestown colony, publishes *A Map of Virginia. With a Description of the Countrey.*

1614 The first colonial English American saltworks is established in Virginia.

1616 John Smith's *A Description of New England* is published. It includes the first detailed and reasonably accurate map of the New England coast.

1620 Founding of the first tannery in the English American colonies, at Jamestown.

1622   Early Virginia industries destroyed by Native American attack.

1624   John Smith's *Generall Historie of Virginia* published in London.

1625   Publication in London of the Reverend Samuel Purchas's (1575?–1626) collection of travel narratives, *Purchas his Pilgrimes*. It includes accounts of America.

1632   Father Gabiel Sagard, a Catholic missionary of the Recollet order, publishes an account of his journeys among the Hurons. To encourage French businessmen to support missionary activity in the area, he gives the first written description of the copper mines of the Lake Superior region, although he does not claim to have seen them himself.

1634   William Wood's *New Englands Prospect* is published. It combines descriptions of New England's topography and natural history with promotion of English colonization.

1635   The French physician Jacques Philippe Cornut (d. 1651) publishes, in Latin, *Canadian Plants*. Based on plants sent to Paris by French explorers, the well-illustrated work is the most scientifically advanced treatment of New World plants yet to appear.

1636   Founding of Harvard College in Cambridge, Massachusetts, the first institution of higher learning in English America.

1638   The first printing business in English America is in operation by early October in Cambridge, Massachusetts.
Founding of the Ancient and Honorable Artillery Company of Boston, the first British American artillery company.

1639   Publication of the first English American almanac in Cambridge, Massachusetts. The author is a sea captain, William Pierce.

1643   John Winthrop Jr., then visiting England, sets up a Company of Undertakers of the Iron Works in New England. Winthrop returns to New England with financial backing, materials, and a company of skilled workers.

1644   Winthrop's Company of Undertakers begins construction of a blast furnace for smelting iron ore in Braintree, Massachusetts. The Massachusetts General Court issues Winthrop a monopoly on iron manufacture.

1645   The Jesuit missionary Father Lallemant learns of the salt springs of the Onondagas.

1646   The Massachusetts Bay Colony issues the first American mechanical patent to Joseph Jenks, giving him an exclusive right for 14 years to his improvements in sawmills and scythes.

1650 The Harvard-educated alchemist and physician George Starkey, frustrated with the difficulty of getting good laboratory equipment in America, relocates to England, where he becomes a leading chemist.

1652 The Massachusetts General Court votes to establish a mint and incorporates a company to provide water to Boston.

1653 The English Royal Navy starts buying pine trees in New England to serve as masts for their ships.

1662 The Royal Society for the promotion of natural knowledge is chartered in London by King Charles II (r. 1660–1685) on July 15. Among its members is the American John Winthrop Jr. On July 16 he gives a talk on the preparation of pitch in New England, the first paper at the Royal Society by a colonial.

The English Parliament requires that merchant vessels be built within the Empire to avoid paying duties. This is a huge boost to the shipbuilding industry in the Anglo-American colonies.

1663 First-known emigration of a professional bookbinder to the English American colonies. John Ratcliff comes to Boston to bind John Eliot's Indian Bible.

1672 John Josselyn's (c. 1608–1675) *New-England's Rarities Discovered* is published. Along with his *An Account of Two Voyages to New-England* (1675), it comprises the most complete natural history of New England produced in the colonial era.

1673 The French explorer Louis Joliet and the Jesuit missionary Jacques Marquette, journeying down the Mississippi, discover coal deposits in the Illinois region. Publication of Augustine Herman's map, *Virginia and Maryland as it is Planted and Inhabited this Present Year 1670.* Herman will receive a large estate from the proprietor of Maryland as a reward.

1680 Thomas Brattle (1658–1713) of Harvard College telescopically observes a conspicuous comet. His records eventually find their way to Isaac Newton (1642–1727), who praises their accuracy in his masterpiece *Mathematical Principles of Natural Philosophy* (1687).

1682 A spectacular comet (which later becomes known as Halley's comet) attracts much interest in America.
Thomas Holme surveys the site of the new city of Philadelphia, setting a new British American standard of precision in the laying out of a city's streets.

1683 Capitalizing on the recent comets, the Reverend Increase Mather publishes *Kometographia, or a Discourse concerning Comets*, exhibiting familiarity with the scientific literature on the subject.

Increase Mather leads in forming the Boston Philosophical Society, America's first scientific society. Other members include his son Cotton Mather. The first official meeting is April 30. The Society's history is largely unknown, but, at the latest, it had ceased to exist by 1687.

1684   Increase Mather publishes *An Essay for the Recording of Illustrious Providences,* calling for an organization of ministers and others to collect accounts of remarkable events in the natural world and elsewhere.

1685   First publication of an almanac in the English colonies outside Massachusetts, the *Kalendarium Pennsilvaniense 1686* in Philadelphia.

1688   John Love publishes the first surveying manual adapted to New World conditions, the frequently reprinted *Geodaesia, or the Art of Surveying and Measuring of Land made Easie.*

The Boston Mint is closed at the orders of the British government.

1690   First British American paper mill constructed at Germantown, Pennsylvania, by William Rittenhouse and William Bradford.

Around this date, large-scale cultivation of rice as an export crop by African slaves begins in South Carolina. Rice will become the colony's main crop.

1691   The South Carolina Assembly gives a patent to Peter Jacob Guerard for a rice-hulling "pendulum machine." It is unsuccessful, but it was one of the earliest attempts to mechanize rice processing.

1692   First appearance of a British American printed work employing color, Benjamin Harris's *Boston Almanack 1692.*

1693   Founding of the College of William and Mary in Williamsburg, Virginia, the first institution of higher education in the southern English colonies.

1694   Establishment of the formal garden at the College of William and Mary, the largest formal garden in the English colonies to that time.

1697   Construction of a three-span stone arch bridge over the Pennypack River in Philadelphia. Now known as the Frankford Avenue Bridge, it is the oldest bridge in North America still carrying traffic.

1700   In December, the English naturalist and surveyor John Lawson is commissioned by the Lords Proprietors of Carolina to explore the Carolina backcountry. He leaves Charleston on December 28, and his expedition lasts until February.

1701   A college is founded at Saybrook, Connecticut. In 1716 it will move to New Haven and become known as Yale College.

First known American copperplate engraving, a portrait of Increase Mather in the frontispiece of his sermon collection, *The Blessed Hope and the Glorious Appearing of the Great God our Saviour.*

1705   Parliament's bounties on naval stores such as tar, pitch, and turpentine lead to a rapid expansion of this industry in the pine-rich Carolinas. The Carolinas soon pass New England as the leading producer of naval stores.

Large fossil bones and teeth are discovered by a farmer near Claverack, New York.

The French monk and government agent Charles Plumier (1646–1704) publishes an eight-volume *American Botany.*

First copper mine opened in British America, near Simsbury, Connecticut. Promoters encourage the immigration of German copper miners.

1707   Act of Union between England and Scotland. This Parliamentary act opens up England's American colonies to Scottish emigration. The Scots will furnish many leaders of eighteenth-century American science and medicine.

1708   Thomas Robie (1689–1729) of Harvard begins publishing an almanac series, *An Ephemeris of the Coelestial Motions.* Several volumes will include discussions of scientific topics, disseminating Newtonian physics to a popular audience.

James Logan of Pennsylvania imports from England a copy of Isaac Newton's *Mathematical Principles of Natural Philosophy,* the first copy known to have been owned by an American. Logan will go on to build the most important private scientific library in early eighteenth-century America.

Publication in London of John Lawson's account of his Carolina trip, *A New Voyage to Carolina.* It includes much new information on Carolina's natural history and resources.

1711   Cotton Mather starts gathering accounts of American curiosities to send to *Philosophical Transactions,* the journal of the Royal Society. Some of the accounts go back to the seventeenth century.
A major fire in Boston, still a wooden town, leads to rebuilding of some of the city in brick.

1712   Traditional date when Captain Christopher Hussey of Nantucket located schools of sperm whales in the North Atlantic, beginning the deep-sea sperm whaling trade.

1713   Copper is discovered on the Schuyler estate in New Jersey. The Schulyer mine will become America's most productive copper mine.

1714   The succession of the Hanoverian ruler George I to the British throne leads to hostility between Sweden, at war with Hanover, and Great Britain. This increases British demand for colonial iron and naval stores, products Britain had imported from Sweden, and leads to further expansion of those colonial industries.

1716   English immigrant Thomas Rutt sets up a bloomery forge for iron in the Manatawny region of Pennsylvania. Rutt will go on to be a leader in the establishment of the eastern Pennsylvania iron industry.

Building of the first lighthouse in Boston Harbor.

1718   Construction begins on the *acequias,* or system of irrigation canals, in San Antonio, Texas, that will become the most elaborate in Spanish America. Indigo cultivation begins in Louisiana.

The French cartographer Guillame Delisle publishes a *Map of Louisiana,* combining advanced cartographic technique with aggressive support of French territorial claims.

1719   On December 11, a spectacular aurora borealis appears over New England. Along with an English aurora of 1716, it will inspire pamphlets by Cotton Mather, Thomas Robie, and the Reverend Thomas Prince (1687–1758). Prince and Robie emphasize that auroras are explainable by natural causes and are not divine signs, while Mather attempts to balance natural and providential causes.

Colonel Alexander Spotswood sets up a blast furnace to smelt iron near Fredericksburg in Virginia. This is the beginning of the iron industry in the Chesapeake region. Spotswood encourages the immigration of German ironworkers with technical expertise.

1720   English mapmaker Herman Moll responds to Delisle with *A New Map of the North Parts of America Claimed by France,* supporting English territorial claims.

Construction begins on the French fortress at Louisbourg on Cape Breton Island, destined to be the strongest fortress on the North Atlantic coast.

Approximate date of the founding of the Principio Company, colonial America's largest ironworks. Located in Maryland, it principally served the British market. Although most of the investors were English, they include Augustine Washington, George Washington's father.

1721   Cotton Mather publishes *The Christian Philosopher,* the work of many years and an ambitious attempt to present current science, as he understood it, in the framework of Puritan theology.

1722 White Pines Act, intended to reserve trees for masts for the Royal Navy, requires a permit to fell white pines with a diameter of more than 24 inches unless on private land.

Mark Catesby (1683–1749) arrives in Charleston from England May 3, with English and American patronage to collect natural historical specimens, seeds of American plants for English gardens, and information to write a natural history of the area.

1724 Founding of the Carpenters' Company of Philadelphia, a group of builders. Parliament's bounty on naval stores expires. The industry quickly collapses in South Carolina, but persists in North Carolina where there are fewer economic alternatives.

1725 Launching of the largest ship built in colonial America, a 750-ton vessel built by the New London shipwright John Jeffery.

1726 Isaac Greenwood (1702–1745) publishes at Boston a prospectus for his forthcoming series of natural philosophy lectures, *An Experimental Course in Mechanical Philosophy.*
Catesby returns to London.

1727 The London merchant Thomas Hollis (1659–1731) endows the Hollis Professorship in Mathematics and Natural Philosophy at Harvard with 1,200 pounds and a gift of scientific equipment. The first holder of the chair is Robie's pupil Isaac Greenwood, who arrives from England and gives a series of public lectures on experimental philosophy, the first of their kind in New England, beginning in January. Greenwood will do much to promote scientific awareness in New England and keep the chair until 1738, when he is removed for drunkenness.

A very strong earthquake in New England leads to many sermons and tracts claiming that the disaster was a result of God's anger at the sinful people of the area, warning people not to miss God's meaning by becoming too interested in the earthquake's natural causes.

French engineers build a levee over a mile long to control Mississippi floods near New Orleans.

James Logan of Pennsylvania carries out experiments on the pollination of corn.

1728 John Bartram establishes a botanical garden.
A group of surveyors from Virginia and North Carolina, including William Byrd of Virginia, establish the boundary between the two states. Byrd will write two accounts of the expedition.

1729 On May 22, Catesby submits the first of the five parts of the first volume of his *Natural History of Carolina, Florida, and the Bahama Islands.* The last part is given to the Royal Society November 23, 1732.

Isaac Greenwood publishes the first mathematical textbook by an American, *Arithmetick Vulgar and Decimal*. It is unsuccessful.

1731   The Baltimore Company, a Maryland group planning to build ironworks mostly to supply the British market, is formed. It will become one of the largest colonial iron manufacturers.

The octant, a navigational instrument, is independently invented by John Hadley (1682–1744) in England and Thomas Godfrey (1704–1749) in Pennsylvania. Patriotic Americans will support Godfrey's claim to priority.

Benjamin Franklin and his associates found the Library Company of Philadelphia. A general-interest institution, it will acquire many scientific books and a collection of scientific instruments.

The first German-language almanac appears in British America.

1732   The first appearance of Benjamin Franklin's *Poor Richard's Almanac*. It will continue until he leaves for England in 1757.

1733   The Trustee's Garden is founded in the new city of Savannah, Georgia, the first public garden devoted to agricultural research in British America. Harmed by neglect, the garden will disappear by 1748.

1734   The founding of the Library of the Carpenters' Company of Philadelphia, a repository of works on building design, mostly printed in England.

1735   The first part of the second volume of Catesby's *Natural History* is submitted to the Royal Society January 20. The whole work will not be completed until April 16, 1747.

1737   Publication in Dublin of John Brickell's *The Natural History of North Carolina*. Although much of it is plagiarized from John Lawson's *A New Voyage to Carolina*, it also contains some new information.

Publication of William Byrd's *Natural History of Virginia* in German, in Bern, Switzerland, as part of an effort to attract Swiss immigrants.

1739   After Isaac Greenwood loses the Hollis Chair at Harvard, his former pupil, the astronomer John Winthrop (1714–1779), a descendant of the seventeenth-century Winthrops, is installed January 2. He will hold the chair until his death, introducing differential and integral calculus into the curriculum.

A French military party discovers a deposit of fossils, including a mastodon, at Big Bone Lick on the Ohio River in the modern state of Kentucky.

The Dutch botanist Johann Friedrich Gronovius's *Flora Virginica* is published. It is based on a manuscript by the Virginia botanist and collector John Clayton (1694–1773). A second volume appears in 1743.

German immigrant Caspar Wistar builds the most successful colonial glass factory, using German workers, in Alloway, New Jersey.

Eliza Lucas begins to experiment with indigo cultivation at her father's plantation in South Carolina.

1740   The College of Philadelphia, later the University of Pennsylvania, is founded. Establishment of the first type foundry in colonial North America. Founded at Germantown, it produces type for German-language presses.

Around this time Benjamin Franklin devises the Pennsylvania Fire Place or Franklin stove, a device for heating rooms more efficiently by minimizing the escape of heated air.

1742   A spectacular shooting star arouses the Reverend Thomas Clap's (1703–1767) interest in meteors, to which he will devote much of his scientific career.

Publication of a pirated edition of Eliza Smith's English manual, *The Compleat Housewife*, in Williamsburg, Virginia. This is the first cookbook and domestic guide published in British America.

1743   Publication of Franklin's broadside "A Proposal for Promoting Useful Knowledge Among the British Plantations in America" in Philadelphia, the first plan for the creation of an American Philosophical Society.

The Scottish electrical lecturer Archibald Spencer, touring America, first arouses Franklin's interest in electricity.

1744   Franklin gives a model Franklin stove to the iron founder Robert Grace and helps publicize them.

Eliza Lucas's first successful production of indigo.

1745   Thomas Clap becomes president of Yale College, a position he will hold until 1766. He reorganizes the curriculum to place more emphasis on science.

The New York natural philosopher and statesman Cadwallader Colden (1688–1776) publishes *An Explication of the First Causes of Action in Matter; and the Cause of Gravitation*, a work of physical theory that attracts some notice, mostly unfavorable, in Europe.

Franklin reads an article on recent electrical experiments in the English periodical *Gentleman's Magazine* and is inspired to begin his own electrical research. First-known advertisement from an American maker of bookbinder's tools appears in Boston.

1746   The College of New Jersey, later Princeton University, is founded.

1748   In September, a Swedish disciple of the great botanist Carl Linnaeus, Peter Kalm (1715–1779), arrives in North America. He will gather plants in Pennsylvania, New York, New Jersey, and New France, and meet many American botanists, natural historians, and other scientists before leaving in February 1751.

The clergyman-physician Jared Eliot (1685–1763) publishes the first of six short treatises, *Essays on Field-Husbandry in New England*. The last pamphlet in the series, which adapts the new agricultural ideas of the Englishman Jethro Tull and other so called improvers to New England, will be published in 1759.

1749   Benjamin Franklin publishes *Proposals Relating to the Education of Youth in Pensilvania*, advocating including natural philosophy in the curriculum. Franklin's friend Ebenezer Kinnersley (1711–1778) commences a tour of the colonies as an electrical demonstrator, lecturer, and showman that will last until 1753. He disseminates Franklin's electrical theories.

The surveyor Lewis Evans publishes *Map of Pensilvania, New-Jersey, New-York, and the Three Delaware Counties*.

The British Parliament agrees to subsidize colonial indigo.

1750   The British Parliament passes the Iron Act, encouraging iron imports from America but forbidding the colonists to construct mills for slitting or rolling iron or to make steel.

A Welsh shoemaker, John Adam Dagyr, arrives in Lynn, Massachusetts. He will introduce improved techniques for mak-ing high-quality shoes to New England, and begin Lynn's prominence as America's shoemaking center.

Edward Pattison, a Scottish tinsmith, settles in Berlin, Connecticut, around this time. He will introduce tinsmithing to the colonies, and Berlin will become the center of eighteenth-century tin manufacture.

A group called the Young Junto starts meeting in Philadelphia to discuss scientific questions as well as other issues.

In the fall, Christopher Gist begins an observational and geo-graphical expedition into the Ohio country for the Ohio Company that lasts to the following spring.

A short canal is built in Orange County, New York, one of the few canals built in the colonies before the American Revolution.

1751 Sugar cane cultivation is introduced to Louisiana.

Benjamin Franklin's *Experiments and Observations on Electricity* is published in London. In it, Franklin puts forth his electrical theory and suggests the use of pointed metal rods to protect buildings from lightning.

The British Parliament removes the tariff from American potash (potassium carbonate), a substance derived from burning wood and used in soap manufacture, glassmaking, dyeing, and bleaching.

Establishment of a system of public streetlights in Philadelphia using whale oil.

Founding of the Society for Encouraging Industry and Employing the Poor, a Boston group that sets up a linen factory to employ poor Boston women and children in spinning while advertising in Ireland for skilled male weavers. The operation never becomes self-sustaining and collapses by 1759.

1752 In June, Benjamin Franklin's famous experiment with a kite and key establishes the electrical nature of lightning.

Along with Britain, the colonies switch from the Julian to the Gregorian Calendar. Eleven days are expunged from the calendar between September 2 and the following day, September 14.

Two surveyors, George Heap and Nicholas Scull, publish *A Map of Philadelphia and Parts Adjacent, With A Perspective View of the State House.*

The Sterling ironworks is established in Orange County, New York.

1753 Obadiah Brown, a leading businessman of Providence, Rhode Island, establishes a spermaceti candleworks at Tockwotton.

Short of funds, the Royal Society withdraws the exemption from fees previously extended to Fellows from the colonies on July 5.

On November 30, the Royal Society awards Franklin the Copley Medal, its highest honor.

The Philadelphia professor Theophilus Grew publishes a textbook, *The Description and Use of the Globes, Celestial and Terrestial.*

1754 The Society of Arts is founded in London. The society is devoted to improving technology in Britain and its colonies by circulating technical information and offering prizes for new ideas.

King's College in New York, later Columbia University, is founded.

Joshua Fry and Peter Jefferson (the father of Thomas Jefferson) publish their *Map of the Inhabited Parts of Virginia*. It will go through several more editions in England and France.

The first system in North America for providing water for household use to an entire community through pumps is built in the Moravian community of Bethlehem, Pennsylvania.

For the first recorded time, a rice-pounding mill is mentioned in a South Carolina plantation sale.

1755   The London Society of Arts announces its first premium for American industry, on silk.

Flooding in the deep shafts threatens the Schuyler copper mine. Mine owners import a steam engine from England to pump the water out. This is the first-known steam engine in America.

On November 18, an earthquake shakes New England. On November 26, the Harvard astronomer John Winthrop gives a lecture in the Harvard Chapel, setting forth the natural explanations of earthquakes and rebuking those who ascribed them to God's anger. The talk is published as *A Lecture on Earthquakes* and sets off a controversy between Winthrop and Thomas Prince, a defender of the religious interpretation of earthquakes, lasting into the next year.

Construction of Braddock's Road, a 115-mile road connecting Fort Cumberland and Pittsburgh for military purposes.

First publication of Dr. John Mitchell's British government—sponsored *A Map of the British and French Dominions in North America*. This frequently republished map will become the standard map of North America until the American Revolution.

Lewis Evans's *General Map of the Middle British Colonies in America* is published.

1756   Benjamin Franklin is admitted as a Fellow of the Royal Society, with fees waived by unanimous agreement.

1757   The Englishman Thomas Stephens tours the colonies, promoting potash making.

The German Moravian community of Nazareth in Pennsylvania opens a vocational school. Initially, 16 youths are taught various crafts. This is one of the first efforts to learn craft skills in a school rather than by apprenticeship.

Daniel Treadwell appointed the first professor of Mathematics and Natural Philosophy at King's College in New York City.

1758 William Small (1734–1775) becomes professor of mathematics at William and Mary. Before moving back to England in 1764, he will be Thomas Jefferson's instructor, impressing Jefferson favorably.

First-known shipment of an apple variety originating in America to Europe when Newtown Pippins are sent to Benjamin Franklin in London.

1759 The Juliana Library Company in Lancaster, Pennsylvania, modeled on the Philadelphia Library and including a museum and collection of scientific equipment, is founded.

Opening of the one of the few lead mines in British America, along the Great Kanawah River in Virginia. Investors hope to find silver as well as lead.

1760 The English natural historian John Ellis (1710–1776), with the approval of Linnaeus, Europe's arbiter of botanical names, names the cape jasmine after his correspondent, the botanist and physician Alexander Garden (1730–1791) of Charleston. The plant is now known as the gardenia.

1761 The first of two transits of Venus across the face of the sun in the mid-eighteenth century occurs on June 6. These rare phenomena provoke worldwide bursts of scientific activity. The transit is not visible in the 13 British colonies but John Winthrop leads a group of observers to Newfoundland in a trip financed by the Massachusetts Assembly with instruments on loan from Harvard. He publishes *Relation of a Voyage from Boston to Newfoundland, for the Observation of the Transit of Venus, June 6, 1761*.

The Association of Spermaceti Candlers is formed. Its purpose is to control the market in high-quality candles made from the whale product, spermaceti. Public street lighting, using whale-oil lamps, begins in New York City.

1762 John Bartram explores the interior of South Carolina in search of new plants. Jared Eliot publishes *An Essay on the Invention, or Art of Making Very Good, if not the Best Iron, from Black Sea Sand*.

1763 A New York Society of Arts is formed with the goal of fostering an independent American linen industry.

Founding of the Ancient and Honorable Mechanical Company of Baltimore, an artisan's group.

The London Society of Arts sends James Stewart to New England to encourage the potash industry, and awards Jared Eliot a gold medal for his success in extracting iron from sand.

Two Englishmen, Charles Mason and Jeremiah Dixon, arrive in Philadelphia in November to begin establishing the borders of Pennsylvania. They start by fixing the latitude of the southern boundary of Philadelphia.

1764   Harvard Hall is destroyed by fire early in the year, and with it the collection of scientific and experimental equipment originally donated by Thomas Hollis and subsequently built up by the Hollis Professors Isaac Greenwood and John Winthrop. Winthrop appeals to the public for funds to replace the collection, and with the help of Franklin, then in England, he is able to build the largest and most up-to-date scientific instrument collection of any colonial institution.

During the summer, Mason and Dixon trace the north-south line dividing Pennsylvania from Delaware.

The College of Rhode Island, later Brown University, is founded.

1765   Benjamin Franklin sponsors John Winthrop's admission as a Fellow of the Royal Society.

In the spring, Mason and Dixon begin establishing the east-west Mason-Dixon Line between Maryland and Pennsylvania.

John Bartram is appointed King's Botanist and explores the southeastern British colonies including Florida, recently acquired from Spain.

Edward Quincy's *Treatise of Hemp Husbandry* is published by command of the Massachusetts Assembly as part of an effort to promote an American hemp industry. It contains material on European and American hemp raising, including an account of a large hemp-raising project at Salem, Massachusetts.

1766   Philadelphia's Young Junto takes on more formal organization and a new name, the American Society for Promoting and Propagating Useful Knowledge.

Construction begins on the King's Road connecting Savannah and St. Augustine. Work will continue until 1775.

Queens College, later Rutgers, is founded.

An anonymous pamphlet published in Boston, *Directions for Making Calcined or Pearl-Ashes*, promotes the manufacture of pearl-ash, a refined form of potash.

1767   The American Philosophical Society is revived in Philadelphia.

George Croghan sends fossil teeth from Big Bone Lick to Franklin and others in London.

On October 9, Mason and Dixon make their last measurement, at the mouth of Dunkard Creek.

Two treatises on potash production and American potash are published in London, Robert Dossie, *Observations on the Pot-Ash Brought from America* and W.M.B. Lewis, *Experiments and Observations on American Potashes*. Dossie is a leader in the Society of Arts.

1768   On November 4, the Philadelphia Medical Society is dissolved as its members are admitted to the American Society for Promoting and Propagating Useful Knowledge. On December 20 the American Society and the American Philosophical Society merge to form the American Philosophical Society for Promoting Useful Knowledge, the first American scientific society to establish itself as a permanent institution. It is usually referred to as the American Philosophical Society.

Henry Wilhelm Stiegel founds a glassworks at Manheim, Pennsylvania, planning to manufacture the highest-quality glass yet made in America.

A chair of mathematics and natural philosophy is established at the College of New Jersey, but it is not filled until 1771, when William Charles Houston is appointed.

A German scholar, Cornelius de Pauw, publishes *Philosophical Researches on the Americans* in Berlin. Following the French natural historian Buffon, de Pauw argues that American animals and peoples are naturally inferior to those of the Old World, particularly Europe. This sets off a controversy lasting several decades and involving Thomas Jefferson and the great German scientist Alexander von Humboldt, among many others.

1769   On January 2, at the first meeting of the American Philosophical Society for Promoting Useful Knowledge, Benjamin Franklin is elected President *in absentia* and Thomas Bond vice-president. In January, a member of the Society, the military officer Lewis Nicola (1717–1807), publishes the first issue of *The American Magazine, and General Repository*. This periodical, which lasts for only nine months, included much scientific material (mostly reprinted from European sources) and unofficial transactions of the American Philosophical Society.

The second transit of Venus June 3 occasions more observations and widespread interest in the American colonies. A French expedition to Baja California, led by the astronomer Jean-Baptiste Chappe d'Auteroche (1722–1769) is nearly wiped out by an epidemic, with only one survivor who brings the data back to Paris. The Royal Society sends an expedition to Hudson's Bay to observe the transit. The American Philosophical Society sponsors and gathers over 20 observations. John Winthrop, America's leading astronomer, turns down an invitation from the Royal Society to observe the transit at Lake Superior for health reasons. He observes the transit from Harvard, communicating his results directly to *Philosophical Transactions*. The Lake Superior expedition is abandoned for lack of funding.

Abel Buell establishes the first American English–language type foundry in Killingworth, Connecticut.

Isaac Doolittle of New Haven is the first American to build a printing press.

Benjamin Rush is appointed professor of Chemistry at the College of Philadelphia.

Dartmouth College is founded.

1770   The physician Benjamin Gale (1715–1790) is awarded a special gold medal by the London Society of Arts for an improved drill-plough, an accomplishment building on the work of his father-in-law Jared Eliot and Thomas Clap.

The first American porcelain factory, Bonnin and Morris, is founded in Philadelphia.

Benjamin Rush publishes the first American chemistry textbook, *A Syllabus of a Course of Lectures on Chemistry.*

1771   The first volume of the *Transactions of the American Philosophical Society* is published in Philadelphia in February. It includes observations of the 1769 transit of Venus.

The London Society of Arts sends James Stewart to Maryland to encourage the potash industry.

David Rittenhouse completes work on an orrery, a mechanical representation of the motions of the planets and moons of the solar system. This is the first orrery built in America, and Rittenhouse had been working on it since 1767. It provokes much interest and is eventually bought by Princeton University.

1772   John Hobday of Virginia invents a threshing machine.

Franklin elected Foreign Associate of the Royal Academy of Sciences in Paris, Europe's leading scientific organization.

1773   The natural historian and scientific illustrator William Bartram leaves on a series of expeditions through southeastern British America that will last until 1776.

The Virginian Society for the Promotion of Usefull Knowledge is founded, with the botanist John Clayton as its first president. It awards a gold medal to John Hobday's threshing machine.

1774 Nearly 300 whale oil–fueled public street lamps are illuminated in Boston.

Economic failure forces Henry William Stiegel to close his glassworks.

British Parliament forbids the export to America of tools and machines used in textile production.

First Continental Congress passes several measures to encourage American manufactures.

William and Mary College institutes its first course in chemistry.

1775 *American Husbandry*, the most complete work on colonial agriculture, is published anonymously in London.

The first architectural book published in British America, a reprint of Abraham Swan's *British Architect*, appears in Philadelphia with 60 copperplate engravings by the American engraver John Norman.

Fourth edition of Mitchell's map published as *A Map of the British Colonies in North America with the Roads, Distances, Limits and Extent of the Settlements.*

The Dutch engineer and surveyor Bernard Romans publishes *Concise Natural History of East and West Florida* along with coastal charts for sailors.

Henry Monzon's *An Accurate Map of North and South Carolina With Their Indian Frontiers* is published.

The United Company of Philadelphia for Promoting American Manufactures is founded. It concentrates on textiles.

Establishment of a business to make lampblack for printer's inks in Germantown by Cabel Fox. The high-quality product eventually becomes known as "Germantown lampblack."

The Yale student David Bushnell invents and builds a one-man submarine for use against the British.

The Continental Congress issues orders to standardize the muskets being manufactured for the Revolutionary War, although manufacturers frequently ignore the specifications.

1776 The American Revolution leads to the suspension of the meetings of the American Philosophical Society, which do not resume until 1779.

The shortage of gunpowder for the American armies leads to increased interest in gunpowder manufacture, particularly the scarcest ingredient, potassium nitrate or saltpeter. Benjamin Rush publishes *Essays upon the Making of Salt-Petre and Gun Powder.*

Around this time, Jeremiah Wilkinson of Cumberland, Rhode Island, devises a technique for making nails out of cold iron rather than forging them.

Responding to America's need for salt, the Continental Congress puts a bounty on salt imported or produced in America of a third of a dollar per bushel. This act encourages a rapid expansion of American saltmaking. John Sears of Dennis opens the first large-scale saltworks on Cape Cod. The operation uses a large vat for evaporation, and begins the salt industry in the area.

1777   The Continental Congress commissions a Corps of Engineers. It is at first composed of four French officers and will remain heavily dominated by foreigners throughout the war.

1778   The surveyor Thomas Hutchins publishes *Topographical Description of Virginia, Pennsylvania, Maryland and North Carolina.*

A great chain, weighing more than 100 tons, is laid across the Hudson as a defensive measure against the British. It was made at the Sterling Iron Works.

1779   In an order dated March 10, Benjamin Franklin follows the French example by directing captains of American ships not to molest the British scientific and geographical expedition led by Captain James Cook. Franklin lacks authority for this order. Unknown to Franklin, Cook had already been killed by Native Hawaiians on February 4, after mapping much of the far northwestern seacoast of North America.

1780   At the urging of John Adams and others, the Boston Academy of Arts and Sciences is founded with a charter from the Massachusetts General Court.

The Pennsylvania Assembly formally charters the American Philosophical Society.

General George Washington of the Continental Army commands the formation of a Corps of Sappers and Miners.

1781   Thomas Clap's *Conjectures upon the Nature and Motion of Meteors,* in which he argues meteors are comets orbiting the earth, is published posthumously.

1

Making a Living:
Agriculture

Like the Europe and Africa from which settlers came, colonial America had an economy based on agriculture. The crops colonists raised and the tools and techniques they used were sometimes indigenous to America, such as corn and squash; sometimes imported from Europe, such as wheat and barley; and sometimes imported from Africa, such as rice. Most crops were grown to be used as food, whether for humans or animals, but many, such as tobacco and indigo, were non-food cash crops, raised to be sold in the colonial, British, or European market.

Agricultural knowledge spread mostly by word of mouth or by demonstrations. Colonists wrote few books on agriculture, although in the eighteenth century they contributed many essays and articles to newspapers and periodicals in Europe and America. Many European technical manuals on agriculture appeared in colonial libraries, some of them quite old and of dubious relevance given the different conditions and different crops in the Americas. The eighteenth-century South Carolina planter and indigo pioneer Eliza Lucas Pinckney regarded the ancient Roman poet Virgil's *Georgics* as a useful source of agricultural advice. Although agricultural societies, bringing together farmers and botanists to discuss ways of improving farming, were becoming increasingly common in Europe during the late eighteenth century, they did not emerge in America until after the Revolution.

AGRICULTURE AND THE LAND

In the Europe from which the original colonists came, a large number of people intensively cultivated a small amount of land. The situation was quite different in America, and was one of the attractions of the new-found land to ordinary Europeans. Land was abundant, and when it was exhausted, many colonists simply moved on. The cheapness of land in America encouraged techniques that quickly exhausted the usefulness of an agricultural plot. Corn, America's staple food crop, in particular took nutrients out of the soil quickly, and many corn farmers moved on after taking a few crops out of a plot. Plowing was also inefficient. Many farm-ers plowed straight up and down hills rather than following the contours of the land. This channeled water down the hill, carrying valuable nutrients with it.

In many wooded areas, the first task of the colonial farmer was clear-ing the land. Even in wooded areas, there were many natural or Native American–made clearings that could be cultivated without being cleared first. These plots of land were snapped up early, leaving later colonists the task of clearing. Many colonists adopted the Native American technique of "girdling," killing a tree by cutting around it under the bark, and then leaving the dead tree to fall or be chopped down in a later year. When the tree died and lost its foliage, enough sunlight could come through to plant beneath it. A quicker technique was firing a stand of trees, although fire was always difficult to control. Once big trees had been cleared, the plot was "grubbed," relieved of small trees and weeds with a hoe, which was back-breaking work. New England farmers faced the additional task of clearing their fields of stones.

The abundance of land, particularly in settlement frontiers, meant that many American farmers spent little time worrying about fertilizing it. When crops had exhausted a patch of land, many farmers simply moved elsewhere and practiced the same wasteful agriculture on their new land. A few fertilization techniques were practiced. Fish and rockweed, a type of seaweed, were used as fertilizer in coastal communities, and in the eighteenth century farmers in the British colonies began to use gypsum as a fertilizer. There was surprisingly little use made, however, of one of the most commonly available fertilizers, human and animal manure. In fact, tobacco farmers claimed that manure ruined the taste of tobacco. European observers, coming from a crowded continent where every bit of agricul-tural land had to be exploited to its maximum potential, were often sur-prised at what they regarded as the slovenliness of American farmers and blamed it on the cheapness of American land. In the early eighteenth cen-tury, the Englishman John Lawson claimed: "I never saw one Acre of Land manag'd as it ought to be in Carolina, since I knew it; and were they as negligent in their Husbandry in Europe, as they are in Carolina, their Land would produce nothing but weeds and straw" (Lawson, *A New Voyage to Carolina*, 75). The anonymous *American Husbandry*, published in London on the very brink of the American Revolution, continued the denunciation of the backwardness of American agriculture: "There is no error in hus-bandry of worse consequence than not being sufficiently solicitous about manure; it is this error that makes the planters in New Jersey and our other colonies seem to have but one object, which is ploughing up fresh land. The case is, they exhaust the old as fast as possible till it will bear nothing more, and then, not having to replenish it, nothing remains but taking new land to serve in the same manner" (*American Husbandry*, 105).

WATER AND IRRIGATION

British colonial farmers faced relatively little difficulty in acquiring the fresh water they needed for their crops. Eastern U.S. areas were quite wet (too wet in many places, where the problem was not irrigation but draining swamps and marshes), even permitting the cultivation of water-intensive crops such as rice with irrigation technologies adopted from West Africa and Europe. Hispanic farmers in the American Southwest shared with many of the English colonists of eastern America a bountiful supply of land and a concentration on corn but faced the additional challenge of a chronic shortage of water. Fortunately, Spain itself, with many dry areas, had developed sophisticated irrigation, and Hispanic farmers and Spanish administrators met the challenge of the dry Southwest with the most developed system of irrigation in colonial America. Farmers in the Southwest relied on vast irrigation works called *acequias*, systems of earthen ditches that took water from a source along a main ditch, the *acequia madre*, and distributed it along smaller ditches to individual farms. Acequias were also used to provide Hispanic communities with water for drinking and household use. The word *acequia* is derived from the Arabic term, *as-saquiya*, indicating the influence of Muslim irrigation techniques during the time that Muslims occupied Spain in the Middle Ages. Spain defined agricultural water legally as communal property rather than individual property, so acequias were administered by governments, religious bodies, or local councils rather than by farmers. So important was water that property ownership in the Southwest was often defined in terms of water rights and the land that went with them, and the acequia was built in a new settlement even before the Catholic Church.

AGRICULTURAL TOOLS

Early immigrants from England came with standard agricultural tools, including the hoe, the forked hoe, and the spade for tilling; the sickle for harvesting; the flail for winnowing; bill hooks for removing underbrush; tongs for weeding; and shovels. The tools were designed to minimize the use of expensive metal. For example, rather than making a whole shovel out of metal, toolmakers usually made the body of the shovel out of a cheaper material, wood, and sheathed the edges in metal to take advantage of its sharper edge.

The earliest technique for breaking up ground to prepare it for planting was spading and hoeing. This was the method used by the earliest

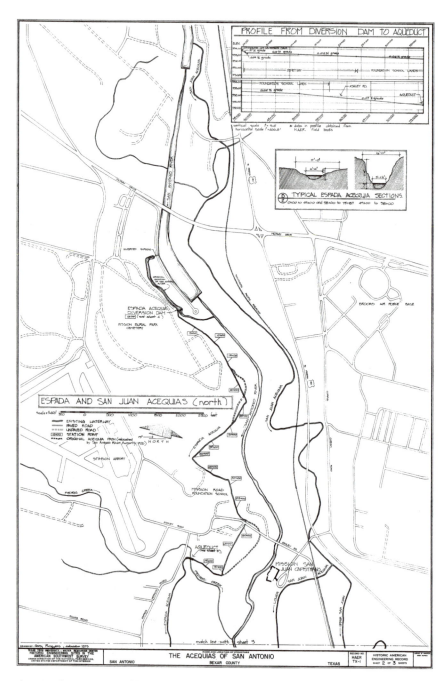

Among the greatest public works in colonial America were the *acequias*, or irrigation systems, of the Spanish cities. Courtesy of the Library of Congress.

settlers, and it required heavy physical labor. A more efficient form of tilling was plowing. Plows substituted animal for human muscle power. They began to appear in New England in the 1630s and 1640s, and were usually heavy, requiring several teams of oxen to draw them. Many farmers could not afford the expense of a plow and team, and either continued to hoe or hired a plow from a wealthier neighbor. Colonists originating in different parts of Europe brought different styles of plows and other farm equipment. For example, English-derived plows had a flat plowshare, a wooden coulter to cut the soil ahead of the plowshare, and two handles, whereas Dutch farmers in America used hog plows with a pyramidal plowshare, no coulter, and one handle. The lighter Dutch plow took less animal power to pull and was better on good soil like that of Holland itself, whereas the English plow took more power to pull but was more effective on poor and rocky soil. Most American plows remained heavy and inefficient until the development of the shovel plow, named after its shovel-shaped plowshare, in the mid-eighteenth century.

The Spanish settlers of New Mexico were also plow users. The principal handicap they faced in employing their light, unwheeled plows pulled by oxen or mules was a shortage of iron. Iron was rare enough to be used only as the tip of a wooden plowshare. It wore away, and there were no local supplies of the metal. Spanish friars wrote back to Mexico, imploring Spanish authorities to send more iron for plows and other tools. The early Spanish missions in Arizona lacked even the iron to tip their plows; their devices were entirely wooden.

In the Chesapeake region, where tobacco was king, ground was prepared for tobacco plants with hoes rather than plows throughout the colonial period. Since Virginia planters relied on the labor of slaves, rather than principally employing their own labor and that of their families, as was the case for New England farmers, labor saving was of less importance to them. Plows only arrived in the region in quantity in the early eighteenth century, when diminishing returns on tobacco inspired planters to diversify into corn and wheat, and even then many farmers went without them. The Virginia tobacco and grain planter Landon Carter used plows but continued to argue for hoes into the late eighteenth century: "Oxen are not the thing to plow with, they are slow at best, and tire every hot day. And the plowmen unmercifull to them by constant beating them... and if I get horses, they are rode out in the nights by the negroes. So that on all accounts hoes are the surest and best way of tending" (Carter, *The Diary of Colonel Landon Carter of Sabine Hall,* 442). In South Carolina, where rice and indigo were dominant, plows were hardly found at all. In West Africa, where the slaves who did the agricultural work of South Carolina originated, the hoe was the dominant tool for turning earth, and they carried hoe cultivation across the Atlantic.

Although the first agricultural tools in the colonies were imported, Anglo-American farmers and blacksmiths soon began creating tools locally. Some smiths in centers of population even specialized in toolmaking. The best tools were still usually imported from England, but most farmers could not afford them and made do with the product of local toolmakers. The growing prosperity of the British colonies meant that good tools, whether domestic or imported, became more widely distributed in the eighteenth century and the overall quality and effectiveness of tools improved. For example, metal spades nailed to a wooden handle replaced the seventeenth-century metal-sheathed wooden ones.

CORN

Perhaps the greatest technological achievement of Native Americans was the slow, centuries-long process by which a wild grass was transformed into a plentiful and adaptable source of food. European colonists quickly adopted corn and many of the Native American practices—and vocabulary—associated with it. The most famous exponent of this cultural transfer was Squanto, the English-speaking Native American who taught the Pilgrims of Plymouth techniques of planting, fertilizing, and raising corn, without which they would have starved. But the Pilgrims were following in the footsteps of previous generations of settlers in taking to corn. The versatile grain was cultivated everywhere from New England to New Mexico, serving as both food for human consumption and, along with the corn plant itself, feed for livestock. Cultivated in nearly every colonial farm, corn could also be grown in small enough quantities to be suitable for small garden plots in the cities. It was an efficient crop, requiring that only a very small amount of corn kernels be set aside as seed for the next planting season.

Corn differed from wheat and other cereals in that it was reared in hills rather than scattered along rows. Thus plowing the land to prepare it for sowing was unnecessary, although it did make it more productive and was increasingly practiced during the colonial period. However, throughout the colonial era, farmers often broke up ground for corn with spades or hoes, like the original Native American corn cultivators, rather than plowing it. Corn was planted in the spring, although the exact timing varied by region. Many settlers adopted the Native American practice of simply poking a hole in the turned-up soil with a planting stick. Another practice adopted from Native Americans was to plant beans or pumpkins between the rows of corn hills. The best corn kernels, as chosen by criteria including the size of the ears, evenness of the rows on the ears, and early ripening, were set aside after each harvest to be planted the next year. Early ripening of corn was important in protecting corn from the first frosts of the fall. By the 1740s, corn in the northern British colonies was maturing in about two and a half months.

One problem with newly sown corn was its attractiveness to animals and birds, who could devour seed corn before it had a chance to germinate. Some farmers protected their crop by soaking their planting kernels in a solution of hellebore before planting. Hellebore produced nausea when eaten, and it was hoped the animals that menaced corn seeds—crows, blackbirds, rodents, and others—would be discouraged after a few unpleasant experiences. Pine and coal tar was also effective for this purpose.

The planted corn was cultivated with the hoe, the basic tool for grubbing the omnipresent weeds. Hoes were also used to break up soil after rains. Excess corn stalks growing from a hill and suckers, secondary stems, were removed and used for animal fodder. Today, corn scientists question the efficacy of removing suckers as useless. Unlike wheat, which had to be harvested all at once, corn could be harvested at different stages in its development, from the baby ear eaten whole to the young and tender roasting ear to the mature ear whose hard kernels were destined to be ground into flour. Leaves, used as fodder for farm animals, were harvested separately, as farmers walked up and down the rows and pulled them from the stalks below the ears, a process called "pulling fodder." The ears themselves were harvested by being cut from the stalks with corn knives.

Once harvested, corn also had the advantage of durability—it could last for years properly stored. Indeed, there are cases of corn retaining its edibility for more than one thousand years. Native Americans stored ears of corn both in underground pits and in small buildings. European settlers, who preferred above-ground storage, adopted from Native Americans the basic design of the corn crib. Cribs were small wooden buildings raised on posts above the ground to keep the corn safe from rodents with walls and floors constructed of loose slats to ensure ventilation.

Unlike wheat, which was always ground into flour and baked, corn could be eaten in many different ways, from straight off the cob to popcorn to cornbread. But first the husk, the green leaf-like bodies that surround the cob, had to be removed or "shucked." Colonists used a wooden tool first developed by Native Americans, the shucking peg. Shuckers peeled the husk off by grasping it between their thumbs and the peg, a sharpened piece of hardwood. Like other parts of the plant, husks had their uses. Corn husks were used to stuff mattresses or even made into paper.

Shelling corn, removing the kernels of corn from the cob, was a tedious process carried out by hand. It stubbornly resisted mechanization throughout the colonial era and for decades after. There were many techniques for shelling ears of corn individually by hand, some taken from Native Americans. Corn was beaten or scraped to loosen the grip of the kernels. A dry corncob itself could serve as a scraping tool. This was not the only use for a corncob. Corncobs were used for purposes as varied as providing a float for a fishing line or a handle for a knife. They made excellent kindling for fires, and children staged corncob fights, throwing cobs at each other because the light cobs were less dangerous than rocks or pieces of wood. Old World practices developed for threshing cereals, such as beating the grain with flails and driving heavy-hoofed animals over it, were also used for shelling corn.

Once the corn was shelled, grinding the hard kernels of the mature ear into flour, if desired, presented few technical problems. Milling technology, developed to grind Old World cereal grains such as wheat, was easily adaptable to grinding hard corn, particularly as the large corn kernels were less likely to clog the works than the smaller cereal grains. Although British colonists sometimes ground corn at large, water-powered mills, these were not necessary, and there were many ways that individual households could grind their own corn. Anglo-American households used the "hominy block," or "saump mill." The saump mill was composed of a hollowed out hardwood tree stump, such as oak or hickory, and a block of wood suspended above it, tied to a flexible tree limb. The hollow stump was filled with the corn kernels to be ground, and the corn-cracker grasped the wooden block and brought it down repeatedly. The resultant corn flour, known by the Algonquian word *hominy*, could be baked into cornbread, cooked and served as grits, or combined with pork in a dish known as hog and hominy. The Hispanics of New Mexico had small stone-grinding wheels in their homes, a technique adopted from local Native Americans, and cooked their corn into tortillas. Slaves in the seventeenth-century Chesapeake region, where mills were relatively scarce, were required to grind corn into flour in a mortar and pestle to feed both their own and their masters' families—adding significantly to their already exhausting workday.

Two food-processing techniques that colonists brought from Europe and enthusiastically applied to corn were fermenting and distilling. Corn was made into beer and ale from very early in European settlement. Corn whiskey was particularly associated in the eighteenth century with the Scots–Irish settlements of backcountry Anglo-America. The Scots–Irish came from a whiskey making and whiskey drinking culture, but distilling was also a solution to the economic problem of what to do with the corn they produced for market rather than for home consumption. Liquid corn whiskey was simply cheaper and more profitable to ship to faraway markets than corn kernels or corn flour.

WHEAT AND OTHER EUROPEAN CEREALS

The cereal crops—most importantly wheat, but also oats, rye, buckwheat, and barley—were transplants to America from Europe where they formed a staple diet for humans and livestock. There were pronounced differences between different immigrant groups in cereal raising; for example, the Swedes who settled the Delaware Valley in the seventeenth century preferred rye to wheat, a preference their English neighbors found puzzling. The technology employed in raising and processing cereals in America was basically similar to that in Europe. Plows were popular with those who could afford them for preparing the ground for sowing. Cereal grains were usually sown by scattering.

The most popular tool for harvesting wheat and other grains in the areas of English settlement was the sickle, a curved metal blade with a short wooden handle. It required bending over to grasp the grain plant by one hand and then swinging the sickle with the other hand to cut it. Dutch farmers in New York and New Jersey used a device called a "mathook" or "reaping hook," which gathered stalks together to be more easily cut and bound into sheaves. When used in conjunction with the sith or Flemish scythe, smaller than the scythe used by English colonists, the mathook enabled reapers to harvest more efficiently without bending over, but this device does not seem to have spread beyond the Dutch farms. By the end of the colonial period, the cradle scythe, much more efficient but heavier than the sickle, had come into use for grain harvesting in New England. The cradle scythe had a long straight blade at the end of the handle, with four wooden fingers about the same length as the blade and parallel to it. When wielded by a skilled practitioner, the cradle scythe not only cut grain more quickly than the sickle, but laid it out in a form suitable for easy binding into sheaves.

Once harvested, cereals had to be threshed to separate the grain from the rest of the sheaf. The basic threshing tool was the flail, which had existed unchanged for many centuries. Two pieces of wood were held together by a strap. The thresher held one piece of wood, and swung the other at the grain. It was slow and exhausting work. The alternative was threshing by having heavy-hoofed animals walk over the grain, an ancient technique that required less labor but was slow and produced unclean grain. John Hobday of Virginia invented a threshing machine in 1772, but it had little impact besides winning him a prize from the Virginia Society for Promoting Useful Knowledge.

Wheat was the king of cereals in both Europe and America, because unlike others (including its new American rival, corn), it contained gluten, enabling it, if leavened, to rise and form the bread so highly prized in the European diet. However, unlike corn, wheat had few ways to be made into edible food for humans. To make bread, by far the most common wheat product, threshed wheat had to be ground into flour. The most efficient way to grind grain was by using a water-powered mill. A mill for grinding grain was called a "gristmill." If no gristmill was available, grain could be ground by hand in a "quern." Querning was exhausting work—about two hours of grinding was necessary to provide a family's needs in a typical day—and produced a coarse, inferior flour.

Wheat, along with gristmills for grinding it, spread to the Chesapeake region as a cash crop in the second half of the eighteenth century. Wheat possessed the advantage for Virginia plantation owners of a production cycle that complemented that of tobacco and offered independence from the vagaries of the tobacco market and debt to London tobacco merchants. Decades of tobacco cultivation had also exhausted the soil in many areas, and returns on tobacco were dropping along with its quality.

The most famous Virginia planter to shift from tobacco entirely to wheat was George Washington.

POTATOES

Corn's only rival as the most important food crop of American origin was the potato. Potatoes and sweet potatoes are examples of another kind of agricultural transfer than that from across the Atlantic—transfers from one part of the Americas to another—carried out by colonial societies. Potatoes originated in South America, and only began to be cultivated in North America in colonial times. The Spanish introduced the sweet potato from the Caribbean to Florida, from whence it spread to the other Continental colonies. (Hispanic settlers also introduced *chiles*, peppers originally found in Mexico, into the American Southwest.) Although important in some regions, potatoes had not yet attained their modern status as a ubiquitous staple food. Potatoes had excellent nutritional value and could be cultivated even on poor soils, but in both America and Europe, they still had something of a social stigma in the colonial era—they were the food of the poor, considered bland and unappealing by society's elite.

The Swedish Lutheran pastor and historian Israel Acrelius described the cultivation of potatoes in eighteenth-century Delaware and Pennsylvania:

Potatoes are quite common, of two kinds—the Irish and the Maryland [sweet potatoes]. The Irish are also of two kinds: the first round, knotty, whitish, mealy, somewhat porous. They are planted thus: upon a smooth and hard ground a bed of dung is formed. Portions of this are thrown upon the potatoes, which are then covered with ground of even the poorest kind. When the stalks have come up about four ells high, they are again hilled up with the same kind of earth, in order to strengthen the roots, which are thus considerably increased in number. The other kind is long, branching, thick, reddish, juicy, and more porous. For these a long ditch, the depth of a spade, is dug; the bottom of which is covered with manure, set with pieces of potatoes, and covered over with earth. When the stalks come up, they are treated as those above mentioned.

Maryland potatoes are long, thick, juicy, sweet and yellow. They are planted from sprouts in hills or round heaps of good earth. When the stalks come up, they are hoed around. These are also wonderfully prolific, so that everywhere around and between the hills the fruit is dug up. (Acrelius, *A History of New Sweden*, 150)

RICE

Rice was the staple crop of South Carolina and the engine that drove the colony's rapid economic expansion beginning at the end of the seventeenth century. Rice growing operated on a very different technological basis than did growing corn, wheat, and the other staple grains. Whereas these crops were grown on dry land and could be watered with rainfall in much of North America, rice could not be profitably raised in such conditions (although some of the early Virginia colonists tried). To do well, rice requires an immense amount of fresh water.

Europeans, with the exception of some northern Italians who did not emigrate to America, lacked experience with rice and the complex technological problems it posed. The know-how had to come from elsewhere. Much of the technology for rice growing, along with the rice itself, came to North America in the knowledge of slaves from West Africa, an area with a long rice-growing tradition. West Africans had over the centuries worked out a number of schemes for growing and processing rice in different settings, including floodplains and swamps. Carolina planters valued this knowledge, and slave-dealer advertisements from the late seventeenth century frequently claimed that the slaves they offered for sale possessed particular expertise in rice.

The eventual system for growing rice as usually practiced in South Carolina and Georgia was most closely related to that practiced in West African mangrove swamps. The work of cultivation, mainly performed by enslaved African women, was physically very debilitating. Not only was the work itself very hard, but so was the environment in which the work was carried out. The fact that Carolina slaves were doing much of their work standing in dirty water made rice cultivators particularly vulnerable to disease.

Rice was the most labor-intensive of all grain crops, requiring a variety of demanding tasks to grow and process. The grain was planted either in a European fashion, in trenches made by a hoe, or in the West African fashion with indentations made in the ground with the heel. Sometimes the rice seed was wrapped in a thin layer of clay before planting to protect it from seed-eating animals and birds, another technique originating in Africa. In addition to preparing the earth, planting the seed, constant hoeing, operating and maintaining the irrigation system, threshing, and winnowing, rice had an additional stage of processing: pounding to remove the outer husk and inner film. This process differed from the milling of corn and wheat, whose purpose was to grind the individual grains into a fine flour. Rice pounding sought to preserve the whole grain in edible form. This made it much harder, although not impossible, to mechanize rice processing. Attempts to devise machines for rice processing began in South Carolina almost as early as rice processing itself, but saw little success until the last decades of the colonial era, when planters invested in large winnowing fans and pounding mills powered by draft animals. The first mention of a pounding mill in an estate sale dates from 1754, and such machines spread rapidly in the following decades.

In the absence of mechanized power, female slaves used mortars and pestles very similar to those used in West Africa to pound rice. A stump was hollowed by fire, and the rice in the receptacle was pounded using a wooden pestle weighing between 7 and 10 pounds. Skillful pounders could keep nearly three-quarters of the rice grains intact. Although women monopolized this work in Africa, Carolina planters eager to maximize their rice production forced slave men to do it as well. Men had the physical strength to process a larger amount of rice, but it was a long time before they could rival the skill of women pounders. Whether done by men or women, rice pounding was work carried on in addition to a full plantation day. This work was extremely draining physically and contributed to the high death rate of South Carolina slaves.

After the rice was pounded, slave women winnowed it to separate the fragments of hull from the grain. They put the rice in shallow, circular baskets made of straw and closely resembling baskets used for the same purpose in West Africa. The baskets were then rotated and tossed to separate the lighter hulls from the heavier grains. The long-grain rice, the famous "Carolina Gold," had to be handled carefully to avoid breakage, as broken rice was of less value.

TOBACCO

Many crops raised in colonial America were used for purposes other than food. These crops often required elaborate processing before they could be used and posed further technological challenges.

Tobacco was one of the great discoveries of the New World. It was used by many different Native American groups, and was one of the first New World crops that Europeans took a liking to. The mariners of Columbus's early voyages were known to have smoked tobacco, and it was one of the most prominent features in many early European descriptions of the Americas. The act of smoking itself was new and shocking to Europeans, and some condemned tobacco smoking as a filthy custom imposed on Native Americans by Satan. However, many more were enthusiastic about the new herb. Some promoters of the new leaf such as Jean Nicot, a French physician after whom nicotine is named, even claimed that tobacco was a powerful medicine, able to cure many diseases. The belief that tobacco was a cure for syphilis, which was commonly believed by Europeans to share tobacco's New World origins, was particularly common. Whether or not tobacco smoke enjoyed this health-giving property, cultivation of the plant undoubtedly made many people rich. The economy of the Chesapeake colonies, particularly Virginia, was based on tobacco growing in the seventeenth century, and even after their economy diversified in the eighteenth century, tobacco remained a major source of wealth and the single greatest export from the British-American colonies. Like rice in South Carolina, tobacco in Virginia was treated as money.

Tobacco comes in many varieties with different characteristics. Soon after the first permanent settlement of Virginia, at Jamestown, the English settlers found that the local tobacco was too bitter to be a profitable export crop. The solution was to import Spanish tobacco, a superior variety, from the West Indies. But the Spanish, who wanted to control the tobacco trade to Europe, forbade others from obtaining their superior seed. The answer, then, was to smuggle the seeds. The settler John Rolfe, best known as the husband of Pocahontas, was the first Virginian to plant seeds smuggled from the Spanish plantations of the Caribbean.

Tobacco growing and processing was a labor-intensive process requiring the tobacco to go through many stages. The seedlings were first grown in flats, then transplanted in early April, after the ground had been prepared by laborious hoeing. Protecting the growing tobacco plants from worms and weeds required great care. The harvesting of the tobacco plants in August was not the end of the process. The leaves then had to be dried in a tobacco house over the next six weeks. The entire plant was hung up in a tobacco house, constructed with loosely connected walls that allowed the moisture to be carried off by the breezes. Many things could go wrong in this process, as the eighteenth-century Virginia tobacco planter Landon Carter well knew. In 1757, much of his tobacco was spoiled while hanging in the tobacco house by a "sweat," which Carter believed was caused by the plants being hung too close together in damp air with poor circulation: "Sweat introduces a kind of putrefaction the leaves grow black and fetid and, being divested of all their proper qualities and indeed moisture when the leaf dries, it remains in a dirty black, starched and stinking state and is never more affected by any moisture but what will carry on its rottenness" (Carter, *The Diary of Colonel Landon Carter of Sabine Hall*, 175). Carter tried to save his tobacco by thinning it out as it hung in the shed and using fire to dry the air but remained pessimistic.

Following drying, the tobacco leaves, the valuable part of the plant, were stripped from the stems and loaded in wooden hogsheads to be taken to tobacco ships that would carry the crop to England. Shipping the tobacco in hogsheads rather than loose both helped keep it in good condition and impeded smuggling—tobacco was a heavily taxed commodity. The Chesapeake region had the advantage of being honeycombed by water-ways, so the tobacco suffered less damage being moved smoothly over water than it would being jostled over land. Tobacco leaves were exported to Europe where they were further processed into consumable form. Tobacco could also be ground into snuff in American mills, which became more common in the eighteenth century.

Not all American tobacco was grown on plantations for the export trade. People also grew tobacco in small lots for their own consumption. The historian of the Swedish settlements on the Delaware, the Reverend Israel Acrelius, described this small-scale cultivation and use: "When the leaves are ripe, they are cut, cured, and twined together like twists of flax, and are used, without any further preparation, by the country people for chewing and smoking" (Acrelius, *A History of New Sweden*, 151). In taking tobacco, colonists followed the example set by Native Americans who not only pioneered the cultivation of tobacco but also the main methods by which it was consumed. North American natives, who had originally received tobacco from Central America, were predominantly pipe smokers. The English and Dutch, both in North America and at home, followed the custom of the North Americans from whom they learned smoking and usually smoked tobacco in pipes. French Canadians were also pipe-smokers, and imitated the Native American practice of mixing their tobacco with red dogwood bark. A type of stone pipe with a hole drilled for a wooden stem, called a "Micmac pipe," after an Algonquian people of the northern coast of North America, was commonly used by Europeans as well as Native Americans. The Spanish settlers preferred cigars, which they learned about from Central American and Mexican Natives. Snuff, powdered tobacco inhaled through the nose and then sneezed out, was the French method and became popular throughout Europe and America in the eighteenth century along with other aspects of French upper-class culture.

CROPS FOR TEXTILES—INDIGO, FLAX, AND HEMP

Many crops were grown for textile uses. One of the most technologically complex of all crops raised in colonial America was indigo, the source of a popular blue dye for which demand was increasing with the expansion of the English textile industry in the eighteenth century. Previously grown in the Caribbean and Louisiana, indigo was introduced as a crop in South Carolina by Eliza Lucas (1722–1793), who administered her family's plantations while her father, a British army officer, was stationed in the Caribbean. Lucas began planting indigo in 1739, but it took several years before she produced a commercially acceptable product. In the 1740s, as more dyes of all kinds were needed to give color to English textiles, indigo cultivation expanded dramatically. The British Parliament agreed to subsidize its production in 1749. Indigo's growing season complemented that of rice, so it was a godsend to South Carolina planters and an additional burden upon their slaves.

The extreme care with which the indigo plant had to be cultivated was matched by the difficulty of refining it into dye. The cut plant had to be placed, as quickly as possible, into a vat of water called a steeper for fermenting. After 12 to 15 hours, the contents of the steeper were placed in a second vat called a beater, where it was stirred. Lime water was poured into the beater to precipitate the sediment. After removal from the beater, the indigo was strained through cloth, cut into blocks, and dried. This process produced an overwhelming stench and attracted masses of flies and other insects. Planters usually built their indigo works at a considerable distance from their homes. Their slaves had no such choice.

The work and stench of indigo refinement was extremely debilitating for the slaves who carried it on. There was also no guarantee of the quality of the final product. The result of processing indigo was dependent on local conditions, the time in which the various processes were carried out, the ratios of the various components, and the strength of the lime water. Expert indigo-makers, even if they were slaves, received much respect on the plantation.

Indigo remained an unpleasant substance as it made its way to the end-user, the dyer of wool or other fabric. Its use was not restricted to large-volume textile operations. New England women bought small cakes of indigo for home use, dissolving the cakes in stale urine, then putting them over mild heat and fermenting them for up to two weeks. The smell was awful, although the home dyer had the considerable advantage over the production or commercial worker of only dealing with a small amount of the substance. Eliza Lucas's daughter, Harriot Pinckney Horry, wrote out a different procedure for using indigo in her collection of recipes. A plantation mistress, she operated on a larger scale than simple housewives:

Take 24 Galls. rain Water free from grease or dirt and put into it 4 lb. copras [ferrous sulfate or "copperas"] and 4 lb. stone lime. Take 2 lb. Indigo grind it as fine as possible (adding rain water to it till you have a quart or three pints of the Indigo and Water) it must be quite an impalpable powder. Then put it in a Bll. [barrel] with the other ingredients and churn it up 3 times a day till you see a foam on the top of a changeable colour and the dye of a dark green streak'd with black then let it stand 2 days to settle. Boil the yarn so as to be thoroughly Wet, wring it very hard dip it in the dye about half the depth of the Baul turning it over the hands three or four times observing never to let it go to the bottom among the grounds wring it and hang it up till you go over the yarn 2 or 3 times a day. When the yarn quits turning green it will dye no more set it with Vitriol and Water made sour enough to drink then rince it thro' one or two waters. (Horry, *A Colonial Plantation Cookbook*, 137)

Whatever the procedure employed, indigo dyers, however, found the end result worth the trouble and stench. Indigo made a beautiful blue that was chemically stable, unaffected by heat or by exposure to other chemicals.

Cotton was only beginning its American career in the late colonial era. Most of the cotton used to make cloth in colonial North America was imported from the Caribbean. A more commonly reared textile crop in colonial America was flax, the raw material of linen. Unlike cotton, flax was frequently grown in small amounts to serve a household's needs, although it could also be grown on large commercial farms. The stalks, which contained the fibers that would eventually become cloth, were pulled from the ground, and seeds were removed with a flail or by drawing the stalk through an iron comb, sometimes called a "hetchel." Then the stalks were moistened, or "retted," either by being submerged in water or by being spread on the ground to absorb moisture from the air or rain. The moistening caused the outer stalk to break down, revealing the fibers and removing extraneous material. The stems were then beaten, a process referred to also as "swingling," to remove the remaining part of the outer shell, short fibers, and other trash. The fibers were then combed with an iron comb until they were soft and smooth enough to be spun into yarn. Although flax could also be eaten, its textile use remained primary.

Hemp was a vigorously promoted crop in the eighteenth century. It was the raw material of rope, a product in constant demand particularly by shipbuilders and sailors. Given the importance of ships and shipbuilding to the British Empire, imperial authorities were concerned about Britain's dependence on Russia for hemp. Parliament sought to promote hemp by enacting a bounty on it, as did local colonial governments interested in their own shipbuilding industries. However, hemp never became a major crop in the colonial era. The main problem was the demands hemp processing made upon labor. Hemp had to be broken by pounding to separate the fibers from other vegetable matter—brutal, physically draining work. Britain used female convicts for this task because free people were unwilling to do it. William Byrd of Westover, the great Virginia planter, was initially enthusiastic about hemp, growing it on his plantation and promoting a plan to grow large amounts using slave labor on reclaimed land in the Great Dismal Swamp. However, he abandoned the crop after several years because processing it took up too much of the time and energy of his slaves, and the profits were too small to justify the labor.

2

Wood, Fruit Crops, and Other Tree Products

In the early days of English colonization, Native North Americans speculating on the motivations of their strange and dangerous new neighbors suspected that the newcomers originally came to the American shores because they had cut down all the trees in their own countries. This suspicion was not very far from the truth. One characteristic of North America that amazed its early English settlers was its wealth of trees. Heavy demand for wood over the centuries had deforested much of Europe and the British Isles, and the bountiful forests of eastern North America were ripe for exploitation in all sorts of ways. Early colonial promoters knew the importance of trees in inspiring potential colonists' and investors' dreams of wealth. John Brereton, a Cambridge-educated clergyman who accompanied Captain Bartholomew Gosnold's expedition to New England in 1602, rhapsodized about the wealth of trees to be found on Elizabeth's island (now Cuttyhunk Island in Massachusetts) and their many potential uses in his promotional tract *A Briefe and True Relation of the Discoverie of the North Part of Virginia*:

This Island is full of high timbred Oakes, their leaves thrise so broad as ours; Cedars, straight and tall; Beech, Elme, hollie, Walnut trees in abundance, the fruit as bigge as ours, as appeared by those we found under the trees, which had lien all the yeere ungathered; Haslenut trees, Cherry trees, the leafe, barke and bignesse not differing from ours in England, but the stalke beareth the blossoms of fruit at the end thereof, like a cluster of Grapes, forty or fifty in a bunch; Sassafrass trees great plenty all the Island over, a tree of high price and profit; also divers other fruit trees, some of them with strange barkes, of an Orange colour, in feeling soft and smoothe like Velvet. (Brereton, *Discoverie of the North Part of Virginia*, 7)

Two of the most basic things trees provided were wood, the principal building material of the early and frontier settlers, and heat, in the form of fire. The domestic fire, giving both heat and light, was often kept ablaze with hickory, but fire had its industrial uses as well, baking brick and ceramic. The dramatic rise of the Anglo-American colonial iron industry in the eighteenth century was literally fueled by thousands upon thousands of acres of American trees, and locating a foundry near a good supply of wood was nearly as important as locating it near a good supply of iron. However, wood and fire were only the beginning of the exploitable resources America's trees provided. Other kinds of tree products included apples and other fruit for eating, fermenting, and distilling to industrial products such as potash, pitch, tar, and tannin.

WOODWORK AND WOODWORKING TOOLS

Eastern North America's bountiful wood resources were exploited from the earliest days of European colonization. In 1622 the Virginia Company, the London-based group of investors in the first Virginia colony, recommended that each immigrant family come equipped with two broad axes, two felling axes, two steel hand saws, one whip saw, two hammers, two augurs, six chisels, two stocked braces, three gimlets, two hatchets, two froes, nails, and a grindstone. If all this equipment had actually been brought along, it would have represented a huge expense for a family of settlers. The Virginia Company was often disconnected from the reality of colonial life, but it was right about one thing—American settlers would need to fell trees and shape lumber.

No woodworking tool was more important to the development of America than the axe. Axes show up very early in the European invasion of North America, since Europeans, whether Spanish, French, or English, frequently exchanged small axes and hatchets for Native American goods. These small axes were known as Biscayan axes if Spanish and Hudson Bay axes if English. Given the Native American lack of sharp metal tools, the axes were quite valuable to them.

A larger axe was the felling axe, made for chopping down trees. Felling axes were among the most common axes settlers used. British colonists improved on the European original. The American felling axe developed by shortening the blade and creating a heavier (and sometimes steel-reinforced) poll, on the opposite side of the handle to the blade, to counterbalance the weight of the blade and make the axe easier to swing. It also made the reverse of the blade a more effective hammer. The body of the blade of the American felling axe was iron with a steel cutting wedge as wide as one and one half inches welded on. When the edge dulled, it was replaced by welding a sheet of steel on one side of the axe, a process known as "steeling" the axe. Another common kind of axe was the hewing or goosewing axe, with the handle bent away from the blade to enable the user to chop wood lengthwise without his hand striking the wood. Goosewing and other broadaxes were used to transform round logs into square beams suitable for building log cabins and other houses. Goosewing axes often had the maker's name inscribed, while felling axes did not. The mortising or posthole axe, with the blade at right angles to the haft, was used to chop square "mortises" into wood for making a mortise and tenon joint, commonly used in house construction.

Another commonly used hand tool was the "froe," used to split wood. A froe was a long metal wedge, extending at right angles to a short wooden handle. The woodworker set the froe where he desired to split off a layer of wood from a block, and then struck it with a one-handed wooden hammer or "froe-club." The operator twisted the froe to break off the wood. Froes had many uses. Builders used froes to split off clapboards for siding houses and shingles for roofing. A curved froe, known as a "cooper's froe," was used for making barrel staves.

To turn logs into boards, the first commonly practiced technique, drawn from Europe, was use of the pit saw. The log to be sawed was laid over a pit about as deep as the height of a man. One man on top and another man in the pit used a long vertical saw to cut the log into boards. Pit sawing was exhausting, particularly because the bottom man (the two "sawyers" changed positions often) was constantly showered with sawdust, even though he protected himself with a wide-brimmed hat. It was also relatively inefficient, taking a long time to turn a whole tree into boards. The abundance of wood in America meant that hand tools and muscle power were not sufficient for exploiting it, particularly since labor was relatively expensive.

Shortly after the first British colonies were established, sawmills powered by water were introduced. Anglo-American workers themselves could not build them, as England, which had been consuming its wood avidly for centuries, had become a wood-poor country and lacked sawmills. Experts from the European continent built the first sawmills in Anglo-America, using straight saws rather than the later circular saw. Germans built the first sawmill in the Chesapeake region, and Danes in Massachusetts Bay. The Dutch settlers of New Netherland used windmills, familiar technology from their own country, to cut wood. However powered, mills wasted considerably more wood than did sawyers or axemen cutting lumber by hand. They more than compensated for this disadvantage by being much faster. The abundance of wood in early America and the ravenous demand for boards for houses and buildings meant that speed was more important than efficiency.

The fact that the water-powered sawmills of Anglo-America had to be situated by a stream was an advantage in that softwood logs could be floated to the mill. Hardwoods sank in water, and had to be carried to the mill. Streams also provided a deceptively easy solution to one problem sawmills created, a problem that would recur many times in the history of America and the world, disposing of toxic waste. The waste sawmills generated took the form of sawdust. Up to one-fifth of the wood a sawmill processed ended up as useless sawdust. The most common solution to the problem of how to dispose of these mountains of dust was for the miller to just dump all of it back into the millstream to be carried downstream. This habit, along with overfishing, eventually killed off the abundant freshwater fish life that had greeted the first settlers.

A WORLD OF WOODS

The experienced colonial woodworker knew exactly what kind of tree the wood he used came from. Different species of trees served different purposes. Hickory burned hot and bright, making excellent firewood. Cedar's lightness and resistance to rot made it the best material for light, maneuverable boats like those used by whalers as well as for roofing shingles and clapboards. The famous cedar swamps of New Jersey served much of the demand for roofing materials in the English colonies in the eighteenth century. Cedar's water resistance also made it useful for pails. Willow's flexibility was valuable to coopers binding together the staves of their barrels and casks. The straight, soaring white pines of the New England forests were prized for ships' masts; the Royal Navy's greed for them angered colonists. Black oak was another nautical wood; it was particularly well suited for the underside of ships because it resisted the attacks of worms. It was also used for barrel making. White oak was used in shipbuilding, and it was also popular for boards and staves. Red oak made fence rails and barrel staves. White ash combined flexibility with strength, making it ideal for making the handles of pitchforks and other tools, as well as oars. Ash's rigidity made it a substitute for expensive imported brass in scientific instruments and a shaft for pikes and pole arms. American beech, or ironwood, produced a strong, rigid wood excellent for levers. Walnut not only provided nuts for eating, but also was prized in furniture making and as a firewood. Maple was another wood commonly used in furniture making and was also used for oars and bowls. Poplar, which could be cut thin, was made into boxes and other light containers by urban specialists called "white coopers." Locust wood was made into "tree-nails" or "trunnels," wooden pegs carpenters used to fasten boards as a substitute for expensive iron nails. The huge cypress tree could be cut down, hollowed out, and made into a canoe. Pine knots, lumps of resinous fiber found in pine trees, provided illumination, and pines generally produced pitch, tar, turpentine, and other naval stores as well as wood.

Some woods, such as oak and pine, were common; others were luxuries and served to show off the users' wealth and status. A builder might accentuate the door of a rich family's house by making it of a special wood not used for walls or roof, such as apple, sassafras, or mahogany, one of the rare woods in use that was not of local origin and had to be imported to North America from the Caribbean or Central America. Cherrywood, which could be polished to a rich red, was used for doors and also prized for furniture.

Bark also had its uses. Canoes were made of birchbark, and the bark of oak trees and spruces was ground for tannin. Sassafras bark was prized for its rather exaggerated medicinal uses as an emetic and fever treatment.

CHARCOAL

A common use of hardwood was to make it into charcoal—essentially a lump of carbon used as fuel. Charcoal burned clean and hot and was essential to the iron industry that emerged in eighteenth-century America. It was also an ingredient in gunpowder. America's abundance of wood meant that American iron foundries continued to use charcoal long after their English rivals had switched to coal.

Charcoal was made from wood by men called "colliers." It was difficult, exhausting, and dangerous work, as a heap of wood had to be carefully burned without being allowed to burst into flame.

FRUIT AND TREE CROPS

Wood and lumber were only the beginning of the bountiful resources of the American forest. One tree resource that the colonists learned how to exploit from the Native Americans was the sap of the maple. The eighteenth-century Massachusetts lawyer Paul Dudley described how Americans made maple sugar in a letter to the Royal Society, England's premiere scientific organization.

Making Maple Sugar

> Maple Sugar is made of the Juice of Upland Maple, or Maple Trees that grow upon the Highlands. You box the Tree, as we call it, i.e. make a hole with an Axe, or Chizzel, into the Side of the Tree, within a Foot of the Ground; the Box you make may hold about a Pint, and therefore it must shelve inwards, or towards the bottom of the Tree; you must also bark the Tree above the Box, to steer or direct the Juice to the Box.
>
> You must also Tap the Tree with a small Gimblet below your Box, so as to draw the Liquor off. When you have pierced or tapp'd your Tree, or Box, you put in a Reed, or Pipe, or a bit of Cedar scored with a Channel, and put a Bowl, Tray, or small Cask at the Foot of the Tree, to receive your Liquor, and so tend the Vessels as they are full.

(Continued)

(Continued)

> After you have got your Liquor, you boil it in a Pot, Kettle, or Copper. Ten Gallons will make somewhat better than a pound of Sugar.
>
> It becomes Sugar by the thin part evaporating in the boiling, for you must boil it till it is as thick as Treacle. Ten Gallons must boil till it comes to a pint and half.
>
> A Kettle of twenty Gallons will be near 16 Hours in boiling, before you can reduce it to three Pints; a good Fire may do it sooner.
>
> When you take it off, you must keep almost continually stirring it, in order to make it Sugar: otherwise it will candy as hard as a Rock.
>
> Some put in a little Beef Sewet, as big as a Walnut, when they take it off the Fire, to make it turn the better to Sugar, and to prevent its candying, but it will do without. A good large Tree will yield twenty Gallons. The Season of the Year is from the beginning of February to the beginning of April. (*Philosophical Transactions* XXXI, no. 364 [1720]: 27–28)

Another tree important to the colonial diet was the apple. Unlike maple syrup, apples were something Europeans were familiar with before the invasion of America. Colonists introduced the apple tree to the Americas. The first apples planted in what is now the United States came from the Mayflower settlers in 1620, but shortly afterward the apple came by the southern route as well from the Hispanic settlers of New Mexico.

European apples had difficulty adjusting to the harsh winters of northern North America. Fortunately, the apple tree develops new varieties easily, and many new, hardy apple strains emerged in the Americas. Smart apple farmers were always on the lookout for the spontaneous emergence of new kinds of apples. Apple varieties of colonial Anglo-American origin included the Roxbury Russet, the Newtown Pippin, the Rhode Island Greening, the Winesap, the Yellow Bellflower, and the Baldwin, at first known as the Pecker apple because the tree attracted woodpeckers. Different apples had different uses. The Baldwin's success was came from the fact that the fruit kept well and was versatile, suitable for eating fresh, for cooking, and for extracting juice. The Fameuse, an apple of Canadian origin known for its good flavor, was cultivated in Vermont and northern New York. The first-known shipment of American apples to Europe occurred in 1758, when Newtown Pippins were shipped to Benjamin Franklin in London. The many varieties of apples could be made into applesauce, apple butter, dried apples, apple pies and tarts, and the ubiquitous apple cider. The eighteenth-century Swedish Lutheran pastor Israel Acrelius described how cider was made and drunk in the Swedish community of Delaware and Pennsylvania:

Apples are ground up in a wooden mill which is worked by a horse. Then they are placed under a press until the juice is run off, which is then put in a barrel, where it ferments, and after some time becomes clear.

When the apples are not of a good sort, decayed or fallen off too soon, the cider is boiled, and a few pounds of ground ginger is put into it, and it becomes more wholesome and better for cooking; it keeps longer and does not ferment so soon, but its taste is not so fresh as when it is unboiled.

The fault with cider in this country is that, for the most part, the good and the bad are mixed together. The cider is drunk too fresh and too soon; thus it had come into great disesteem, so that many persons refuse to taste it.... The common people damask the drink, mix ground ginger with it, or heat it with a red-hot iron. (Acrelius, A *History of New Sweden*, 160–61)

Acrelius went on to describe the two kinds of cider royal, one mixed with brandy and sugar, the other with mead, and mulled cider, heated with sugar, egg yolks, allspice, and sometimes rum.

Another Swede, the eighteenth-century traveler Peter Kalm, described an apple drink found in the Philadelphia area that he called apple ale: "Some apples—which need not be the best—and apple peelings are taken and dried. Half a peck of this dried fruit is then boiled in ten gallons of water and when removed from the fire the solid part is taken out. Then yeast is added to the water, which is allowed to ferment, whereupon it is poured into vessels like any other drink" (Kalm, 643).

The apple was the king of colonial fruits, but other fruits also played a prominent role in colonial culture. Peaches were particularly common in the southern British colonies. William Byrd, the eighteenth-century Virginia planter and immigration promoter, praised the fruit, describing the many ways it could be processed:

Unbelievable amounts are dried. These are, however, first peeled, and afterwards mashed in a mortar until a thick paste is formed, from which one makes cakes or bread, and dries them afterwards for sometime in the sun. They may then be kept for any need. Such bread is very good, as also healthful to eat and to cook. Good fancy cakes are likewise made from them, as well as beer, which is very pleasant and refreshing, [it] is also good for fever. From the juice of these peaches a drink called Mobby can be produced. It is much more agreeable than apple juice or pear juice, and, when it is distilled, yields a very good brandy. (*William Byrd's Natural History of Virginia*, 48)

GRAPES AND WINEMAKING

Winemaking was never a major colonial industry, but it was actively carried on in some parts of the South. The French colonists of Louisiana brought skills and stocks of wine grapes with them. The vintages they produced were consumed locally but were not competitive with the wines of France itself. The Spanish produced wine in their missions and settlements in Arizona and New Mexico. These Catholic societies had a particular incentive to produce wine—priests needed it to perform the Mass. Britain, on the other hand, a Protestant country with no domestic wine industry, was interested in promoting winemaking in some of its colonies to reduce its dependence on imports from actually or potentially hostile Continental European states. The problem was that the British lacked the expertise and skills of grape growers and winemakers. All British plans to promote wine culture in America required luring the French, Italians, or others from lands experienced with winemaking to their colonies.

PITCH AND TAR

Not all tree crops were eventually meant for human consumption. From early in North American settlement, pitch, tar, and turpentine were important commodities. They were particularly vital for shipbuilders, which meant that the Royal Navy took an active role in securing these products. They were often referred to as "naval stores." The first paper ever given by a colonial resident to the Royal Society, England's premiere scientific society, was John Winthrop Jr.'s description of how pitch was made in New England.

Before the establishment of the American industry, England had relied on imports from the vast forests of the Baltic Sea in northern Europe. These resources were controlled by Sweden in the seventeenth and eighteenth centuries, and the English government was very interested in breaking this dependency by exploiting American resources. The insatiable need of the navy and merchant shipping for naval stores became particularly acute in the early eighteenth century, when the great Baltic war between Sweden and Russia interrupted supplies. Throughout the eighteenth century, the ups and downs of Britain's relationship with Sweden would affect the government's interest in American resources.

The anonymous author of *American Husbandry*, published in London on the eve of the American Revolution, described how North Carolinians extracted turpentine, one of the province's most important exports, from pine trees:

Pitch, tar, and turpentine are made throughout this province, which is a proof, among others, that the country is very far from being well settled even yet. These commodities are the produce of that species of pine called the pitch-pine; they are all made by different preparations from the resin of this tree. Turpentine is this resin or gum as it flows from the tree through holes cut for that purpose, the heat of the sun assists this extraction, and the operation of it is performed while the tree is growing. It is well known that oil of turpentine is a distillation from it. From the holes cut to gain the turpentine, little channels are made in the trees to conduct the resin down to the foot of them, where boxes and bowls are placed to receive it. After the oil is distilled from the turpentine, the residuum is the resin in a very thick consistence, which is dried, and then is in the lumps we have it in England. (*American Husbandry*, 244)

Tar was made by a different process. Pine logs were heated in an enclosed space, which prevented them from burning. The heat forced the tar out of the logs, where it was collected in a pipe running off from the bottom of the chamber in which the logs were burning.

Pitch was made from tar by boiling it. William Bartram, the eighteenth-century Philadelphia naturalist and traveler, contrasted the practice of the French colonists around Mobile, Alabama in boiling tar into pitch in huge iron pots with those of the British colonists: "In Carolina the inhabitants pursue a different method; when they design to make pitch, they dig large holes in the ground, near the tar kiln, which they line with a thick coat of good clay, into which they conduct a sufficient quantity of tar, and set it on fire, suffering it to flame and evaporate a length of time sufficient to convert it into pitch, and when cool, lade it into barrels, and so on until they have consumed all the tar, or made a sufficient quantity of pitch for their purposes" (William Bartram, *Writings*, 339).

POTASH

Wood burned to ashes was the raw material for the creation of the most important alkali of the early modern chemical world, a crude form of potassium carbonate called potash. The word *potassium* is derived from potash. Large-scale potash making in America began as a profitable side-line to the necessary work of clearing trees from land for farming. Potash was also made from domestic ashes but on a far smaller scale, and the resulting inferior product was usually restricted to household use. In the decades before the American Revolution, there was an attempt in Virginia to make potash from tobacco waste, but it failed. Potash was made by burning logs and other wood to ashes, then placing the ashes in a barrel lined with twigs and straw. (Unlike the carpenter or the cabinetmaker, the potash maker did not distinguish between types of wood: ashes were ashes!) Potash makers poured water on top of the ashes, dissolving out the salts. If lye for soapmaking was desired instead of solid potash, the process would stop here. Otherwise, the water, potash lye, was then evaporated in an iron kettle and the remaining substance, "brown salt" was heated in a smaller kettle until most of the original organic material was gone. The result, potash, was packed in casks for the market. Potassium carbonate usually made up less than a quarter of the mass, but it found a variety of uses, from household soapmaking to glass manufacture. Small amounts were even used in baking to help cakes rise.

A form of potash that contained a much higher concentration of potassium carbonate was pearlash. It was formed by dissolving crude potash in just enough cold water to dissolve the potassium carbonate while leaving the other substances undissolved. The resulting liquid was then filtered and heated again. Pearlash could contain as much as 95 percent potassium carbonate and was more expensive than crude potash.

3

Making a Living: Manufacturing and Industry

Manufacturing in the American colonies covered a broad range of goods made for local and distant consumption and use. Workers made barrels, clothing, teapots, and a huge range of other items in workshops, households, and plantations. American manufacturing was shaped both by the traditions colonists brought with them from many parts of Europe and by the unique conditions and needs of the colonies. Although American manufacturers were not usually as technically advanced as the best European artisans, colonists were innovative and willing to try new methods. Manufacturing took place in many colonial societies, but the developed urban societies and economies of British North America were far advanced over the Spanish and French colonies.

Anglo-American colonial promoters were eager to import technically knowledgeable people from different areas of Europe. The importance of Continental workers for industrial technology in the Anglo-American colonies can be seen as far back as the first ventures of the Virginia Company in the early seventeenth century, and it continued through the eighteenth century and beyond. The Virginia Company drew upon Continental glassmaking knowledge, bringing first Polish and Dutch and then Italian glassmakers to get a glassworks up and running. A few decades later, the first sawmill in Massachusetts Bay was built by Danes. The creation of an iron industry in early eighteenth-century Virginia was built on the immigration of skilled German and Swiss miners and ironworkers.

MANUFACTURING IN THE FIRST ENGLISH COLONIES

The most industrially minded of the early English colonization companies was the Virginia Company, which wanted to diversify the economy of the Virginia colony beyond tobacco monoculture. The company's ambitious plans included ironworks, silkworm cultivation and silk manufacture, and the first colonial glassworks, founded in 1608, for which Dutch and Polish workers were imported. After the failure of the first glassworks, a second attempt was made with Italian workers. These efforts were unsuccessful for many reasons, including the attacks of the Native Americans and other disasters that struck the colony and the ever-present lure of quick wealth in tobacco. The technical problems also proved more formidable than the company's optimistic promoters first thought.

The New England Company was somewhat more cautious—and more successful—in founding industrial enterprises. The first large-scale American cloth enterprise was founded in 1638, as 20 Yorkshire families with textile experience were settled in Rowley, Massachusetts, and a fulling mill was established. The following year a glassworks was set up at Salem. In the 1640s, John Winthrop Jr., an enthusiast for science and technology, attempted to establish an ironworks, first at Braintree and then at Lynn. The works produced wrought iron suitable to be made into bolts, nails, and tools. Despite the technical ingenuity of the project, high labor costs and other economic factors eventually brought it to a halt. Another of the largest American manufacturing efforts in the seventeenth century began around 1685, when the first large colonial potworks was set up in Burlington, New Jersey, by the physician and proprietor of New Jersey Daniel Coxe. Coxe claimed to have spent about 2,000 English pounds on the plant, and planned to export stoneware to the neighboring colonies, as well as Barbados and Jamaica. However, the project was abandoned shortly afterward, when Coxe sold his interest in New Jersey.

SALT

One of the simplest, yet most necessary, substances to manufacture was salt. In the colonial period, salt was viewed less as a seasoning and more as a preservative, especially for fish. The great New England cod fishery was utterly dependent upon salt to preserve its catch for the international market. Salt was also used to preserve meat and poultry and in the preparation of furs, another vital early American export industry. Most of the salt that came into British North America was imported from Europe, often in exchange for colonial salt fish, but colonists from the earliest days of colonization had attempted to create their own sources of salt. Early colonial saltworks, such as the one set up at Cape Charles in the Virginia colony in 1614, followed the traditional European practice of catching seawater in shallow pools, then relying on the sun to evaporate the water, leaving the salt. Although some colonial saltworks were carried on in this manner for decades, most were economic failures, particularly in New England, which had a great need for salt to treat its cod but could not evaporate it effectively because of its cold, wet climate. The great salt producers on the American mainland were found much farther south, where the Spanish had taken over the Maya saltworks in Yucatan. The Dutch in New York, facing climate problems similar to those of New England, also had little success in salt manufacture. Boiling sea water, an obvious alternative to evaporation given America's bountiful supply of wood, required too much labor to be profitable, particularly given the heavy regulation imposed on saltworks by colonial governments, who wanted the salt to be affordable.

The greatest obstacle to American salt manufacturing, however, turned out to be economic rather than technological. British authorities favored British colonists using British salt, a cheap but mediocre product that supplied much of the need for salt in the colonies while keeping them dependent on Britain. The Caribbean, which had a thriving salt industry on small islands where pools and small lakes of trapped seawater evaporated, leaving salt on their shores, also provided salt to the mainland colonies. Cheap foreign salt drove out American manufacture.

Colonists had more success finding natural salt springs or outcroppings of salt than they did manufacturing it from seawater. Although Native Americans had exploited such resources for centuries, the first major encounter with salt resources by a European occurred in 1645, when the French Jesuit missionary Jerome Lallemant discovered that the land of the Onondaga people of what is now upstate New York included a salt spring. The Onondaga later adapted French saltmaking techniques and built a profitable business. Other deposits of salt were found in Virginia and Louisiana. America's overall salt shortage persisted, however, to the point where one of the major problems of the American Revolution was breaking or circumventing the British blockade on imports of European and Caribbean salt.

TANNING

One of the most important colonial American industries was the making of animal hides into leather by tanning. Uses for leather included boots and shoes, saddles and bridles, carriage parts, breeches, and the covers of bound books. Although some farmers tanned leather in small amounts as an adjunct to livestock raising, most leather was not produced in households but by artisans called "tanners" in special buildings usually positioned far away from habitations. Tanneries were shunned because of their horrible smell. Tanners were necessary, however, both to produce leather for immediate domestic use and for export. Commercial tanneries were some of the first manufacturing businesses to be established in Anglo-America, and were encouraged by colonial legislatures.

Many types of animals provided hides for tanning. Wild animal skins, particularly deerskins, were traded particularly in the early days of colonization and in frontier areas. One of the most important exports of Spanish New Mexico was wild animal hides from buffalo, antelope, and deer. In the English-settled regions, most tanned hides came from domestic animals.

Tanners had to put their hides through several different treatments. When hides were received from a farmer or butcher, the tanner first trimmed the extremities such as the head and legs. Cowhides, because of their large size, were usually cut in half down the middle. The tanner also removed whatever flesh remained on the hide. The skins were then washed, preferably in running water, for as long as a day. The next step was removing the hair. This was done by immersing the skins in lime, which loosened the hair. The process could take as long as a year. Lime vats were made of wood or masonry and held about 125 cubic feet. Once the skins were removed from the lime and the hair had been scraped off, the lime itself had to be removed. This was done by rinsing in water (tanneries relied on a supply of fresh, clean water and were often situated by streams). A common but not strictly necessary procedure after this was "bating." Hides were immersed in a mixture of chicken or dog dung, salt, and water to remove the lime and soften them.

All of this had been preliminary work for the actual tanning. An alternative process, "tawing," was used for some light and thin skins. Tanning relied on a chemical reaction of hides with tannin, a substance usually found in plants. Tannin was secured by crushing bark or other plant material in an animal-powered mill. Such bark mills were frequently part of tanneries. The most common sources of tannin were the bark of oak, including black, white, and red oak in the north and hemlock bark in the South. Sumac leaves were also a common source. The hides were laid in a tanning vat, usually dug into the ground and about 6 feet cubed. Tanners alternated a layer of crushed bark with a layer of hides, along with water. The tannin tended to settle to the bottom, so the bottom hides got the most. Tanners equalized the exposure of the hides by rotating them. Tanning was a slow process, and the highest-quality leather could be tanned for well over a year. Once removed from the vat, the tanned leather was hung up to dry.

Once the leather was dried, the manufacturing process continued. Although some leather, such as that for the bottoms of shoes, could be used as is from the drying rack, much of it had to be softened and trimmed. Preparing leather for use was called "currying." In most places, tanning and currying was carried on at the same place, but in some large cities currying emerged as a separate trade. Curriers used several methods to soften and polish leather, including soaking it in water, shaving it with a special knife for even thickness and a smooth surface, beating it, stretching it, or treating it with oils. The ultimate goal was a soft, lustrous piece of leather.

FOOTWEAR

American colonists solved the problem of shoeing themselves in a range of ways, from elaborate boots to nothing at all. Spanish colonists and French traders adapted the comfortable leather moccasin from Native Americans in place of the European shoe and boot. At the other end, some aristocrats in British America, particularly in the South, continued to import their shoes from Europe through the colonial period. But most leather shoes were made in the colonies themselves.

Unlike clothing, shoes were not usually made in the home but by specialized artisans called "cordwainers" or shoemakers. Workers who repaired shoes were called "cobblers." Shoemakers made up one of the largest bodies of colonial craftspeople. They tended to concentrate in urban areas. Shoes were made from two kinds of leather: hard, rigid, thick leather for the soles and lighter, more flexible leather for the uppers. The uppers were made in two parts, held together with buckles or "lachets." The uppers were sewn to the soles with waxed linen or hemp. To protect the soles, some shoes had iron plates attached, or additional soles held onto the main sole with "hobnails."

Some shoes were "bespoke"—the customer brought in the leather, and the shoe was molded to a wooden last in the shape of the customer's foot. There were no distinctions, however, between left and right shoes. Other shoes were made without a specific customer in mind. Over time, this became the standard mode of business for shoemakers. By the last decades of the colonial era, shoemaking had become one of America's first centralized industries. Lynn, Massachusetts, where techniques of mass production had been introduced by a Welsh immigrant named John Adam Dagyr, displaced the Boston shoemakers and became the shoemaking capital of British America.

FUR

One of the most important early American export trades was that in furs. The French and Dutch colonies in North America depended for their very existence on the fur trade with Native Americans, and although the British colonies had a more diversified economy, the fur and hide trade was also important for them. Originally, much of the processing of fur and hides was done in Europe, but as the colonial economy developed more of it was done in America.

One of the great growth industries following the discovery of America was hatmaking. The most common material used to make hats was felt, a product of the underfur of fur-bearing animals, most commonly beaver. In many areas, the beaver was hunted to extinction to provide hats. A hat-maker took a beaver skin and pulled all the long hairs, the visible fur from it, and then shaved the remaining underfur off the skin. The underfur was then compacted until it held together in a solid mass of felt. Beaver underfur held together naturally, one of the reasons it was the preferred material. Another common hat material, wool, had to be helped with glue. Felt was processed in hot and cold water to compact and shape it. Finally the felt was blocked—molded over a wooden form in the shape of a hat. Originally, the role of America in the hat trade was to supply beaverskins to European makers, but, inevitably, American cities developed their own industry. The British tried to control the competition from colonial hatmakers with the Hat Act of 1732, placing restrictions on exports of colonial hats and the size of hatmaking workshops. Never well enforced, the act proved ineffectual.

METAL PRODUCTION

Although colonial North Americans did not share in the wealth of silver and gold exploited by the Spanish colonists of Mexico and Peru, metal was essential to their economies and lives.

Central to the early European colonists' establishment of their settlements in the face of Native American opposition was the colonists' use of iron, a metal that Native Americans had no tradition of employing for tools or weapons. The eastern North American combination of readily available iron ore and abundant wood meant that Anglo-American colonial promoters envisioned an iron industry from the beginnings of permanent colonization. Iron in North America was not deep mined—indeed little deep mining of any sort took place—but refined out of relatively common iron ore. In the seventeenth century, iron was smelted out of iron ore by heating with charcoal made of hardwoods. Although English ironworks switched from charcoal to coal in the mid-eighteenth century, Americans, blessed with an abundance of wood, continued using charcoal until the nineteenth century.

The crudest way to refine iron was "blooming." The resources required for a bloomery were little beyond those available to a blacksmith. A charcoal fire heated with a bellows was used to reduce an iron oxide to iron. The bloom, composed of iron and "slag," or waste material, was repeatedly pounded with a hammer to drive out the slag. Bloomeries produced small amounts of iron and demanded heavy labor, but they were cheap to set up and met the needs of small communities seeking iron for domestic and farming uses.

High-volume iron operations used the blast furnace. Blast furnaces stood between 20 and 30 feet high, clothed on the outside with granite or some other local stone and on the inside with imported stone capable of withstanding the intense heat. Colonial American blast furnaces used charcoal as fuel and a rock with a low melting temperature such as limestone as a flux to take away rock and impurities from the ore. The carbon monoxide gas produced by the charcoal reduced the iron oxide to iron,

This massive blast furnace was part of the Principio Iron
Works in Maryland, one of colonial America's largest iron
enterprises. Courtesy of the Library of Congress.

and the extreme heat of the blast furnace, whose oxygen was provided by
water-powered bellows, liquefied the metal. The metal could be poured
out in long bars called "pigs." This pig iron was then refined to remove
the carbon it had absorbed in the furnace. This was done by repeated
meltings at a refinery hearth. Then the iron was hammered into shape.
The resulting product was wrought iron.

The Swedish Lutheran pastor Israel Acrelius, who visited America in
the mid-eighteenth century, praised American iron while comparing it
unfavorably to the product of his native country. His *A History of New
Sweden*, published in 1759, was written in Swedish for a Swedish audience and recounts the careers of the Swedish settlements on the Delaware
during Swedish, Dutch, and English rule. It contains extensive discussion
of American ironworks, indicating that some eighteenth-century Swedes

were concerned about potential American competition. "The American iron is generally soft and tough, and is regarded as most suitable for house and ship-building, for which also it is employed; but for use in horse-shoes and wagon-tires it is far inferior to the Swedish iron. But good iron can also be smelted at many points, whereof edge-tools, and all sorts of implements, are made in the country, such as axes, scythes, sickes with file-like edges for reaping, spades, shovels, hoes, plows, with other articles, all of which are obtained in the country better made than they could be brought from England" (Acrelius, *A History of New Sweden*, 167).

Steel was a different problem, presenting greater technological and political challenges. Steel is iron with the just the right mixture of carbon, which gives it metallurgical properties different from cast or wrought iron. Steel had been known for many centuries, but it was made in small quantities, and was not the ubiquitous material it has become in the modern era. Small quantities of steel, however, were extremely useful. Its ability to hold a keen edge made it indispensable for cutting implements like knives, razors, and axes. Usually steel was used for the cutting edge only, rather than for the whole implement. Steel tools were included in the supplies of the earliest Anglo-American colonists in Virginia and New England, but for many decades steel had to be imported. Steel production in America began around 1730, but American steel was of relatively poor quality. The best steel in America continued to be that imported from the Sheffield region of England, a traditional steelmaking center. The idea of colonists not needing the mother country for steel and steel products alarmed British manufacturers, who goaded Parliament into passing the Iron Act in 1750. The act encouraged Americans to export pig iron to Britain but forbade them to make steel. This act seems to have been widely ignored, but steel's technical challenges remained daunting.

SMITHS AND METALWORKERS

The most essential and versatile metalworker to American colonists was the local blacksmith. Blacksmiths had been represented among the earliest Anglo-American colonists, and plied their trade in cities, towns, and villages throughout the colonies. The blacksmith's tools and workshop were not very complicated. A charcoal-fed fire, the hearth, was kept very hot with a bellows. Indeed, the heat of the blacksmith's fire made his shop a popular gathering place in cold weather! When iron laid on the coals was sufficiently softened to be malleable, the blacksmith pulled it off the hearth with tongs and placed it on the anvil, a solid block of iron, where the iron to be worked was beaten into the desired form with hammers. Finally, it was tempered by being plunged into freshwater or saltwater. An endless array of iron products for farm, home, and workshop, ranging from mundane but indispensable horseshoes and nails to the elaborate decorative grillwork found in the homes of the wealthy in Philadelphia and Charleston poured forth from the hundreds of blacksmith shops in the colonies. Even the blacksmith's tools themselves, the hammer and tongs, were made by blacksmiths; anvils, however, had to be imported from Europe until late in the colonial era.

Blacksmithing, like other forms of metal work, required great technical knowledge, but this was primarily passed on through apprenticeships rather than printed books and manuals. Most blacksmiths were general workers, but with the more diverse economy of the late colonial period came more specialized iron craftsmen, working mostly in cities. Iron specialists included locksmiths, "cutlers," who made fine blades out of steel that was mostly imported, and "whitesmiths." Whitesmiths made complex iron machinery, such as scale balances, and their work involved the filing and polishing of iron to a high (for the period) degree of precision. Another high-end blacksmith specialist was the maker of ornamental grillwork. A common type of specialist smith likely to be found in the country as well as the city was the wheelwright, who made iron parts for wagons and carts, including chains and brake levers.

Although no metal rivaled iron for use, other kinds of metal were more decorative or had specific useful properties. Metalworkers specializing in a variety of metals were common in colonial cities, particularly in the eighteenth century as genteel culture spread. Accoutrements like tea sets and silver candlesticks became increasingly necessary for the self-defined upper classes: the ladies and gentlemen of colonial cities and rural mansions.

Silversmiths were increasingly prominent in Dutch New York and the Anglo-American colonies. The most celebrated early Anglo-American silversmith was John Hull, the minter of the famous Pine Tree shillings of the Massachusetts Bay Colony. Colonial silversmithing culminated in the career of Paul Revere, artisan, businessman, and patriotic hero of the early Revolutionary War. Like many silversmiths, Revere was of French origin, the descendant of exiled Huguenots, French Protestants. Unlike iron, silver was valuable not chiefly for its practical uses but because it was beautiful and represented wealth. Silver coins, many originating in the Spanish colonies, circulated throughout the Americas in the seventeenth and eighteenth centuries. The growing wealth of urban colonists in the eighteenth century led to an increase in the silver supply as well as ever-present fears of being robbed. Silversmiths responded by working silver into massive plates (easier to keep safe than silver coins) and easily distinguishable silver spoons.

Unlike iron, silver had a low enough melting temperature to be actually liquefied in colonial furnaces. Following melting, silver was alloyed with copper to strengthen it. Silver ingots could be shaped and decorated using a variety of techniques, from cold-hammering to engraving. Silver was soft enough to be marked using stamps or dies, necessary in mints and commonly used to decorate items like spoons and table knives. Unlike most blacksmiths, the silversmith had to keep up with fashions in decoration, often using stylebooks printed in England or the Continent.

A more rare, specialized metalworker was the coppersmith. Copper was valuable enough to be deep mined, but it was also in scarcer supply in the areas of European settlement in America than iron or silver. The British and the Dutch sought copper deposits with avidity, but the major copper resources of North America were located in the Great Lakes region, dominated by France. Jesuit missionaries among the Native Americans of the region attempted to get French businessmen and administrators interested in exploiting it, but the remoteness of the area prevented copper mining from developing there. Lack of experienced copper miners and workers was also a limitation. Even after the establishment of the first Anglo-American copper mine in Simsbury, Connecticut, in 1705, German copper workers had to be lured to immigrate to the area to fully exploit the mine's resources. Simsbury proved a successful mine, but most refined copper suitable for making into useful products still had to be originally imported from England in the form of copper sheet. Of course, like other metals, copper was also frequently recycled. Simply throwing away a metal item would be unheard-of waste!

Many uses of copper took advantage of its ability to transmit heat quickly and evenly. Copper utensils such as kettles, skillets, frying pans, and teakettles were common among wealthier settlers, and copper kettles were a common item traded with Native Americans. Copper vessels were also used in industrial processes such as brewing, distilling, and dyemaking. "Tinkling cones," cones ranging from about half an inch to an inch and a half and commonly worn in strings by fur traders and Native Americans in the Northwest, were made of copper. Copper's ductility meant that such simple objects could be made by people other than skilled metalworkers. Copper was also used for making plates for engravers.

The uses of copper increased when it was alloyed with other metals. Common copper alloys included brass, an alloy of copper and zinc, and bronze or gun metal, an alloy of copper and tin. Neither zinc nor tin were found in America, so brass and bronze had to be imported. Brass founders were another specialized group of craftspeople. Brass was distorted very little under heat, which made it a preferred metal for precision goods such as clock parts, surveying instruments, and bookbinder's stamps and rolls. Its decorative qualities and durability also made it desirable for doorknobs and doorknockers, and brass wire was traded with the Native Americans. Like iron, brass could be made into points for spears and arrows, particularly valued in trade with those fur-trading Natives who lived far from the colonial frontier and had not switched to firearms. Brass was also used in "brazing," a procedure for soldering two pieces of iron together.

Pewter, an alloy of tin and other metals including antimony, was imported from Europe and commonly used in Anglo-American households for

This copper "tinkling cone" was manufactured to be traded to Native Americans. Courtesy of the Flowerdew Hundred Foundation.

cups, plates, tankards, coffeepots, candlesticks, and other domestic goods. Pewter items, of less value and status than silver, were usually cast rather than hammered into shape. There were few specialized pewterers in the colonies, however, as the lack of tin and antimony in America meant that most pewter goods were imported from England. Tinsmithing was even rarer, and was a relatively late arrival to the colonies. The first successful colonial tinsmith was a Scottish immigrant, Edward Pattison, who settled in Berlin, Connecticut, around 1750. The area of Berlin became the center of American tinsmithing, but the trade only took off after the American Revolution.

POWER TECHNOLOGY AND MILLS

Like all preindustrial societies, the colonies of North America principally ran on the power of muscle, whether human or animal. One of the most important technological advantages European settlers possessed over Native Americans was the muscle power of domesticated horses and oxen. However, the colonists also suffered from a shortage of human muscle relative to their contemporaries in heavily populated, labor-rich Europe. They therefore made somewhat greater use proportionately of inorganic power sources than did Europeans, although the technology they used was no different.

For power technology, the colonists used a technology widely used in Europe since ancient times, the mill. Mills could be powered both by human or animal muscle power and by inorganic power, notably wind and water. Although Americans drew on all these sources of power for their mills, water-powered mills were particularly suited for eastern North America due to the shortage of labor and the presence of easily exploited quick-running streams. They became the most common form of mill. All three forms of water mill—the horizontal mill with the wheel on its side, the undershot mill with the water turning the mill running along the bottom, and the most efficient, the overshot with the water running along the top of the mill—appeared in colonial America. Mills had many uses. Two of the most important were gristmills for grinding grain and sawmills for cutting lumber into boards. Sawmills, which used straight saws rather than the later circular saw, wasted considerably more wood than did sawyers cutting lumber by hand (sawdust also polluted mill streams when not properly disposed of), but they were also much faster. The abundance of wood in early America and the demand for boards meant that speed was more important than efficiency. Another use of mill power was fulling woolen cloth. Fulling mills, mostly animal-powered, were found in New England from the 1640s, spreading to the mid-Atlantic and southern states after 1700. Animal-powered mills also crushed oak and spruce bark for tannin and apples for cider. By the mid-eighteenth century, mills were grinding tobacco into the newly popular product, snuff. Thousands of mills dotted the colonial landscape, to the point that a shortage of millwrights became a problem.

LOCAL, HOUSEHOLD, AND PLANTATION MANUFACTURING

More modest manufacturing activities serving local needs emerged in the first decades of colonization and persisted throughout the colonial period. Kilns for the manufacture of crude earthenware appeared shortly after colonization, and home-based industry was common in the American colonies, as it also was in Britain and Europe. The Spanish settlers used ceramics made by Native Americans.

Manufacturing increased on Chesapeake plantations in the late seventeenth and early eighteenth centuries, when the growing exhaustion of the land meant that returns on labor in tobacco farming were diminishing. Planters seeking to shrink the amount they were paying for imports encouraged the manufacture of shoes, cloth, and simple tools. This work was mostly carried out by waged or indentured white workers rather than by slaves.

While women worked on preserving and cooking food, spinning, and weaving, European and Native American men in the Anglo-American colonies filled in periods when the labor demands of agriculture were low by availing themselves of America's abundance of wood to make potash, roofing shingles of cedar, and barrel staves of red and white oak, although the barrels themselves were made by specialists called coopers. In addition to their use in American storage and shipping, barrels and casks were also exported to the wood-poor West Indies. Rather than being sawed, shingles and barrel staves were cut from blocks of wood using a metal wedge with a handle, a once-common tool called a "froe." Gourds and calabashes, or "bottle gourds," were dried and made into containers and vessels.

4

The World of the Sea

The sea was both a path and a resource for early modern Americans. In addition to being the road by which the first Europeans arrived in the Americas, the sea was also exploited by some of the earliest colonial industries, such as codfishing and whaling. These industries continued to be important to the colonial economy through the eighteenth century.

COMING TO AMERICA: CROSSING THE OCEAN

The early colonization of America benefited from navigational and design improvements in European ships and posed new challenges. The principal navigational improvement was the magnetic compass, used to find the direction of a ship. The compass had originally been invented in China. It had reached Europe and was in general use in the late medieval period. The large, three-masted oceangoing ship was developed in the fourteenth and fifteenth centuries.

Centralizing and disseminating navigational and cartographic information was part of the discovery of the Americas. The Casa de Contratación, founded in 1503 to regulate Spanish movement to and from the New World, trained pilots and captains in the arts of cartography and navigation, systematizing the information Spanish captains gathered from the Americas. The Casa de Contratación and other institutions helped make oceanic navigation a more textual procedure. Sea captains and pilots now made greater use of maps and charts, as opposed to passing down and receiving navigational knowledge orally. But information was disseminated only within strict limits. It benefited Spain for Spanish captains to know the routes to America; it hurt Spain if French or English captains had the same knowledge. The earliest European explorers realized the importance of excluding rivals from navigational knowledge, and therefore, the wealth of the Americas. This strategy ultimately failed, as not for the first or last time it proved impossible to permanently keep information from active rivals.

SHIPBUILDING

Some of the earliest ships built in North America were the products not of high technology but of desperation and ingenuity. Álvaro Cabeza de Vaca, survivor of a disastrous Spanish expedition in southern North America in the early sixteenth century, described in his memoir how at one point the desperate Spanish explorers fashioned ships:

We had no tools, no iron, no smithery, no oakum, no pitch, no tackling, in sum, nothing of what was indispensable. Neither was there anyone to instruct us in shipbuilding ... The next day, God provided that one of the men should come and say he would make wooden flues and deerskin bellows, and since we were in such a state that anything with the appearance of relief seemed acceptable, we told him to go to work, and agreed to make from our stirrups, spurs, crossbows and other iron implements the nails, saws and hatchets that we so greatly needed for our purpose.... We gathered plenty of palmettos, twisting and preparing their fiber and husk and using it for the boats instead of oakum. The work on these boats was done by the only carpenter we had, and owing to great effort, progressed so rapidly that, begun on the fourth day of August, on the twentieth day of the month of September five boats of twenty-two cubits were ready, calked with palmetto oakum and tarred with pitch, which a Greek called Don Teodoro had made from some pine trees. From the husk of palmettos and the tails and manes of horses we made ropes and tackles, from our shirts we made sails, and from the junipers that grew there we made oars, which we believed were necessary. The land into which our sins had placed us was such that only with great difficulty could we find stones for ballast and anchors for the boats, since we had not seen a stone in the whole country. (Cabeza de Vaca, *Chronicle of the Narvaez Expedition*, 23–24)

Shipbuilding emerged from these modest beginnings to become one of colonial North America's most important industries. British-American colonists, the only ones to establish a shipbuilding industry, had the advantages of ready access to the coast and most important, an abundance of wood. Shipbuilding was a top concern of the early colonization companies. The cod fishery, central to the early Massachusetts economy, and trade, whether across the Atlantic, along the coast, or to the Caribbean, required vessels that could be created locally. The first vessel built in the English colonies of North America was the *Virginia*, a 50-foot pinnace built by colonists of a short-lived colony at the mouth of the

Kennebec in Maine in 1607. A "pinnace" was usually a coast-hugging vessel, movable under either oars or sails but capable of ocean voyaging. The colony was abandoned the next year, but the *Virginia* sailed between Virginia and London for 20 years before being wrecked on the Irish coast. In 1622, the Virginia Company sent out Captain Thomas Barwick and 25 ship's carpenters to construct small vessels for coasting. Barwick died shortly after he arrived, though, and the plan came to nothing. There was a more successful effort at Plymouth, where a ship's carpenter was sent in 1624.

The leading shipbuilding colony in the early seventeenth century was New England. The New England Company sent six shipwrights to Salem in 1629 to build "shallops," small undecked vessels, for fishing. John Winthrop Sr.'s "bark," a small decked sailing ship built for fishing and coastal trade, *Blessing of the Bay*, was launched on July 4, 1631. New England was building oceangoing ships in the 1630s—the 60-ton *Rebecca* was launched from Medford in November 1633, and the 120-ton *Desire* from Marblehead in 1636. To encourage shipbuilding, the General Court of Massachusetts exempted ship's carpenters from militia training in 1639.

The centers of New England shipbuilding in the late seventeenth century were Charlestown, Salem, Salisbury, Portsmouth, and particularly Boston. Boston was not advantageously situated for access to the wood and iron shipbuilders needed, but its capital and good harbor facilities enabled it to dominate the trade. Connecticut also acquired a shipbuilding industry, centered in New London. The largest merchant ship ever produced in colonial America—720 tons—was built by the New London shipwright John Jeffrey, and launched in 1725.

New England shipbuilders were building not only for local needs, but for British shippers as well. Shipbuilders in New England had an advantage over their English competitors not only in the supply of wood but in design. English shipbuilders were still building dual-use ships, capable of being used as cargo ships or warships. This meant that English ships, unlike the Dutch *fluyts* or flyboats, were not designed for optimum carrying capacity. The *Susan Constant*, leader of the Jamestown expedition, had had so little capacity for carrying supplies that she had been obliged to stop in the West Indies for food and water on the way to North America. New England ships were pure cargo ships, capacious in comparison. So successful was the New England industry that some English mercantilists were concerned that it was draining wealth from the mother country. New England shipbuilding was further stimulated by the need to replace the considerable English losses in the war of the League of Augsburg and the War of the Spanish Succession (Queen Anne's War). Other foreign markets for American ships included the French and Spanish West Indies as well as Spain and Portugal.

The second major shipbuilding center to emerge in British America was Philadelphia. William Penn encouraged shipwrights to settle in his new colony. The late seventeenth century saw a boom in Philadelphia ship-building, which completely dominated the industry in Pennsylvania and the Delaware Valley. By the early eighteenth century, Philadelphia was second only to Boston as a builder of ships. The types of ships Americans built were also changing. The pinnace disappeared in the late seventeenth century, replaced by the "sloop." The sloop, a single-mast vessel of Dutch origin, came in two main forms: small vessels between 20 and 40 tons that specialized in coastal trade, and West India traders of 50 tons or more. Unlike the pinnace, it was a pure sailing vessel.

By the early eighteenth century, Boston was by far the leading harbor in the British Empire outside of England, with a 1,600-foot wharf constructed between 1710 and 1713. (A 2,000-foot wharf was later built at Newport.) New York, with a merchant fleet mostly composed of sloops, was a distant second. Although shipbuilding, along with the rest of the economy, slumped after Queen Anne's War, the American shipbuilding industry was still a formidable competitor to Britain's. In 1724 the master shipwrights of the Thames, the center of British shipbuilding, petitioned the board of trade to restrict American shipbuilding, claiming that the emigration of British shipwrights to the Americas would threaten the home industry. The board refused to intervene, preferring an American shipbuilding industry rather than American textile exports paying for imports from Britain.

Ships made technological demands far beyond wood, rope, and sail. The development of the colonial iron industry in the eighteenth century aided American shipbuilders, although cordage and sailcloth would continue to be imported until the American Revolution. Many areas of colonial America produced the pitch, turpentine, and tar needed to build and maintain ships. These products were all derived from pine trees, and the industry moved from one area to another as pines were exhausted. North Carolina, an agriculturally backward province sand-wiched between the Chesapeake Bay area and the South Carolina Low Country, replaced New England in the eighteenth century as America's leading producer of naval stores.

One great resource America presented to shipbuilders were its tall trees, which could be made into excellent masts. In the British-American colonies, the Royal Navy attempted to establish a monopoly over the best trees, marking them with the broad arrow as reserved for naval use. This inspired considerable resentment from colonists, who wished to profit from the trees themselves. No matter who made them, masts were physically impressive objects. The seventeenth-century Boston lawyer Samuel Sewall recorded in his diary a special trip he had made to see a mast hauled: "Ride into swamp to see a Mast drawn. Of about 26 inches or 28. About two and thirty yoke of Oxen before, and about four yoke by the side of the Mast, between the fore and hinder wheels. "Twas a very notable sight" (Sewall, *Diary of Samuel Sewall*, 189).

FISHING

America's seas, rivers, and lakes offered a bounty of fish and seafood for local consumption and export. One fish in particular, the cod, was one of the earliest links between Europe and North America, and in the sixteenth century, the cod fishery of the North Atlantic rivaled the Spanish mines of Mexico and Peru as a source of wealth for Europeans. Throughout the colonial era, European, and later American, fishing fleets gathered in the waters off Newfoundland and New England to take its bountiful harvest of cheap protein and trade with the Native American peoples along the coast. The first English voyage of exploration, that of the Italian in English service John Cabot in the late fifteenth century, revealed to Europeans the richness of the North Atlantic fishing grounds. Cabot left a legacy of English involvement with the fishing trade, although the English were far less prominent than the French and Portuguese until the second half of the sixteenth century. The English captain Bartholomew Gosnold gave Cape Cod its name from the wealth of the fish he found there in his voyage of 1602.

With the European settlement of the Americas, fishermen based in the colonies began to rival their Old World contemporaries. New England, an agriculturally poor land but one with many good harbors and active codfishing areas only a dozen or so miles from shore, was by far the most active center of commercial fishing. The cod industry had been an economic necessity since the early colonial days, and the importance of fishing actually increased in the eighteenth century. Like other cod fishers, New England fishermen used lines used to catch fish individually rather than nets as the cod were too large and too deep in the water to be netted. (Smaller fish caught for bait like herring and capelin were netted.) The technology of codfishing was not very advanced from the Middle Ages—iron fishhooks were baited and cast to the bottom where the cod usually fed. Lead sinkers weighted the lines. Codfish are not dainty eaters; they are omnivores who swim around with their mouths open, and so they were vulnerable to the baited hook. Cod also does not fight on the line, and once hooked, need only be hauled up.

Small-scale fishing for personal or local consumption was even more widespread than commercial fishing. In South Carolina, "fishing Negroes" used nets and boats adapted from West African designs to catch fish. Freshwater fishers used a variety of techniques, from the eel-pot, a basket trap made of willow and baited to hold eels, to stretching nets over streams to catch salmon. Nets could also be fixed to one point on the bank with the other end held in a boat. The boat would sweep along the stream, a technique called "seining." Some fishers used simple scoop nets attached to a wooden hoop at the end of a handle as well. Freshwater fishing with a hook and line was also widely practiced. The eighteenth-century naturalist William Bartram in his account of his travels in Florida described early fly fishing for trout as "curious and singular":

They are taken with a hook and line, but without any bait. Two people are in a little canoe, one sitting in the stern to steer, and the other near the bow, having a rod ten or twelve feet in length, to one end of which is tied a strong line, about twenty inches in length, to which are fastened three large hooks, back to back. These are fixed very securely, and covered with the white hair of a deer's tail, shreds of a red garter, and some particoloured feathers, all which form a tuft, or tassel, nearly as large as one's fist, and entirely cover and conceal the hooks: this is called a bob. The steersman paddles softly, and proceeds slowly along shore, keeping the boat parallel to it, at a distance just sufficient to admit the fisherman to reach the edge of the floating weeds along shore; he now ingeniously swings the bob backwards and forwards, just above the surface, and sometimes tips the water with it; when the unfortunate cheated trout instantly springs from under the weeds, and seizes the supposed prey. Then he is caught without the possibility of escape. (Bartram, *Travels and Other Writings*, 106–7)

PRESERVING FISH AND SHELLFISH

If fish or shellfish were not consumed soon after being taken from the water, they had to be preserved. In a world without freezer technology, the ways of preserving fish and seafood were various. Turtles, the main ingredient in turtle soup, a popular dish in the Tidewater region of Virginia and Maryland, had the simplest preservation technique of all—they were simply kept alive until immediately before being cooked. Most fish and seafood presented a tougher challenge. After the heads were chopped off, the guts removed, and the fish split along the backbone, cod, by far the most important fish economically, was preserved through a combination of salting and drying. Livers were set aside for their oil, which was known as train oil and used as a mechanical lubricant. Cod-liver oil was also used in lamps and to prepare leather.

The cod fishery vastly increased the demand for salt. Salting was skilled work, as too much or too little salt could make the final product worthless. Cod cured with heavy salting and relatively little drying was called green or wet-cured. Green curing was a strategy employed with larger, thicker cod whose insides might begin to rot before drying thoroughly, and by those fishing nations, such as France and Portugal, with ready access to cheap salt. The French put a layer of cod in the holds of their ships, covered it with a layer of salt, and so on, pouring off the brine and recovering the excess salt after three or four days. Newfoundland fishers also wet-cured the last few catches of the season, which they lacked time to dry properly. The usual practice in the English colonies, though, was to use less salt and make heavier use of drying cod, which required a large area exposed to the sun for the cod to dry. (At the end of the Seven Years War in 1763, when France lost all of her North American possessions, she was allowed to keep two small islands, St. Pierre and Miquelon, for drying cod. They remain French to this day, the last remnants of European rule in the Americas.) Cod dries particularly well, since it has no fat to turn rancid. After English or Anglo-American cod workers had salted their fish for a few days, it was rinsed in seawater and spread out to dry on rock or on wooden beds called flakes. If it rained, the cod had to be hurriedly turned skin-side-up to protect it from the water. In less than a week, the cod was dry. It was then stacked for storage or transportation. Dry-curing hurt the flavor of the cod less than heavy salting, and made the fish rigid and easy to transport. It was necessary to dry cod for export to the tropics, the Caribbean, or Africa, as it was particularly difficult to preserve it from the heat. This became known as the "West India cure." Generally, the Caribbean islands, where the primary market for cod was as food for slaves, received the poorer grades of fish.

Shellfish was preserved in several different ways. Peter Kalm, the mid-eighteenth century Swedish scientist and traveler, described oyster-pickling as it was done in New York City, which exported many barrels of oysters to the West Indies:

As soon as the oysters are caught, their shells are opened and the fish washed clean; some water is then poured into a pot, the oysters are put into it, and they are boiled for a while; the pot is then taken off the fire again and the oysters taken out and put upon a dish until they are almost dry. Then some nutmeg, allspice and black pepper are added, and as much vinegar as is thought sufficient to give a sourish taste. All this is mixed with half the liquor in which the oysters are boiled, and put over the fire again. While boiling great care should be taken to skim off the thick scum. At last the whole pickling liquid is poured into a glass or earthen vessel, the oysters are put into it, and the vessel is well stopped to keep out the air. In this manner, oysters will keep for years, and may be sent to the most distant parts of the world. (Peter Kalm, *Peter Kalm's Travels in North America*, 125–26)

Kalm also described an alternative method of preserving oysters for export in which the oysters were fried in butter, then packed in glass or ceramic containers filled with butter so as to protect them from the air.

WHALING

Like codfishing, whaling had a long history in the involvement of Europe with North America. Some of the earliest encounters of Europeans and the indigenous peoples of North America in the sixteenth century were connected to whaling voyages. Sixteenth- and seventeenth-century whalers sought their prey close to coasts. When colonists started whaling on their own, they followed the same practice. Female and young right whales, the most commonly hunted kind of whales in the seventeenth century, came to the shores of North America between Long Island and

Cape Cod in the winter. Beginning in the late seventeenth century, they were hunted by men in whaleboats. Men in observation stations, or whale houses, maintained a lookout on shore, and when a whale was sighted, the whaleboat and its crew set out.

The whaleboat was a narrow wooden boat, about 20 feet long. It was constructed of cedar clapboards. Cedar had the advantage of being light, and speed and maneuverability was important for whalers. The whaleboat was rowed and was manned by six men. The usual pattern in Nantucket was for crews to consist of five Native Americans and one English captain. Although the construction of a whaleboat was completely different from that of a Native dugout canoe, the two kinds of boat were very similar in shape, and Native experience with dugouts may have been an asset on a whaleboat as well.

The most demanding job a whaler could have was harpooning. The barbed harpoon had to be planted firmly in the whale to secure it. The practice of early New England whalers varied from that of their European contemporaries. Europeans connected the harpoon by a line to the boat, which then served as the drag to exhaust the whale so it could be killed with handheld lances. The danger was that the whale would drag the boat under or destroy it in some other way, so whalers had an axe on board to cut the rope in an emergency. Early Nantucket whalers attached the harpoon to a large, square piece of wood called a "drogue." This was less dangerous, but also less effective. The drogue had some European precedents, although the exact reason why it was taken up by New England whalers is unknown. By the late eighteenth century, American whalers shifted to the European method.

In the eighteenth century, Colonial America's whaling center was the Quaker-dominated island of Nantucket and the boom industry was deep-sea sperm whaling (the coastal whale fishery was exhausted by 1760). There was some precedent for going out to sea for whales, as Nantucket whalers had sometimes gone out to hunt whales on the shoals, using a sloop that carried two whaleboats. Although the exact sequence of events that led to the rise of deep-sea whaling on the open ocean is unknown, the traditional story is that in 1712 Captain Christopher Hussey of Nantucket, blown out to sea, had located, killed, and recovered sperm whales. Beginning in the late 1710s, at any rate, Nantucket whalers set out to roam the world's deep seas. Whaleboats were still used for the actual hunting and killing of whales, but now they were carried in ships rather than being launched from the shore.

Killing whales at sea or along the coast was not the only way people could economically benefit from cetaceans. A dead whale that washed up on the beach could be a bonanza for a coastal community. Whichever way the whale fell into human hands, finding and/or killing it was only the beginning of the process by which the wild creature was turned into profit. Ironically from our point of view today, turning dead whales into valuable commodities in those days was called "saving the whales." Hector St. John de Crèvecoeur described how Nantucket whalers attacked the body of a whale after it had been killed and the body recovered: "The next operation is to cut with axes and spades every part of her body which yields oil; the kettles are set a-boiling; they fill their barrels as fast as it is made; but as this operation is much slower than that of cutting up, they fill the hold of their ship with those fragments, lest a storm should arise and force them to abandon their prize" (Crèvecoeur, *Letters from an American Farmer*, 138–39). By the mid-eighteenth century, whale ships had taken on the guise of factory ships, as blubber was reduced to oil aboard ship.

Many parts of the whale had economic value. Whalebone was not actual bone but "baleen," a substance found in the jaws of some whales (the most commercially important being the right whale) who used it to strain the plankton they ate. Strong and flexible, it was used in furniture and the supports of women's skirts. Poorer-quality baleen, such as that found in humpback whales, was used to make buttons. Whale fat also found a particularly valuable export market in Catholic countries where eating meat was forbidden during Lent. Since the Church classified whales as fish, their meat and fat was permissible for cooking during the season (beavers were also classified as fish due to their aquatic habitat). Whale oil was a lubricant, a lamp oil, a component in soap, and food. It was made by melting and rendering the blubber, a layer of fat from 12 to 18 inches thick, in copper vessels fueled by wooden fires. It had the advantage over many other organic oils of remaining liquid even in cold temperatures. Thomas Jefferson sang its praises, focusing on its value in illumination:

Whale oil enters, as a raw material, into several branches of manufacture, as of wool, leather, soap: it is used also in painting, architecture and navigation. But its great consumption is in lighting houses and cities. For this last purpose however it has a powerful competitor in the vegetable oils. These do well in warm, still weather, but they fix with cold, they extinguish easily with the wind, their crop is precarious, depending on the seasons, and to yield the same light, a larger wick must be used, and greater quantity of oil consumed. Estimating all these articles of difference together, those employed in lighting cities find their account in giving about 25 per cent. more for whale than for vegetable oils. (Jefferson, *Writings*, 379)

Sperm whales are toothed whales, hunting giant squid rather than eating plankton. They had no baleen, but they were valuable for other reasons. "Spermaceti," a white, paraffin-like substance found in their heads, was superior to any other material available for making candles and underlay the eighteenth-century boom in deep-sea whaling. Spermaceti's resemblance to semen was what gave the sperm whale its name. Whereas regular whale oil burned with a heavy odor, spermaceti was clear and virtually odorless. So valuable was it that in 1761 the Association of Spermaceti

Candlers, a manufacturer's group, was formed to discourage competition and regulate the product. Another valuable sperm whale product was "ambergris," concretion formed in the intestines of sick sperm whales, often around the undigested hard parts of squid. It was very valuable as a fixative for perfumes. Ambergris was too irregular to be the basis of a whaling industry, but it did increase the potential profit from a whale.

5

Technology in Domestic Life

THE WORK OF THE HOUSEWIFE

Some of the most important technological activity was carried on in the home. For American colonists, as for their European contemporaries, the home was particularly the sphere of activity of the women of the household. Some wealthy households, particularly in the eighteenth century, could shift much of this burden to servants or slaves, but for all except the very rich, the housewife's work was a constant cycle of activity.

TRANSMITTING DOMESTIC KNOWLEDGE

Much of the knowledge of how to run a household, large or small, was passed down from mother to daughter or in other ways handed down from older women to younger women. The apprenticeships of girls frequently required their new masters or mistresses to see to their training in basic needlework and other housewifely skills. More advanced needlework, practiced more as an art than as a household skill, was taught by the governesses and in the boarding schools that catered to the daughters of the eighteenth-century elite. However, there was also a printed and manuscript literature devoted to household management, including domestic technology, the "housewifery manuals." These works represent the largest body of technical writing by women in the early modern period. Most of the printed volumes available in the colonies had been originally published in England and were either physically brought over to the colonies or reprinted there. In 1742 *The Compleat Housewife* by Eliza Smith was the first to be published in America, long after its first publication in England in 1727. Much of the English literature was not adapted to the differing situation of America, with its different foods such as corn and pumpkins. The first cookbook devoted to specifically American resources and conditions, Amelia Simmons's *American Cookery*, was not published until 1796, and even it includes unacknowledged borrowings from English sources.

PRESERVING FOOD

The home was a site of endless activity in the preparation, cooking, and serving of food. Food presented a variety of technological challenges. For early modern people, food was seasonal because different kinds of food

This glass bottle, imported from Europe, was originally carried in a wooden case. Courtesy of the Flowerdew Hundred Foundation.

became available at different times. When a particular kind of food became available, what there was of it that was not prepared immediately had to be stored until needed. Often, this was for long periods and required complicated processes. Much of the colonial housewife's constant labor was directed not toward cooking food but preserving it in a society without refrigeration. Heat, cold, vermin, and the ceaseless process of decay were all threats to the edibility of food. Fruit had to be preserved, vegetables pickled, meat salted or smoked, and flour preserved from the hungry jaws of insects and mice.

Most of these methods involved salt, which had no peer as a drying agent. One of the differences between our own time and most of human history is that earlier generations thought of salt primarily as a preservative rather than as something to add flavor.

PRESERVING MEAT

Meat, whether obtained by hunting or by livestock raising, was essential to most American diets. Of course, animals provided other kinds of food than meat. In addition to dairy products, French Canadians used rendered bear fat as a substitute for butter or as a salad oil. Preserved meat was both an important part of the domestic economy and a major export item. Lacking refrigeration, colonists could eat fresh meat only when it was newly slaughtered, so most meat consumed had been pickled, smoked, salted, or preserved in some other way. Salt was essential to most forms of meat and fish preservation, as it drew the moisture out of the meat. Another technique, often used in combination with salting, was smoking, exposing meat to smoke for long periods. In addition to subtly enhancing the flavor, smoking permeated meat with mildly toxic compounds that inhibited the growth of bacteria. Although early modern people knew nothing of bacteria, they did know, as people had known for many centuries, that smoked meat was far less subject to rot than fresh meat.

Harriot Pinckney Horry, a South Carolina plantation lady, wrote down the following recipe for making bacon, a word often used to refer to meat from any part of a pig. This recipe combines salting and smoking:

Cut up the hogs the day they are killed, and then salt them well (but do not rub them) with a peck of salt to each hog, the next day take 2 lb. sugar and 1/4 lb. Salt peter to each Hog and a little more salt added to what salt hangs about them mix it all together and rub well with it particularly hams or legs put them all in a Tub together and let them lie three days (if the weather is very cold they may lie a day or two longer) then take them out of the tubs and rub them well with salt alone and put them back in the tubs with the bloody brine from which you took them and let them lie eight days longer, then take them out pour away all the brine or pickle from them and rub them a third time with the salt that is unmelted about them and a little more added and about 1/2 pint of red pepper powderd let them remain in the tubs two weeks then smoke them till they are well dried making in the whole less than a month from the killing to the smoking them. The Hogs I cured were very large. (Horry, *A Colonial Plantation Cookbook*, 130)

Other methods, particularly common for beef, skipped smoking. Wet-cures relied on prolonged immersion in brine. "Jerky," which settlers learned how to make from Native Americans, was beef or buffalo meat cut into very thin strips and held over a slow fire that dried it out. Jerky's portability made it very useful to travelers, although some found it unpleasantly dry to eat. German settlers in Pennsylvania made meat into sausages, following the tradition of their native land by grinding it and stuffing the raw meat into casings made of intestine.

PRESERVING VEGETABLES AND FRUIT

Vegetables presented a particular challenge for preservation. Pickling, a process using the ability of vinegar (dilute acetic acid) to control the multiplication of bacteria was one of the most common ways to preserve vegetables, even though, at the time, the colonists did not understand the process. A manuscript carried from England to Virginia and passed down through generations of Virginia aristocratic women contained the following recipe for pickling cucumbers: "Take white wine vinegar and clarret, of each a like quantety, and some salt. Boyle them together and make good brine of it. Scum it clean and when it is cold put in your cowcumbers. Keep it close and look to it once a week that they lack not brine" (*Martha Washington's Booke of Cookery*, 168). There were other techniques besides pickling suited for individual vegetables. The same manuscript describes one method of preserving peas that also employed salt but not pickling: "To Keep Pease all the year. Take Pease, shell and boyle them. Then strow a good deale of salt amongst them; dry them well, then melt as much butter as will cover them in an earthen pot and strow on good store of salt on them, and soe ye may keep them all the yeare" (*Martha Washington's Booke of Cookery*, 162). Sealing items in jars with butter was called "potting."

Fruit, due to its moisture and high sugar content, was even more of a challenge. One common way of dealing with excess fruit was to dry it, removing the excess moisture that promoted decay. This procedure was easier in drier climates, but was also practiced in wetter ones. The South Carolinian Harriot Pinckney Horry described her method for drying peaches in her handwritten collection of recipes: "Take cling stone peaches, pare them and cut them into as large thick slices as you can cut, put them into a stew pan (say about 4 lb) pour 1/2 pint of water to them and sprinkle on them two heaped spoonsful of powdered sugar, put them on the fire and let them scald (but not boil) then pour them into a sieve and let them drain well, then spread them thin on dishes and put them in the sun to dry, remove them on clean dishes every day and put them in the sun till they are dry" (Horry, *A Colonial Plantation Cookbook*, 119). Another method of keeping fruit was to employ the preserving powers of alcohol, which like vinegar, is hostile to many decay-causing micro-organisms. Brandy was commonly used. The first cookbook published in America by an American, Amelia Simmons's *American Cookery* (1796) gave a recipe for making peach preserves with brandy:

Take half a peck of clingstone peaches, wipe them with a flannel cloth, put them in an earthen pot sufficient to contain them, fill it up with brandy, let them stand two days covered, then pour off the brandy, to which add half a pint of the same liquor and four pound sugar; cut two oranges very fine, which add to the sirrup, and when boiling hot pour over the peaches: the next day set them into a hot oven, let them stand half an hour, then set them away in a cool place. If the weather should be warm, the sirrup must be scalded again in six or eight days, adding thereto another half pint of brandy and one pound sugar, pouring it boiling hot upon the peaches, then set them again in a cool place; This method of procedure will give them a more fresh and agreeable flavor, than any mode yet discovered. (Simmons, *American Cookery*, 61–62)

Of course, one very common way of preserving fruit was by making it into alcoholic drinks. Apples were made into cider, an increasingly popular drink in the eighteenth century. Peaches were made into peach brandy, a common drink particularly in the South.

COOKING AND SERVING FOOD

Colonists brought European cooking traditions with them to the New World, but had to adapt them to the different circumstances—and different foods—of their new homes.

Cooking in the Spanish colonies was more directly influenced by Native American culture than that in the British colonies, partly because Native American women were more likely to work in Spanish kitchens as wives or servants than in British ones. Whereas Anglo-American colonists ate bread, the corn tortilla, originated by Native Americans, was a staple of the Hispanic diet and the flat griddle used to prepare it was ubiquitous in Hispanic kitchens. French colonists, who were also more likely to marry Native Americans than were the settlers of the British colonies, were also influenced by Native American corn traditions. French fur traders before their long trips into the North American interior soaked corn in lye to remove the hulls, then washed the kernels to remove the taste of the lye. The kernels were mixed with the fat of bears, deer, and hogs. The resulting substance was boiled, then eaten, and along with game, served to feed a trader.

Although the Anglo-American Benjamin Franklin omitted mention of tortillas and bear's fat, he paid generous and patriotic tribute to the culinary versatility of the ubiquitous American grain, corn:

1. The family can begin to make use of it before the time of full harvest; for the tender green ears, stript of their leaves, and roasted by a quick fire till the grain is brown, and eaten with a little salt and butter, are a delicacy. 2. When the grain is riper and harder, the ears, boil'd in their leaves, and eaten with butter, are also good and agreable food. The green tender grains, dried, may be kept all the year, and, mixed with green *haricots* [beans], also dried, make at any time a pleasing dish being first soak'd some hours in water, and then boil'd. When the grain is ripe and hard, there are also several ways of using it. One is, to soak it all night in a *lessive*, and then pound it in a large wooden mortar with a wooden pestle; the skin of each grain is by this means stript off, and the farinaceous part left whole, which, being boil'd., swells into a white soft pulp, and eaten with milk, or with butter and sugar is delicious. The dry grain is also sometimes ground loosely, so as to be broke into pieces the size of rice, and being winnow'd to separate the bran, it is then boil'd and eaten with turkies or other fowls, as rice. Ground into a finer meal, they make of it by boiling a hasty-pudding, or *bouilli*, to be eaten with milk, or with butter and sugar; this resembles what the Italians call *polenta*. They make of the same meal with water and salt, a hasty cake, which, being struck against a hoe or any flat iron, is plac'd erect before the fire, and so baked, to be used as bread. Broth is agreably thickened with the same meal. They also parch it in this manner. An iron pot is fill'd with sand, and set on the fire till the sand is very hot. Two or three pounds of the grain are then thrown in, and well mix'd with the sand by stirring. Each grain bursts and throws out a white substance of twice its bigness. The sand is separated by a wire sieve, and return'd into the pot, to be again heated and repeat the operation with fresh grain. That which is parch'd is pounded into a powder in mortars. This, being sifted, will keep long for use. (Franklin, *The Ingenious Dr. Franklin*, 76–77)

BOILING, ROASTING, AND BAKING

The basic source of heat for cooking was the kitchen fire, although for most people the kitchen fire was the same as the main hearth fire. Only the well-to-do could afford separate kitchens with their own fire. Of course, not everyone was lucky enough to be able to cook the food in a kitchen. Joseph Plumb Martin, a Revolutionary War soldier from Connecticut, remembered decades later how he had cooked his flour and beef ration: "The flour was laid upon a flat rock and mixed up with cold water, then daubed upon a flat stone and scorched on one side, while the beef was broiling on a stick in the fire" (Martin, *Private Yankee Doodle*, 77).

One of the most common ways to cook food was in water, by boiling or stewing. This was particularly common among the poor, who could not afford separate ovens in their fireplaces or the expensive cuts, or joints, of meat that benefited from roasting or baking. The kettle was the most basic item of the colonial kitchen.

Colonial people distinguished between cooking meat in the open air—roasting it—and cooking it in an enclosed oven—baking it. Roasted meat, which was viewed as preferable, was impaled by a spit above or in front of the fire, and had to be turned—a monotonous, exhausting task that exposed the turner to the fire's full heat. One way to alleviate this drudgery was to use a mechanical turner. The "clock jack" was a mechanism of weight-driven gears, while the "smoke jack" worked by harnessing the power of the heated air rising from the fire itself. A dish lay beneath the roasting meat to catch the drippings, which were then used to baste the meat.

The oven was built of brick and separate from the hearth. Spanish-American ovens in the Southwest, known as *hornos*, were built from adobe brick. The primary purpose of the oven was to bake breads, cakes, and pies. A fire was built in the oven, and the door left open to provide air. In order to keep the heat in the oven, a flue or chimney was omitted, so the door was the only opening. When the fire was out, the items to be baked were placed in the oven. Because the door would not be opened until the cook thought the item was ready to be taken out, baking required an ability that depended on experience to judge the relationship between the items to be baked, the temperature of the oven, and time needing for baking. Ovens were not found in the houses of the poor or much of the middle class, as they represented a substantial investment. Other ways of baking included small, portable enclosures that could be placed on a cleared space on the hearth. One way of baking that was unique to English America was the "hoe-cake." A cake was held in the fire on a hoe to be baked. Ingredients of the hoe-cake varied—the New England "johnny-cake" was more likely to be made of wheat flour and molasses, while the southern version was made of unsweetened corn meal.

SWEETENERS

The most important sweeteners in colonial America included molasses, maple syrup, and honey. Molasses was a sugar-derived product made in the Caribbean and imported to the British colonies in vast quantities, mostly to be distilled into rum. It was the cheapest sweetener and became the most commonly used, but the others remained important throughout the colonial period.

Beekeeping had already had a long history in Europe before the first colonists arrived. Bees came along with European settlers, but colonists also gathered wild honey. Hector St. John de Crèvecoeur described how he gathered wild honey:

I proceed to such woods as are at a considerable distance from any settlements. I carefully examine whether they abound with large trees; if so, I make a small fire on some flat stones in a convenient place; on the fire I put some wax; close by this fire, on another stone, I drop honey in distinct drops, which I surround with small quantities of vermilion, laid on the stone; and then I retire carefully to watch whether any bees appear. If there are any in that neighbourhood, I rest assured that the smell of the burnt wax will unavoidably attract them; they will soon find out the honey, for they are fond of preying on that which is not their own; and in their approach they will necessarily tinge themselves with some particles of vermilion, which will adhere long to their bodies. I next fix my compass, to find out their course, which they keep invariably straight, when they are return-ing home loaded. By the assistance of my watch, I observe how long those are returning which are marked with vermilion. Thus possessed of the course, and, in some measure, of the distance, which I can easily guess at, I follow the first, and seldom fail of coming to the tree where those republics are lodged. I then mark it; and thus, with patience, I have found out sometimes eleven swarms in a season; and it is inconceivable what a quantity of honey these trees will sometimes afford. It entirely depends on the size of the hollow, as the bees never rest nor swarm till it is all replenished; for like men, it is only the want of room that induces them to quit the maternal hive. (Crèvecoeur, *Letters from an American Farmer*, 59–60)

Maple syrup was a product requiring much labor. It was principally found in the northern British colonies and Canada. The French of Quebec were particularly notorious for their love of maple syrup, even boiling whole hams in maple sap.

SOUTH CAROLINA'S RICE CULTURE

Different colonial societies prepared and consumed different foods. Influences in developing regional foodways included culture, whether indigenous or imported, and the availability of different kinds of food. For example, the South Carolina Low Country, where rice, the renowned "Carolina Gold," was the staple export crop, also ate rice itself and devel-oped a distinct regional cuisine. The Low Country was the only English-speaking community in the world to consume rice as a staple. Before rice cultivation began in South Carolina, what little use of rice existed in English cooking focused on making puddings and porridges. Often English cooks simply boiled rice until it burst. Since their own tradition offered little help with how to prepare the grain, white South Carolinians adopted many of the techniques introduced by the African slave women who toiled in their kitchens. The technique of making plain, long-grain rice, with every grain separate, was adapted from African sources.

DRINK

Early Americans were quite fond of alcoholic drinks and had many to choose from. Although religion condemned drunkenness, no one con-demned the drinking of alcoholic beverages *per se,* and moderate drinking was a necessary part of daily life. Alcohol was a "good creature" of God, and even the grimmest Puritans could relax with a glass of ale or cider.

The teetotaler movement against drinking any kind of alcohol didn't come along until the nineteenth century. Some drinks were imported, such as most wine, while others were made in works dedicated to the purpose, such as the ubiquitous rum made from the sugar of the Caribbean (and distilled in lead pipes, which caused lead poisoning, known as the "West-India dry gripes").

The most common alcoholic drink in colonial America was apple cider. Apples were not the only fruit to be fermented, though; peach brandy was a common drink in the South. Cider was made both at home and in commercial cider mills, which became more common in the eighteenth century. Apples were first mashed to a pulp, then the resultant mash was pressed into cakes separated by layers of straw. Further pressure was applied to draw out the juice, which after straining was placed into wooden casks to ferment. There was no need to add a fermenting agent, as wild yeast was already present. In the winter, the alcoholic content of cider could be increased by letting it freeze. The water rose to the top as ice and was broken off and removed. What was left had a greater concentration of alcohol, forming a drink known as hard cider.

SOAPMAKING

One of the most important and arduous of the housewife's tasks was soapmaking. Rural housewives were particularly likely to make their own soap, as the needs of urban households were served by the large-scale commercial soapmaking operations that spread in eighteenth-century American cities.

Soap is essentially a combination of fat and lye. Lye is a solution of potash, made from wood ashes, in water. One way of making lye was to put wood ashes into a bottomless barrel, then pour water over it until a brownish liquid oozed from the bottom. There were other arrangements, but the principle was the same—the water dissolved the salts in the ashes.

The second ingredient after lye was fat. Animal or vegetable fats can be used for soap, but the British-American colonists, like northern Europeans, lacked olives or other sources of vegetable fat and made their soap from the fat of livestock, beef tallow, or hog lard. Because tallow was also used for candles, it was common for commercial soapboilers to also be tallow chandlers. Among those who combined these trades was Josiah Franklin of Boston, Benjamin Franklin's father. Producing acceptable animal fat for soapmaking was a long and unpleasant process, called "rendering." Rendering removed impurities from fat, whether fragments and traces of meat if animal fat from the butcher was being used, or kitchen waste if old cooking grease was used. If the fat was not rendered properly, the soap would smell horrible! Rendering was done by boiling the fat with an equal amount of water. The purpose of heating the fat with the water was to liquefy it, thus easing the separation of the waste matter. After being left overnight to cool, the fat formed a solid layer on top of the water, while the impurities remained at the bottom of the kettle.

Once the lye and rendered fat were on hand, the making of soap, or soapboiling, began. Soapmaking, or "saponification," is a complex chemical process, which colonial soapmakers did not understand. What they knew is that fat and lye, if boiled together for several hours, formed a new substance. The tricky part was combining the right amount of lye with the fat. Since the strength of lye varied, there was no set formula for the ratio of fat to lye. Colonists had a crude way to measure the strength of lye, by seeing if an egg or a potato would float in it. But mixing lye and fat remained an intuitive art, and it was not at all uncommon for a batch of soap to fail.

Once the fat and lye boiled into a white froth, the soap was allowed to cool. The final produce was a brown jelly that was treated as an all-purpose soap for cleaning clothes, bodies, and all the other legion of things that needed to be cleaned around a home, workshop, or farm.

Soap made for domestic use was soft soap. Urban commercial soapboilers, interested in preserving and transporting their product, made hard soap. Hard soap was made by adding salt to boiling soap. A hard crust formed on the top, which was then cut into large bars. Slices were taken off the large bar for individual customers. At the high end of the market, the bars of hard soap were scented.

TEXTILES AND CLOTHING

In textiles, the most important category of expenditure in household goods, domestic American household production coexisted with imports from Europe. The two most important textiles in colonial British America were wool and linen, made from the flax plant. But not all American flax was processed locally; much of it was exported to Ireland, the center of fine linen production. Although not grown in the mainland colonies, cotton was imported from the Caribbean to the colonies, and was a fabric of increasing importance in the colonial period. In addition to use as clothing or bedding, textiles were also used to make sacks, wagon covers, and other tools. Like food preparation, textile production was a gendered activity. Women spun wool or flaxen fiber into yarn, and in New England and the Chesapeake Bay area, they took over weaving, previously a male task, in the early eighteenth century. In the middle colonies, to which many male weavers from Continental Europe emigrated, weaving remained a male trade. In all cases, spinning was a more widely dispersed activity than weaving. Studies of wills and inventories in Chester County, Pennsylvania, a center of flax culture, from 1773 to 1776, reveal that two-thirds of the households possessed spinning wheels but less than 8 percent had looms for weaving. Much of the cloth and garments produced by Americans were either worn by members of the household or exchanged with neighbors as part of a local barter economy. In the late eighteenth century, the growing need for cloth production to clothe servants and slaves led many owners of large plantations in the Chesapeake Bay area, including George Washington, to require slave women to learn spinning and weaving. Cloth manufacture was unusual in that it was one of the few alternatives to field labor for slave women, as most skilled occupations on a plantation were monopolized by male slaves.

By the period before the American Revolution, capitalist production for the market had begun to transform textile manufacture and move it out of the household. In areas where free labor dominated textile production, the development of communications and transportation networks between colonial communities enabled more centralized household production. Certain communities became identified with a particular kind of manufactured good, which was then sold over a wide area. Germantown, Pennsylvania, was known for Germantown stockings, of which many thousands of pairs were made annually.

Tools used in domestic textile manufacturing changed very little in the colonial period. Spinning wheels were uncommon in the early phases of English colonization, but more common later. They were divided into two types: the walking wheel for spinning wool into yarn, and the foot-operated treadle, variously called the Dutch, linen, or foot wheel, for flax. Both were made of wood. The yarn was gathered and measured by hand on wooden reels, known as "niddy-noddys." There were also hand-cranked reels. The thread was then woven into cloth on wooden looms. The large-scale mechanization of textile production, which would revolutionize the American economy, did not occur until after the American Revolution.

The Puritan poet Edward Taylor, whose devotional poetry abounds in metaphors taken from science and technology, used the spinning and weaving process as a metaphor for the soul's relation to God:

> Make me thy Spinning Wheele of use for thee,
> Thy Grace my Distaffe, and my heart thy spoole
> Turn thou the wheele: let my affections bee
> The flyers filling with thy yarne my soule.
> Then weave the web of Grace in me, thy Loome
> And Cloath my soul therewith, its Glories bloome.
> Make mee thy Loome: thy Grace the warfe therein,
> My duties Woofe, and let thy worde winde Quills.
> The shuttle shoot. Cut off the ends my sins.
> Thy Ordinances make my fulling mills,
> My Life thy Web: and cloath me all my dayes
> With this Gold-Web of glory to thy praise.
> (Taylor, *Poems of Edward Taylor*, 468)

TEXTILES AND GENDER

For Europeans and their American descendants, spinning was not just another household activity. It carried profound symbolic meaning. Although both men and women were weavers, spinning was a quintessentially female occupation. The distaff and spindle were not just tools for spinning yarn, they were symbols of womanhood. Spinning also symbolized frugality and good management, as the home spinner supplied the needs of her family without forcing them to spend their hard-earned money to buy cloth. The always-busy spinning woman was contrasted with the idle, vain woman who gossiped and indulged herself rather than providing for her husband and children. In a sententious letter accompanying a present to his sister Jane, Benjamin Franklin declared that "I had almost determined on a tea table, but when I considered that the character of a good housewife was far preferable to that of being only a pretty gentlewoman, I concluded to send you a spinning wheel" (Franklin, *Writings*, 424).

The woman's spinning wheel was a symbol of the home, but on some occasions, the virtue of the spinning woman could cross over from the private to the public sphere. In New England in the years preceding the American Revolution, spinning parties were one way for women to demonstrate their patriotism and virtue at a time when everyday domestic spinning was declining. By gathering, often in the home of a local minister, and spending all day spinning skein after skein of yarn, women demonstrated that there was no need for America to be dependent on British cloth (and by implication other British imports) and that women were equally, if not more, prepared to sacrifice for the patriotic cause as men. Some went so far as to unfavorably contrast the drinking parties of the Sons of Liberty and other patriot organizations of men with the women's decorous and productive spinning parties. Women in other parts of the country also increased their spinning, but in areas more resistant to women's participation or more rural, they did it in their own households rather than gathering together.

Once the cloth had been woven, it had to be made into useful goods for the family and household. Again, this was principally the work of women. Women cut and sewed undyed cloth into sheets, pillows, napkins, and other useful items, as well as the majority of the clothing people wore on everyday occasions. One exception to this rule was leather clothing, which was made by men outside the household economy. Some high-quality clothes such as formal coats were made by professional tailors, who had the tools and skills to make buttonholes and attach buttons properly, as well as fitting clothes to the individual. However, making repairs to clothes, fixing tears, and reattaching lost buttons, for example, was quintessentially women's work. Needlework extended from these kinds of elementary repairs to embroidering, which at the highest levels was practiced by upper-class women as an art form. Advanced needle-work was one of the few technical skills taught women in an academic setting; the genteel academies teaching upper-class girls included it as one of their subjects. Women also carried out the physically demand-ing task of washing and cleaning clothes, whether as housewives or as laundresses.

6

Architecture and Housing

American colonial housing developed from primitive temporary structures to a wide range of styles, materials, differentiated by ethnicity, economic class, and region. Immigrants from Europe and Africa brought the housing traditions of their native lands with them, and then modified them in the new conditions of America. Besides shelter, one of the most basic of human needs, housing also provided comfort, not such an important value in the early modern period as it is now, and a sense of identity. The big house of the rich landowner, merchant, or official, sent a message of social preeminence, while the shack or shanty of the very poor was socially stigmatizing as well as miserable.

THE FIRST SETTLERS' DWELLINGS

The earliest colonial housing was very simple in its design and sparing in its demands on labor and natural resources in keeping with the poverty of the early colonists. The first dwellings erected in a colony were often planned merely to provide basic shelter while the colony was established, and then to be abandoned in favor of more sturdy housing. One common temporary solution to the housing problem in both Virginia and New England in the early seventeenth century was digging a rectangular hole in the ground about seven feet deep, walling it with timber, flooring it with planks, and putting a wooden roof over the whole. During the first settlement of Philadelphia, some people lived in caves dug into the banks of the Delaware. These persisted as homes for the very poor or the criminal into the eighteenth century. This phenomenon of cheap temporary shelters was repeated in subsequent expansion of the colonial frontier. Eighteenth-century pioneer settlers of the backcountry also built temporary structures, huts, or "English wigwams" constructed of animal skins, bark or sod. Despite their name, these structures had European as well as Native American precursors.

THE EARLY AMERICAN HOUSE

Even when more permanent structures began to be built, many colonists did not put much effort into them, perhaps believing that they would have the opportunity to better themselves by moving again. Early permanent dwellings in the Anglo-American colonies were usually one-room buildings, a story or a story and a half high. Early English-American colonial houses were based on English models, though English houses themselves varied between the different regions that colonists came from. This difference was reflected in the different houses colonists from different English regions built in North America. Puritan immigrants from East Anglia, whose traditional housing was marked by extensive use of wood and second floors that jutted out, built similar houses in New England. The houses of the Chesapeake gentry, with great halls running through the house, resembled gentry manors in the south and west of England, where many of them originated. A similar pattern obtained in Spanish North America. Large houses in New Mexico were arranged with rooms surrounding a central courtyard, in the manner of southern Spain, while Spanish houses in Florida had shade-covered balconies and arcades, like houses in northern Spain.

The general trend in the first few decades of English settlement was for housing patterns to settle down into a few types, as some English varieties ceased to be built. More enduring houses, with waterproof foundations rather than just posts driven into the ground, began to appear in New England after 1650, and in the Chesapeake Bay area around 1700. Whereas the earliest houses were built mostly by those who planned to dwell in them, these houses were more likely to be built by specialized craftsmen. The most common construction material in the seventeenth century English colonies was eastern North America's abundant wood, particularly oak. There were only a dozen or so brick houses in seventeenth-century New England. To avoid the expense of iron nails, many houses were held together with dried wooden pegs known as "tree-nails" (pronounced trunnels). The Spanish in the Southwest, a very wood-poor region, built in the adobe that local Native Americans already used, or when they could afford it, in stone. The Spanish colonists, however, did introduce the technique for forming adobe into bricks, whereas the Natives had puddled it and shaped it directly. Wooden buildings began to appear more frequently in Spanish America once Spain had worked its way up to California and its forests in the eighteenth century.

Clapboard houses, common in English-settled areas, were built around four wood posts pounded into the ground at the corners. The standard size of the single room was around 18 by 20 feet. Walls were short planks, about five or six feet long, called "clapboards," placed horizontally. The common use of clapboards distinguished Anglo-American architecture from that of England, where wood was scarce. Even a small house required as much as a ton of wood. Jaspar Danckaerts, a seventeenth-century Dutch visitor to America, described the shoddy clapboard houses in Delaware:

They first make a wooden frame, the same as they do in Westphalia and Altona, but not so strong; they then split the boards of clapwood, so that they are like cooper's pipe staves, except they are not bent. These are made very thin, with a large knife, so that the thickest end is about a *pinck* (little finger) thick, and the other is made sharp, like the edge of a knife. They are about five or six feet long, and are nailed on the outside of the frame, with the ends lapped over each other. They are not usually laid so close together, as to prevent you from sticking a finger between them, in consequence either of their not being well joined, or the boards being crooked. When it is cold and windy the best people plaster them with clay. (Dankers and Sluyter, *Journal of a Voyage to New York*, 173)

Many people envision the early English settlers in America living in log cabins. As it happened, this much snugger and better-built alternative to the clapboard house was introduced to America by the Swedish colonists of Delaware and for several decades had little influence on Anglo-American houses. Swedish settlers, coming from a part of Europe that was still heavily wooded, also made churches and other buildings out of logs. Danckaerts found the log houses far superior to clapboard: "The house, although not much larger than where we were the last night, was somewhat better and tighter, being made according to the Swedish mode, and as they usually build their houses here, which are block-houses, being nothing more than entire trees, split through the middle, or squared out of the rough, and placed in the form of a square, upon each other, as high as they wish to have the house; the ends of the timbers are let into each other, about a foot from the ends, half of one into half of the other. The whole structure is thus made, without a nail or a spike" (Dankers and Sluyter, *Journal of a Voyage to New York*, 175). The log cabin design began to spread with the settlement of Pennsylvania, when German and British settlers copied the houses of their new Swedish neighbors. From there the log cabin diffused through the settlement of the backcountry in the eighteenth century. By the middle of the century, Virginia planters were constructing log houses for their slaves.

Another local variation in housing was the "stone-ender," a form of wooden house common in Rhode Island, which unlike the other New England colonies had access to good stone for building and lime suitable for mortaring. The stone-ender featured a massive stone chimney that furnished most of the wall on one end of the building. The greater separation of the chimney from the wooden part of the house meant that stone-enders had considerably less risk of burning than all-wooden buildings.

In the early stages of colonization people often roofed their houses with thatch or sod, but eventually shingles, which lessened the danger of fire, became common. Thatch roofs disappeared by about 1670. Cedar, due to its lightness and durability, was the most popular material for shingles—so popular as to rapidly deplete the stock of cedar trees. White pine and fir were also used for shingles. The lightness of cedar shingle roofing contributed to the American tendency to build houses with very thin walls without much load-bearing capacity. Clay tiles nailed to the roof were also used and in the eighteenth century replaced shingles in many areas. They offered still better protection from fire. Benjamin Franklin was among those recommending tile roofing for fire protection; he was also intrigued by the idea of covering roofs with copper. Copper never caught on, but slate roofs were also used for fire prevention. Faced with the problem of heavy snow-fall, houses in the northern English colonies also developed steeper roofs so that snow would slide off easily.

The windows of early colonial houses were slits designed to minimize the loss of heat, and sometimes covered with cheap translucent paper or cloth rather than expensive glass. Early Swedish settlers in the Delaware Valley made windows out of the transparent mineral mica. Heat loss was further minimized through the use of shutters. External privies, or houses of neces-sity, were ever-present, and chamber pots rare until the eighteenth century. Additions to the house, if necessary, often took the form of "lean-tos," one-story wooden structures attached to the back of the building that were an American innovation without English precedent. Lean-tos could be used for cooking or storage. A few houses belonging to the wealthiest members of the community were distinguished by enclosed and gabled two-story porches.

The interior layout of most early American houses was simple. The bulk of the ground floor was taken up by a single large, multifunctioned room called the hall. This room was used for cooking, eating, working, praying, and sometimes for sleep. As people prospered, they added a second room, or parlor. This room was used for visitors and to provide the master and mistress of the household with a separate sleeping area. In eighteenth-century New England, the parlor became a necessity for all those aspiring to respectable status. One-room houses became a mark of poverty, and rooms became more differentiated by function. The lean-to also became a more integral part of the house. The combination of the two rooms and the lean-to led to the classic New England saltbox house, so-called because its shape resembled that of a salt container of the time. The one-room house persisted for much longer in the South, where poor white independent farmers thought it no disgrace.

Some of the shoddiest housing in the British colonies was built for slaves, particularly those field workers on plantations who lived in small groups in simple wooden huts with dirt floors close to where they worked. Many slaves, particularly on small farms and in the early days of settlement, lacked any dedicated housing and slept in barns, tobacco houses, or kitchens. Slaves also slept in large dormitories in some outlying plantations. Where African Americans, whether free or enslaved, were able to build their own houses, they often incorporated African features, such as small rooms around 12 by 12 feet of mud construction, with pounded dirt floors and palmetto-leaf thatching. African housing technologies, like other features of African culture, were particularly marked in South Carolina, where the high death rate of slaves meant that masters continued importing slaves from Africa in large numbers throughout the colonial period. In the Chesapeake tobacco-planting region, where the slave population was more self-sustaining, African cultural survivals were fewer.

Slave housing in South Carolina improved somewhat in the eighteenth century, with sturdier buildings with foundations and plank floors. In the other center of the North American slave population, Virginia, slave housing (including the miserable huts George Washington provided for his slaves at Mount Vernon) was usually shoddier because slave tobacco workers had to follow the crop as fields became exhausted and new ones were planted. South Carolina rice growers, cultivating the same fields year after year, were willing to provide better, more permanent housing for their enslaved workers.

URBAN HOUSING AND BRICK CONSTRUCTION

Urban houses differed in several ways from rural dwellings. A large proportion of the few truly rich people in seventeenth-century America lived in cities, and sometimes had large houses with several rooms. City houses were also constructed differently, with a greater reliance on brick rather than wood. Brick offered less vulnerability to fire, a constant danger particularly in large cities, than wood. Adobe bricks were also common in the Spanish settlements of the wood-poor Southwest. From its founding in 1682, Philadelphia broke with the Anglo-American tradition of timber houses and built its middle-class dwellings and other buildings mostly of brick. Many Quakers who had settled here came from the north of England, with a tradition of building in stone. Brick houses in Philadelphia were both taller—some extending to three stories—and more cramped than wooden houses in New England. Although wooden houses predominated at first, the Dutch also built much of their housing in New Amsterdam in brick or stone. The Dutch houses of colonial New York also put the gable end to the street, while the broad front of the house faced an alley. The Virginia Assembly, prompted by governor William Berkeley, enacted in 1662 a requirement that each county support the building of a brick house in Jamestown as part of a program to expand and modernize the capital of the province. The program was unsuccessful due to the general indifference of

Virginia planters to urban centers. New England, on the other hand, stuck more stubbornly to its wooden housing.

The cities also had a poor population, housed in crowded wooden buildings in back alleys, vulnerable to epidemic disease and fire. A calamitous fire, such as the one that swept Boston in 1679, sometimes led a town to replace its destroyed wooden housing stock with brick. The fire that raged through Spanish New Orleans in 1788 also led to the construction of new, more fire-resistant buildings. Severe weather damage could have the same effect. In Charleston, houses were originally wooden and built in the manner of the West Indies, where many of the city's first colonists originated. These houses had high ceilings and large windows, a style developed to minimize heat, and one that would become characteristic of the American South. The city suffered a severe hurricane in 1713 with much damage to its housing stock. The South Carolina Assembly then ordered that subsequent building be in brick, although this requirement was frequently ignored. Charleston also had a distinctive, French-influenced style of brickwork, a contribution of the town's large French Protestant, or Huguenot, population.

Although some bricks were imported from England, most bricks used in English colonial buildings were American-made. Some areas, such as Tidewater Virginia, boasted clay deposits that made excellent bricks. Bricks were also recycled as old buildings fell into ruin or were demolished. Ivor Noel Malcolm, an archeologist specializing in colonial Virginia, has estimated that the average eighteenth-century Anglo-American colonial brick was 8 3/4 inches by 4 inches by 2 5/8 inches. Seventeenth-century bricks were slightly smaller.

As brick and stone houses advanced, cheaper wooden housing dropped in status. The mid-eighteenth century Swedish traveler Peter Kalm, describing the town of New Brunswick, pointed out that many of the houses had only one brick wall, facing the street, while the rest of the building was of wood. Someone passing through rapidly, he claimed, might think most of the town brick—exactly what the passing stranger was intended to think.

THE GEORGIAN HOUSE

As the Anglo-American colonies prospered in the eighteenth century, rich Americans increasingly followed the latest European fashions in architecture and furnishings, as in other areas. In the seventeenth century, economic differences among Americans had been expressed principally in the size, rather than the style, of their houses. The classically influenced Georgian style of eighteenth-century England provided a way to distinguish between houses by style rather than size. The English Georgian house found many American imitators, beginning with wealthy men who immigrated from England, such as Peter Sergeant of Boston and Richard Whitpaine of Philadelphia. Official residences like the Governor's Palace in Williamsburg, Virginia, built in the early eighteenth century were also trendsetters. The grand house of the late seventeenth and eighteenth century was marked by brick construction, painted clapboards, and large, symmetrically arranged sash windows with ornamental wooden frames and crown glass rather than inferior broad glass. Staircases were broad, straight, and unenclosed. The front room was transformed into a parlor, without bedding or work tools, and given over to the best-quality furniture and display items. Rooms were laid out in a symmetrical pattern. The huge central fireplaces of the seventeenth century were abandoned in favor of smaller, more efficient fireplaces. Seventeenth-century features such as tall gables, broad glass windows with lead casements, and overhanging second floors disappeared, sometimes through remodeling of existing structures.

Whereas building an early American house was a matter of craft knowledge, the Georgian house required more book knowledge. Pattern books were imported from England and widely used. One of the first groups of homebuilders formed in the colonies, the Carpenters' Company of Philadelphia, established a library in 1734 to provide access to imported works of building design. Books on architecture made great demands on printers, as they were required to accurately reproduce detailed illustrations. The technical challenges were such that architectural books were not printed in America until the last years of the colonial era. Among the first of these American architectural publications was Abraham Swan's *A British Architect*. Originally published in England, Swan's book was

This magnificent eighteenth-century house, called "Westover House," was built by the Virginia planter, politician, and scientist William Byrd. Courtesy of the National Library of Medicine.

reprinted in Philadelphia in 1775 with numerous copperplate engravings by the American engraver John Norman.

The Georgian style's basis in a portable body of texts, rather than the experience of individual builders and the customs of local communities, gave Georgian buildings more uniformity across the colonies and between the mainland colonies, the Caribbean colonies, and Britain than previous Anglo-American building styles. Like the homes of the English gentry on which they were modeled, American Georgian homes, often built on the top of a hill or in another prominent position for lesser folk to see and admire, proclaimed both the owner's high social status and participation in an elite transatlantic culture. Sometimes an owner who wanted to claim membership in the Georgian culture but lacked the wealth to build a true Georgian house erected a Georgian facade, visible to the passing public, which concealed a non-Georgian house. In addition to the Georgian style, other architectural features becoming more popular in elite and middle-class houses of the eighteenth century were open verandahs and porches.

The need for housing in the settled areas of the colonies led to the development of construction industry of carpenters, joiners, bricklayers, and stonecutters. The most expert of these workers found their services in high demand, as towns or individuals actively recruited them. Skilled workers also emigrated from England and Europe in pursuit of the greater professional mobility and higher wages America offered. Professional architects did not exist in America, but many American gentlemen with intellectual ability learned architecture and applied it to their own residences. Two of the best-known examples of gentlemanly architecture are Thomas Jefferson's Monticello and George Washington's modifications to Mount Vernon. The most active gentleman-architect of the eighteenth century was Peter Harrison (1716–1775) of Newport, Rhode Island, a merchant and customs officer by profession. Harrison worked on both private and public buildings, including several churches and one of the first dedicated synagogues built in America, the Touro Synagogue of Newport, built in 1760 and still standing today.

HEATING THE HOME AND OTHER BUILDINGS

A great problem for dwellers in early colonial houses in the North was heating them, a problem exacerbated by the coldness of the winters compared with those in Britain. Early colonists took advantage of the bountiful supply of wood to build large, centrally located fireplaces, twice the size of those they had known in England. In addition to the standard tendency of fireplaces to send much of their heat up the chimney, heat also escaped through the many cracks and openings in wooden walls, although stone and brick homes, if well plastered, retained heat better. If a person was not close to the fire, he or she often derived little warmth from it, and fireplaces and open hearths were also dangerous for children. The fireplace's insatiable hunger for wood contributed to deforestation and meant that people spent much of their daily labor chopping down trees, preparing wood for the fire, and tending the flames. It wasn't only private dwellings that consumed firewood—the New England schoolhouse, once established, was a prodigious devourer of wood, particularly since its principal time of activity was in the winter. The requirement that the townsfolk and parents supply the school with wood caused great resentment. A supply of firewood was also a common perquisite of ministers. The Reverend Samuel Parris, later to become infamous as a leader of the Salem witch hunt, had bitter disputes with his parishioners for years over what he alleged was their failure to keep his house adequately supplied with firewood.

Finding and preparing firewood was a task that grew more demanding with the decades, as people exhausted the timber resources close to their dwellings and had to go farther and farther afield for wood. Many Anglo-American colonial leaders of the eighteenth century were acutely aware of the shortage of wood and what it portended. Benjamin Franklin claimed: "Wood, our common fewel, which within these 100 years might be had at every man's door, must now be fetch'd near 100 miles to some towns, and makes a very considerable article in the expence of families" (Franklin, *The Ingenious Dr. Franklin*, 64). The demands of the cold winter of 1770 drove the Virginia planter Landon Carter to fear for the future: "I must wonder what succeeding years will do for firewood. We now have full 3/4 of the year in which we are obliged to keep constant fires; we must fence our ground in with rails, build and repair our houses with timber and every cooking room must have its fire the year through. Add to this the natural death of trees and the violence of gusts that blows them down and I must think that in a few years the lower parts of this Country will be without firewood but pines have a quick growth and we must find out a way of burning them unless we shall be happy in discovering mines of coal" (Carter, *The Diary of Colonel Landon Carter of Sabine Hall*, 382).

Finding an adequate supply of firewood was a particularly pressing problem for cities, given their population concentrations. Boston, which had no native timber, was perpetually bedeviled by a shortage of wood and eventually turned after 1730 to importing coal from Britain. Some Bostonians still depended on firewood, however, since coal had to be burned in a grate, and not everyone could afford one. New York City had to pass strict laws regulating the fees that could be charged for hauling wood to prevent exploitation by haulers during the winter. America's firewood situation improved with the development of better houses and eventually the introduction of the more efficient stove for heating. German colonists are often credited with bringing heating stoves to America. They spread only slowly to the Anglo-American population.

Although stoves were introduced from Europe, they were capable of further improvement in America. Both of the two great physicists produced by colonial America, Benjamin Franklin and Benjamin Thompson (best-known

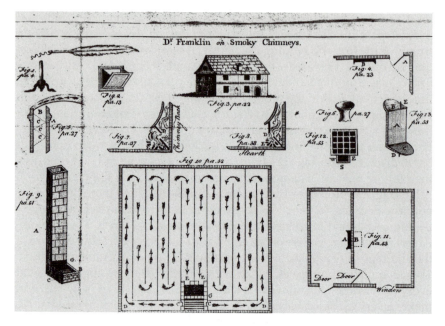

Among the many Americans concerned with the ventilation problems of fireplaces was Benjamin Franklin. Unlike many, he had ideas for what to do about it. Courtesy of the National Library of Medicine.

by his later title as Count Rumford), were fascinated with the problem of efficiency in fireplaces and stoves and originated stove designs. Franklin pointed out that one reason why stoves had not become more popular is that, unlike fireplaces, they did not allow people to actually see the flames. He combined a visible fire with the heating advantage of the stove in his Pennsylvania Fire Place, which he hoped would held conserve America's wood.

The Swedish traveler Peter Kalm described an efficient way of keeping individuals warm, one used by the Dutch women of Albany, New York:

At this time of year since it was beginning to grow cold, it was customary for the women, all of them, even maidens, servants, and little girls, to put live coals into small iron pans which were in turn placed in a small stool resembling somewhat a footstool, but with a bottom upon which the pan was set. The top of the pan was full of holes through which the heat came. They placed this stool with the warming pan under their skirts so that the heat therefrom might go up to the *regiones superiores* and to all parts of the body which the skirts covered. As soon as the coals grew black they were thrown away and replaced by like coals and treated as above. (Kalm, *Peter Kalm's Travels in North America*, 605).

Kalm viewed this custom as weak and self-indulgent.

Of course, heat was not always a blessing. Because a fire was necessary for cooking even on hot days, early colonists in the South faced the problem of dissipating heat during the summer. One solution was to put the fireplace at the end of the house rather than at the central location common in northerly climes. Eventually, many southerners physically separated the kitchen from the rest of the house.

LIGHTING THE HOME

The problem of lighting the home was solved in many ways. The most common source of light, of course, was the sun, and many adapted to it simply by going to bed when the sun set. One of the advantages of the shift from seventeenth-century domestic architecture to the eighteenth-century Georgian house was that the latter's larger windows let in more light. The domestic fire, particularly when in an open fireplace rather than an enclosed stove, also provided some light. Dedicated light sources were more rare. Anglo-American settlers seized on the Native American practice of using pine knots, which could burn in a corner of the fireplace and light the room. The pine knots were also called candlewood or pine torches.

Candles were too expensive to be a source of light for the poor, but were more often used by the middle-class and rich. The wealthiest Americans sought to dazzle visitors to their homes with rooms illuminated by dozens of candles. Candles could be made of many substances, but the two most common were animal fat, or "tallow," and wax. Tallow, which was also used for soapmaking, was most commonly made from the fat of domestic cattle, but all kinds of animal fat could be used. In the fall, tallow was melted in great vessels and skimmed. Tallow candles were made either by dipping, repeatedly lowering the wicks in the tallow, and allowing each layer to cool before dipping again, or in candle molds.

Vegetable fat tallows were unusual but not unknown. The insatiably curious eighteenth-century Swedish scientist and traveler Peter Kalm described how in Pennsylvania tallow for candles was made from the bayberry, or "candleberry," bush:

The berries grow abundantly on the female shrub, and look as if flour had been strewn upon them. They are gathered late in autumn, being ripe about that time, and are then thrown into a kettle or pot full of boiling water. By this means their fat melts out, floats at the top of the water, and is skimmed off into a vessel. The skimming is continued until there is no tallow left. The latter, as soon as it is congealed, looks like common tallow or wax, but has a dirty green color. It is for that reason melted over again and refined, by which means it acquires a fine and rather transparent green color: this tallow is dearer than common tallow, but cheaper than wax. (Peter Kalm, *Peter Kalm's Travels in North America*, 102)

The bayberry candles also had the advantage of giving off a pleasant aroma when snuffed. Myrtle-berries were also used for candle wax, and valued for their scent.

Wax candles burned with a clearer, steadier flame than tallow candles, and given their greater expense, carried more social status. The top of the line candle, however, was the spermaceti candle. Spermaceti, found in the heads of sperm whales, produced a hard candle that did not melt in the hands, and which burned cleanly and brightly. Spermaceti candles were the highest priced, and the profitability of the spermaceti trade made candlemaking and deep-sea whaling boom industries of the mid-eighteenth century.

External lighting was another problem, particularly in cities. In the eighteenth century, cities shifted from a system whereby individuals voluntarily or involuntarily kept lights in front of their dwellings to publicly maintained night lighting systems. Whale-oil lamps were used for public lighting in Boston and Philadelphia.

WATER

Next to air, there is nothing human beings require more than water. Although many shunned water as a drink, it was necessary as the base for other drinks such as tea as well as for cooking, washing, and firefighting. Every household required water, but getting it could be a formidable challenge. Sources varied from streams, which had water in profusion although it was often dirty, to wells, which were more work but which produced water many preferred. Despite the proximity of the Delaware River, Philadelphia drew most of its water for domestic use from wells. Springs and cisterns for catching rain were also commonly used, but presented many difficulties in getting water from one place to another. Cities had neighborhood pumps in some areas, but not central water. A centralized system set up in Boston beginning in 1652 combined a small, gravity-fed reservoir with pipes made from hollow logs to carry water for household and firefighting use, but this early attempt at centralizing water for a city proved a failure.

The first American town that had a system pumping water to every household was the Moravian town of Bethlehem, Pennsylvania. Bethlehemers had depended on a single well at the bottom of a hill near the town gate. Water for household use had to be carried by hand up the hill. The new system was completed in 1755 under the direction of Hans Christopher Christensen, a Danish immigrant millwright, with some help designing the pump from John Boenher, a missionary stationed in the West Indies but visiting Bethlehem. The completed system used a water-powered wheel to pump water from a cistern fed by a local stream. The water was conveyed through a system of hemlock logs bored to form pipe to a water tower constructed in the middle of town. The water was then carried by gravity to Bethlehem homes. The system attracted notice outside of the town itself, and Bethlehem became a destination for curious visitors, including General George Washington. Moravians also spread the idea for this system to their other American communities. The Bethlehem system was later upgraded with multiple iron pumps and pine pipes.

TRASH AND SEWAGE

Another huge problem was disposing of waste. Like other people before the twentieth century, colonists generated far less trash than people do today (for one thing, packaging had not become the ubiquitous source of stuff to be thrown away that it is in the twenty-first century), but they did generate much, and it all had to be disposed of somehow. The most common solution was a trash pit, dug in the ground in the land surrounding the house. Trash pits took all kinds of refuse, including human and animal waste, garbage, and broken crockery (making them, once centuries had passed, an excellent source for archeologists). People urinated and defecated in outhouses or necessities, sometimes with a pit dug below to hold wastes, sometimes not. In either case, the outhouse had to be moved after a period. The presence of all this trash and waste generated horrible odors, particularly in areas of concentrated population. The major cities of northern North America, Boston and New York, began building public sewers around 1700, although Philadelphia was a laggard. New York and Boston in the eighteenth century built their streets with a slight concavity, so that water would run down the middle, while Philadelphia built convex streets, creating gutters on the side.

7

Transportation

FRESHWATER AND INLAND TRAVEL

Although travel was not as common an experience in the colonial period as it is today, colonial people did need to travel for many purposes—business, social, religious. They also needed to ship goods. Although much movement was done by vessels traveling along the coast, there were many modes of travel on land and on inland waters, ranging from walking to coaches to riverboats.

FRESHWATER TRAVEL AND SHIPPING

Transporting goods and people by water was far quicker and cheaper than movement by land. The vast majority of the early colonists who lived away from the sea were close to a river or stream. The ease of transporting goods over water was a boon to the domestic as well as to the export American economy, but personal transportation was a more complex matter. Many ordinary Americans could not afford boats and often lacked the skills to sail them. Some colonists turned to a Native American invention that impressed many Europeans, the canoe. *Canoe*, a word deriving from the indigenous people of Hispaniola, was the first Native American word adopted into European languages. Dugout canoes could be made of the trunks of several different kinds of trees, although red cedar was widely preferred for its lightness and durability. The canoe's opening was either burned or hacked out of the wood. Another type of canoe adopted by settlers was the bark canoe, usually but not always, made of birch bark. Bark boats had the advantage of lightness but also the disadvantage of fragility. Many canoeists carried an extra supply of bark and other boat-making materials in case their craft needed repairs on the way. The mid-eighteenth century Swedish scientist and traveler Peter Kalm described how a bark canoe was made out of elm:

To make such a boat they pick out a thick tall elm, with a smooth bark, and with as few branches as possible. This tree is cut down, and great care is taken to prevent the bark from being hurt by falling against other trees or against the ground. With this view some people do not fell the trees, but climb to the top of them, split the bark and strip it off, which was the method our carpenter took. The bark is split on one side, in a straight line along the tree, as long as the boat it intends to be. At the same time the bark is carefully cut from the trunk a little way on both sides of the slit, that it may more easily separate. It is then peeled off very carefully, and particular care is taken not to make any holes in it. This is easy when the sap is in the trees, and at other seasons they are heated by fire for that purpose. The bark thus stripped off is spread on the ground in a level place [with the smooth side down, later] turning the inside upwards. To stretch better, some logs of wood or stones are carefully put in it, which press it down. Then the sides of the bark are gently bent upwards to form the sides of the boat. Some sticks are then fixed into the ground, at the distance of three or four feet from each other, in a curved line, which the sides of the boat are intended to follow, supporting the bark intended for them. The sides are then bent in the form which the boat is to have, and according to that the sticks are either put nearer or further off. The ribs of the boat are made of thick branches of hickory, these being tough and pliable. They are cut into several flat pieces, about an inch thick, and bent into the form which the ribs require, according to their places in the broader or narrower part of the boat. Being thus bent, they are put across the boat, upon the bark, or its bottom, pretty close together, about a span of ten inches from each other. The upper edge on each side of the boat is made of two thin strips of the length of the boat, where they are to be joined. The edge of the bark is put between these two strips and sewed up with threads of bast, of the mouse wood [probably "moosewood," leatherwood or striped maple] or other rough bark, or with roots. But before it is thus sewed up, the ends of the ribs are likewise put between the strips on each side, taking care to keep them at some distance from each other. After this is done, the strips are sewed together, and being bent properly, both their ends join at each end of the boat, where they are tied together with ropes. To prevent the widening of the boat at the top, three or four transverse bands are put across it, from one edge to the other, at a distance of thirty or forty inches from each other. These bands are commonly made of hickory, on account of its toughness and flexibility, and have a good length. Their extremities are put through the bark on both sides, just below the strips, which form the edges. They are bent up above those strips and twisted round the middle part of the bands, where they are carefully tied by ropes. As the bark at the two ends of the boat cannot be put so close together as to keep the water out, the crevices are stopped up with the crushed or pounded bark of the red elm, which in that state looks like oakum. Some pieces of bark are put upon the ribs of the boat, which may be trod upon with more safety. The side of the bark which has been upon the wood, thus becomes the outside of the boat, because it is smooth and slippery and cuts the water with less difficulty than the other. (Kalm, *Peter Kalm's Travels in North America*, 363–64)

Because canoes were paddled rather than sailed, they required less specialized skill to use. Canoes, both dugout and bark, were particularly indispensable for explorers and Native American traders on America's inland waterways. The expansion of the French in the interior of America, as well as that of their rivals, the Iroquois, depended on canoes. By the eighteenth century, the French and their Native American allies were moving entire armies in flotillas of canoes. On a visit to the French stronghold of Fort LeBouef in the opening stages of the Seven Years War, the young George Washington counted around 220 canoes, plus more being made for French forces.

Canoes were not always comfortable or secure to ride in. Kalm warned that to board a bark boat with shoes on was to court disaster because of the fragility of the boat's bottom. An early eighteenth-century Boston businesswoman, Sarah Kemble Knight, described her experience being ferried in a canoe, exaggerating her fearfulness for comic effect: "The Canoo was very small and shallow, so that when we were in she seem'd ready to take in water, which greatly terrified mee, and caused me to be very circumspect, sitting with my hands fast on each side, my eyes stedy, not daring so much as to lodg my tongue a hairs-breadth more on one side of my mouth then tother, nor so much as think on Lott's wife, for a wry thought would have oversett our wherey" (Knight, *Journeys in New Worlds*, 92). Not all women, however, were intimidated by canoes. The English surveyor John Lawson praised the women of North Carolina: "Many of the women are very handy in canoes, and will manage them with great Dexterity and Skill, which they become accustomed to in this watry country" (Lawson, *A New Voyage to Carolina*, 84).

Many other types of craft were used in colonial America's waterways. African American slaves in South Carolina, the so-called fishing Negroes, used shallow boats adapted from West African designs for fishing and transportation. Ferries in the Chesapeake area, particularly rich in rivers, streams, and inlets, included flat-bottomed boats rowed, poled, or pulled through shallow waters, and small sailing ships or package boats for deeper waters. On the Delaware River, a particular kind of boat designed to transport cargo in relatively shallow water was developed in the eighteenth century. This was the Durham boat, named either after the town of Durham or a boatbuilder named Robert Durham. Durham was a center of iron production, and the Durham boat was developed to move iron to Philadelphia. It was pointed on both ends like a canoe, 66 feet long and 6 feet wide, and usually maneuvered by a boatman pushing along the bottom of the river with a steel-tipped pole. A Durham boat could carry more than 10 tons of cargo. The Durham boat's moment of historical glory, however, came when

George Washington's army used Durham boats to cross the Delaware during the Revolutionary War. Durham boats resemble the kinds of boats used for river transportation in Scandinavia, and one possible explanation for their origin is that they were introduced by the Swedish and Finnish boatmen who dominated Delaware River trade. Similar flat-bottomed boats spread to other river transport systems in northern British America.

No area of British North America was more shaped and dominated by water transport than the Chesapeake Bay region. From the earliest days of colonization, visitors were much impressed by its many waterways. The ease of moving hogsheads of tobacco by water, a process far easier and gentler on the tobacco than land transport, was essential to the development of the Chesapeake tobacco industry. (Wheat was denser, and hogsheads of wheat were harder to move.) The ability to anchor ships in deep freshwater helped protect them from the worm (*teredo navalis*) that attacked ships' bottoms. Because transportation in the Chesapeake region depended on the ability to cross water, boating skills and boats were widely distributed among the population, particularly in the eighteenth century, and roads often served merely to link ferries and landings. The ease of transporting goods and people directly to ships on the bay from plantations helped retard the growth of cities in the region.

The further expansion of the colonies in the eighteenth century meant that inland water transportation assumed an even more prominent role. The last decades of colonial rule saw a concerted yet almost completely fruitless effort to improve internal waterways by means of canals. Canals, though, served other purposes as well. A British military engineer suggested that a canal between the Ashley and Cooper Rivers would be a barrier protecting Charleston against attack by land, although nothing came of the project. Aware of the canal building going on at the same time in England, Americans saw canals as a route to economic development. The leaders in these projects were usually urban merchants interested in increasing the ease of trade. Philadelphia, the economic star of eighteenth-century America, was the most active center of canal promotion. Philadelphia merchants subscribed 140 British pounds to surveying possible routes, while Baltimore merchants charged the Philadelphians with planning to divert trade from their city. The scheme was supplemented by another one to connect the Susquehanna and the Schuylkill Rivers. The plans led to much activity by the Philadelphia-based American Philosophical Society (America's first successful scientific society), the Pennsylvania Assembly, and individual Philadelphia merchants. In addition to commercial rivalry and the difficulties of raising capital, canal building was also bedeviled by America's lack of the technical expertise of experienced canal builders. Benjamin Franklin, in London, suggested in a letter to Samuel Rhoads, a member of the Pennsylvania Assembly, that the Americans hire an experienced English canal builder rather than try to build it themselves. However, neither canal was actually built until the early nineteenth century, and no canals of appreciable size were built in the colonial era.

LAND TRAVEL

One challenge facing early American colonists was maintaining communications across a space much larger than that which they had known in England or Europe. The distance between Boston and Charleston was more than twice the distance between London and Edinburgh. Even attending Sunday Services, carrying goods to market, or courting could require traveling many miles. Although travel by water was the main mode of transport, many Americans did not own boats or live close to navigable waterways and had to travel on land. Colonial Americans, like their Native predecessors and contemporaries, were willing to travel long distances by foot, although as forests were cleared and more horses brought to the colonies, those who could afford it traveled on horseback. Travel was more difficult in winter, but one Native American invention that the colonists eagerly adopted was the snowshoe, made of a bent ash frame crisscrossed with strips of rawhide. The paths used by the colonists often followed old Native American routes. One such path that became a major thoroughfare in early colonial America was the Bay Path, which went from Cambridge to Springfield and the Connecticut River.

Although a path could be clearly visible in open ground, woods often presented a challenge. One way of marking paths in forests was by blazes, sections cut out of the bark of trees along the way—hence the term "trailblazing." These bright patches were intended to show the traveler the way, but they did not always work. The seventeenth-century Dutch visitor Jaspar Dankaerts found blazed trails highly unsatisfactory: "These marks are merely a piece cut out of the bark with an axe, about the height of a man's eyes from the ground; and by means of them the commonest roads are designated through all New Netherland and Maryland; but in consequence of the great number of roads so marked, and their running into and across each other, they are of little assistance, and indeed often mislead" (Dankers and Sluyter, *Journal of a Voyage to New York*, 175).

ROADS

Early colonization often followed the easy route along waterways. But once the riverbanks were settled, subsequent expansion took colonists into areas that were more difficult to get to, particularly as traffic grew heavier. Road building, rather than trailblazing, became a necessity, and many of the new roads were laid out by surveyors rather than following Native trails. However, roads remained poor or virtually nonexistent in most of colonial America. They frequently crossed private property, making it necessary to dismount and mount to open and close gates. Passage in wheeled vehicles over rocky country was jarring and unpleasant. Roads were also unmarked, making it easy for people to get lost.

There were several ways to cross water, the simplest being ferries and fords. Bridges were mostly logs on the surface of the water, either sunk on pilings or free floating. One exception was the fine stone bridge over the Pennypack River in Philadelphia, built in 1697. Now known as the Frankford Avenue Bridge, it is still in use. Whether on pilings or free float-ing, bridges presented problems, as pilings could block the course of the water and floating bridges were unstable.

The gap between planning and surveying a road and actually build-ing it could be immense. In addition to finding the money, differences between governments also hindered road building. A plan to institute a postal service between Boston and New York during the Second Dutch War (1665–1667) came to nothing, partly because there was no road between these two major cities of northeastern America, one English and one Dutch. Nor did the building of a road end the work. Once roads were built, they had to be maintained, and this responsibility fell into the hands of local authorities. The British government took no responsibility for the state of roads, and even provincial assemblies usually deferred to local bodies. Labor was found for road maintenance by means of a draft, a method with

The Frankford Avenue Bridge over the Pennypack River, built in 1697, is a rare example of a colonial bridge; moreover, it's still in use. Courtesy of the Library of Congress.

a long tradition in Europe. For example, in Pennsylvania, where roads were somewhat better than in the rest of the colonies, before 1762, all male inhabitants were legally required to spend a few days each year on road work. In 1762, a system was established whereby men could buy their way out of the obligation, with the money used to hire laborers.

Despite the poor quality of the roads, early American travelers had some advantages over their European contemporaries (many European roads were equally bad). Early America had little highway robbery, although Native Americans might attack travelers from time to time in certain places. Farmhouses often offered hospitality in areas that lacked inns or taverns, and travelers were essential in circulating news to isolated farmers in a society without mass communications.

VEHICLES

By the eighteenth century, in addition to foot travel, Americans could travel in wagons, in carriages, and during the winter, on sledges and sleighs. With the exception of some top of the line coaches, all of these vehicles were American-made. Coaches were the most prestigious vehicles, restricted to persons of the highest social status. The earliest coach to be mentioned in the British colonies was the one that the governor of New Netherland Anthony Colve presented to Sir Edmund Andros, the incoming governor as the colony passed from Dutch to British rule. Some of the first to be seen in America were vehicles of state employed by colonial governors sent from England, from whom they diffused to the American upper classes. Private coaches remained restricted to the elite—the Massachusetts tax list of 1753 includes only six. Of somewhat lower status was the two-wheeled calash. Another vehicle, the chaise, or as it became known in America, the shay, a light two- or four-wheeled carriage, was introduced between 1710 and 1730. All of these horse-drawn vehicles were usually found in colonial cities and towns, except for a few owned by wealthy rural southern planters. Evidence of the spread of coaches and other vehicles in the South is the fact that the Virginia ferry law of 1702 mentioned rates for people and horses only, but the revision of the law in 1720 added rates for two- and four-wheeled vehicles.

Use of horse-drawn vehicles was not restricted to their owners and their families. Stagecoaches and other forms of public transportation emerged in the early eighteenth century. By 1716, there was a fortnightly run between Boston and Newport, although it only lasted a few years. Regularly scheduled wagon-based transit began in New Jersey, building on the freight wagons that traveled between the coast and the Delaware River. By 1750, there was a regular New York–Philadelphia run, traveling by land and water and taking about three days. Philadelphia–Chesapeake lines emerged in the 1760s, taking various routes to different endpoints, although over time, Baltimore dominated. The first successful New England

stage route was between Boston and Portsmouth in 1761, and a Boston–
New York stage was finally established in 1772. In addition to these inter-
city routes, there were also local routes in the areas of Boston, New York,
and Philadelphia.

WAGONS AND CARTS

Not only people but also goods moved overland on horse-drawn vehicles.
Wagon and cart technologies differed among the different European groups
that settled in North America. English settlers made greater use of carts,
Germans of wagons. The Swedes had a unique practice of using cross sections of tree trunks as cart wheels. Spanish settlers, following traditions of
their native country, made less use of wheeled vehicles and more of pack
animals than did other European colonists. The muledriver was as characteristic a figure of the Spanish American Empire as the Franciscan friar or
the hidalgo—and more essential to its functioning than either. One vehicle
that originated in America and came into widespread use in the late colonial
period and beyond was the Conestoga wagon. The Conestoga is named for
the Conestoga River Valley in Lancaster County, Pennsylvania. The term
first appeared in the early eighteenth century in Philadelphia. There was a
Conestoga Wagon Inn on Philadelphia's Market Street by 1750. The defin-
ing features of the Conestoga wagon included a cloth cover held up with
8 to12 wooden hoops stapled at both ends to the side rails with iron, a
curved body with an upswept front and back, rear wheels with a diameter
of 54 inches or greater, and wooden axles. The wagon was pulled with a
team of four, five, or six horses, although by the early nineteenth century,
six became accepted as the standard number. The sturdy draft horses
who pulled the wagons eventually became known as Conestoga horses,
although they were never formally recognized as a breed.

Manufacture of these wagons was concentrated in southeast
Pennsylvania, home of the German settlers who were some of the most
skilled artisans in the colonies. The Conestoga incorporated much metal
in its design and made heavy demands on the skills of the blacksmith
as well as the wagon builder. The design itself seems to have originated
among German-American farmers as a way of carrying their goods to
markets in the towns. The necessity of protecting farm produce from
the weather during the four-day journey from Lancaster to Philadelphia
encouraged covering the wagon. The Conestoga received wider exposure
in 1755 when General Braddock hired more than 150 farm wagons for the
advance against Fort Duquesne. Increasing use of large wagons led to the
widening and smoothing of roads to accommodate them.

Many journeys, even short ones, required a combination of land and water
conveyance with the attendant loading and unloading. Thomas Jefferson
described the route lead ore had to take from one of colonial America's few

lead mines, Great Kanawhay, to the poorly sited refining furnace and the distribution center:

The present furnace is a mile from the ore-bank, and on the opposite side of the river. The ore is first waggoned to the river, a quarter of a mile, then laden on board of canoes and carried across the river, which is there about 200 yards wide, and then again taken into waggons and carried to the furnace. This mode was originally adopted, that they might avail themselves of a good situation on a creek, for a pounding mill: but it would be easy to have the furnace and pounding mill on the same side of the river, which would yield water, without any dam, by a canal of about half a mile in length. From the furnace the lead is transported 130 miles along a good road, leading through the peaks of Otter to Lynch's ferry, or Winston's, on James river, from whence it is carried by water about the same distance to Westham. (Jefferson, *Writings*, 150–51)

ROAD IMPROVEMENTS

The increasingly technological wars of the British, the French, and their Native American allies in the eighteenth century meant new roads had to be built and existing ones widened and improved. Wide roads were necessary to move large bodies of regular troops, their supplies, and siege cannon.

Another force driving improvement of roads in the mid-century was the improvement of postal service after British authorities finally established a postal service covering all the Continental colonies in 1751. (The postal service itself was considered to be contributing to the military organization of the colonies.) Benjamin Franklin, appointed co-deputy postmaster in 1753, was particularly active, traveling extensively through the northern colonies, inspecting post offices and suggesting new routes and procedures. He devised a crude cyclometer that he hitched to the back of his chaise for measuring the distances along the roads and laid out, or encouraged others to lay out, milestones. Improvement of land communication between the colonies was one force contributing to colonial unity before and during the Revolution. The publication of a full atlas of America's roads, however, waited until several years after the Revolution, when Christopher Colles's *A Survey of the Roads of the United States of America* was published in 1789.

8

Reading and Seeing: The Technology of Words and Images

One of the longest-running stories in human technological development has been the increased speed and volume of communications—from the first spoken words to e-mail and the Internet. Colonial people, like their early modern European contemporaries, thought of themselves as beneficiaries of a technological revolution in communications—that of the printing press. Like paper, gunpowder, and the compass, the printing press was originally a Chinese invention. Before its arrival or reinvention in Europe during the fifteenth century, multiple copies of written documents had to be made laboriously—and often sloppily—by hand. Reproducing images was even more time-consuming and difficult, and images degraded quickly over generations of copies. The press, combined with means for mechanical reproduction of pictures, enabled the written word and images to spread far more quickly and accurately. Benjamin Franklin, a printer himself, praised printing and its ability to preserve knowledge in a way typical of early modern writers: "The Improvements made within these 2000 years, considerable as they are, would have been much more so, if the Ancients had possess'd one or two Arts now in common Use, I mean those of Copper Plate- and Letter-Printing. Whatever is now exactly delineated and describ'd by those, can scarcely (from the Multitude of Copies) be lost to Posterity" (Franklin, *Writings*, 480). Of course, printing did not solve every problem of communication—as Franklin well knew, copyist's errors were replaced by printer's errors. He expressed this truth in made-up Latin, *printerum est errare*—to be a printer is to err (Franklin, *Writings*, 143).

PRINTING TECHNOLOGY

Printing presses worked by forcing together sheets of paper and type made from an alloy of lead and antimony, covered with ink. Lead was suited for making type due to its softness and malleability. However, as Franklin realized, the close handling of lead that being a pressman required endangered the health. The individual pieces of type, each bearing a letter, punctuation mark, or space, were put together on an iron rod called a composing stick by a composer, the most highly skilled worker in the printing shop. Requiring literacy, this task was particularly difficult because the text had to be loaded backward so as to be the right way on the printed page. Groups of lines were set in galleys, or wooden cases, which were then set into an iron chase, which collected the lines for an entire page. The type in the chase was smeared with ink, and the chase securely fastened to the stone bed of the press. The moistened sheet of paper was placed in a wooden frame hinged to the chase, and the two brought together. A pressman brought down the platen, which forced the chase and the paper together so that the ink was transferred to the paper. He did this by pulling a lever that turned a screw. While the compositor was a skilled worker, the pressman's primary qualification was the muscular strength needed to bring the platen down with sufficient pressure. The paper was then removed from the press and hung up to dry.

The British colonies were actually latecomers to printing; the earliest surviving Spanish-American printed text, from Mexico City, dates from 1540, nearly a century earlier than the first printing from English America in 1638 in Cambridge, Massachusetts. The first printing press in Pennsylvania was established in 1685, and the Philadelphia printing industry dominated eighteenth-century American publishing. The limitations of the American market meant that colonial American printing was not technically advanced by European standards. Anglo-Americans seeking the services of fine printers and bookmakers—for example, cartographers looking for printers for their maps—continued to turn to London. By contrast, cheap publications with a ready local market, almanacs and newspapers, poured out in torrents from American presses. Printers also branched out into related activities such as papermaking. However, the presses themselves still usually had to be imported. The first American printing press was not built until 1769, when Isaac Doolittle of New Haven made one. Type fonts, the tiny lead and antimony blocks that carried the actual letters and punctuation, were also extremely difficult to make. Until the very end of the colonial period, the British colonies in America had to import their type fonts from England. Ironically, the first successful type foundry in the British colonies was not produced for English-language presses, but for German ones at Germantown, Pennsylvania. English types would not be produced in America until 1769, when Abel Buell established a manufactory in Killingworth, Connecticut, for making type by a process he had invented with encouragement from the American Philosophical Society, colonial America's leading scientific and technological society.

PAPER

The rise of the press increased the demand for paper. The first paper mill in colonial British America was established in 1690 at Germantown, Pennsylvania, one of the most active technological centers in the Americas. Pennsylvania would remain the center of American papermaking throughout the colonial period. The master of the mill was a German immigrant, William Rittenhouse, and the enterprise was financially backed by a leading printer, William Bradford, seeking a reliable supply for his press. Many paper mills, which multiplied rapidly in the eighteenth century, were built or owned by printers. Paper in the colonial period was made out of rags, preferably linen rags, and papermakers and printers were constantly trying to get hold of the raw material. White paper of the kind now familiar was unknown in this period, as paper was not bleached. A fine paper had to be made by hand-sorting the rags and was cream-colored rather than pure white.

The watermark, visible when the paper was held up to the light, was made by putting a wire outline on the mold. The mold was held in place, with tiny, threadlike wires. Watermarks usually served to identify the papermaker, but some rich men like George Washington had a personal watermark on their letter paper.

BOOKBINDING

Unlike modern times, when books are sold already bound, early modern books were sold unbound from the printer. Book printing required that multiple pages be printed on both sides of a large sheet, which was then folded into sets of 2, 4, 8, or 16 pages (called signatures), depending on the size of the book.

Bookbinding was a separate profession, although often combined with printing or bookselling. The most artistically and technologically sophisticated bookbinders worked for the wealthy in Europe, for whom a set of well-bound books with their own personal markings was a source of pride and social status. As a luxury craft, it took awhile for bookbinding to arrive across the Atlantic. The first-known bookbinder to emigrate to practice his trade in North America was John Ratcliff, who came to Boston around 1663 to bind John Eliot's Indian Bible.

On receiving a set of signatures making up a book from a printer, the bookbinder or one of his apprentices compiled them in the order that made up the book and then beat them flat with a hammer. The backs of the signatures were then sewn together with linen thread, which was anchored on horizontal hemp cross threads in larger books.

The front and back covers of a leather bound book were made of thin, rigid boards covered with leather. Although European bookbinders mostly used stiffened paper or pulp, many American bookbinders used a thin piece of wood called "scabbard." The most common leather used for colonial bookbindings was made from sheepskin. Imported calfskin was used more rarely, and pigskin bindings, common in Germany, were rare even in those areas of America settled by Germans. The most prestigious form of leather for binding was a specially treated goatskin called "morocco." Some morocco was imported to America for particular prestige bindings, but it was not made in America itself. The dampened leather was decorated by pressing down on it with heated brass stamps and rolls that laid down patterns. These tools were mostly imported. The first newspaper advertisement for an American maker of bookbinder's tools did not appear until 1745.

Specially valued books could receive special treatments with extra ornamentation and metal inlays to protect the corners or locks across the front of the book for protection. There was a shift around 1760 from decorating boards and leaving spines plain or with little ornamentation toward leaving boards plain and decorating spines. This was probably caused by the greater popularity of shelving books spine out, so that the covers were not normally visible. This was a more efficient way of shelving in larger libraries than the previous way of leaving books on tables or in presses.

PEN, INK, AND PENCIL

Although steel pens had been known for centuries, they were still rare in the early modern period. The most common form of pen by far remained the quill. Many birds were exploited for their quills, but the most common was the goose quill. Quills were usually taken from the wings during molting times (feathers from the left wing were better suited to right-handed pen users) and cut into shape with a penknife, a small, very sharp steel blade. The resulting pen had to be kept moist in a holder, as a dry pen made it difficult to write. The use of a quill pen was a skill that had to be learned. The importance of good penmanship increased in the eighteenth century, as having a good hand became one of the marks of so-called gentle status.

Words on paper, whether printed or flowing from a pen, were made of ink, a complex chemical product. The most common kind of ink in the period was made from oak galls, lumps in oak formed by wasps that laid eggs there. Combined with iron salt (hydrogenated ferrous sulfate, also known as "copperas" or "green vitriol"), the tannic and gallic acids in oak galls produced a purplish-black compound. Some gum arabic was added to help fix the ink to the paper, and the whole dissolved in water. The dyes logwood or indigo were also sometimes added to ink. Printer's ink was particularly difficult to manufacture, as it had to be strongly black in order to show up well. Carbon was added in the form of "lampblack." By the beginning of the American Revolution, the leading American center for the manufacture of lampblack for printer's inks was Germantown, Pennsylvania, home of Germantown lampblack.

The modern wood-cased, graphite pencil had been devised in the seventeenth century, but was not common in colonial America. The only known source of graphite, or black lead, was in the Cumberland district of England, and there were no commercial pencil makers in America. Pencils had to be imported. In the absence of graphite pencils, some Americans used an earlier form of the pencil, relying on metallic lead to mark the paper. Even in the early nineteenth century, Americans were making pencils by melting lead bullets and pouring the molten metal into a quill cut two inches short.

WRITING AND THE COLONIAL CONQUEST OF AMERICA

The technology of written communication, ranging from the alphabet to print, was an area that Europeans had developed and Native North Americans had not. In agriculture, crafts, and food preparation, Europeans had tools that Native Americans lacked, but Native Americans quickly learned to understand that the function of a gun was the same as that of a bow and to use guns themselves. Writing, with no close analogy in the highly oral culture of Native North Americans, produced some of the most notorious examples of Native American culture shock. The first English scientist and technological expert to visit America, Thomas Harriot, described the fascination of the Native Americans with his printed Bible, although he tried to explain to them that the physical book itself was not as important as the message it contained. Harriot claimed that the Natives seemed to crave physical contact with the book, embracing and kissing it. A French missionary complained that such was the desire of Native Americans to turn the pages and look at the pictures in his Bible that they eventually destroyed it. The ability of European missionaries and settlers to communicate precisely across vast distances by means of writing also seemed supernatural to the first Natives to encounter it. Written pieces of paper were viewed as having magical power, and some Natives blamed the epidemics that often followed first contact with Europeans on the pieces of writing the newcomers carried.

The cultural gap between European colonists and Native Americans was particularly wide in the area of religion. Conversion of Native Americans to Christianity was conversion to a "religion of the book," requiring acceptance of the written word. Although Protestants are sometimes viewed as placing more emphasis on the Biblical text than Catholics, both Catholic and Protestant missionaries to Native Americans relied on written documents. Early Jesuit missionaries to the Native peoples of eastern North America sought to persuade their prospective converts by emphasizing the fixity and permanence of the written record of Christianity in comparison to the unreliability of the oral traditions of the Native Americans.

Of course, not all writing was on paper or in books. The Southwest saw a case where Spanish conquerors literally "wrote their names on the land." This is the famous inscription rock of El Morro in New Mexico, where Native Americans had already inscribed petroglyphs long before the Spanish arrival. The conspicuous sandstone mesa was located near a supply of freshwater, which made it an excellent campground. Spanish explorers and conquistadors who left their names on the rock included Don Juan de Onate and the reconqueror of New Mexico, Don Diego de Vargas.

ENGRAVING AND REPRODUCING IMAGES

Not only words but images were reproduced, in a process known as engraving. Engravers could be a disreputable lot, because their skill was easily corrupted to serve one of the most common crimes in colonial America, counterfeiting. One of the most ingenious engravers and inventors of the whole colonial period, Abel Buell (1742–1822), was also a counterfeiter, convicted of altering Connecticut notes in 1764 and sentenced to be branded and have part of his ear cut off. He was productive in prison, though, where he invented a lapidary lathe for grinding and polishing gems.

The oldest form of engraving, indeed the oldest form of printing in Europe, was woodcut. A block of wood was marked with an image, and those parts of the wood not incorporated in the image were cut away. The image could then be printed on a regular printing press. Woodcuts were relatively easy to cut and produce, but most of them were crude. In the hands of a master like the German artist Albrecht Dürer, woodcuts could achieve an astounding level of detail, but such persons were rare in Europe and unknown in colonial America. Fine, detailed printing in America required other techniques, the most common of which was copperplate engraving, an art introduced to Europe in the fifteenth century. The engraver cut lines to hold ink into a copper plate with a sharp steel tool. Only lines were reproduced on a copperplate engraving, so crosshatching was used to simulate depth. The actual production of a copperplate image, which required forcing the paper into the inked lines of the plate, could not be done on a conventional printing press, which worked by impact. Instead, a special press was used that squeezed the plate and the paper together with rollers. Copperplate work was complex and demanding and came to North America rather late in the colonial era. The oldest surviving American copperplate engraving, a portrait of Increase Mather in the frontispiece of one of his books, dates from 1701. Among the most famous copperplate engravings of colonial America was Paul Revere's 1768 depiction of British soldiers landing at Boston's Long Wharf to enforce new government decrees—an influential piece of propaganda.

PAINTING

Painting was a marginal profession in colonial America, which lacked the established personal or institutional concentrations of wealth that supported many European painters. All but the elite of American painters (who mostly emigrated to Europe) had to travel constantly in search of new customers. Portability was important. Painters could not carry their own backing surfaces, having to make do with what was available. Lacking the medium of canvas, they painted on many fabric surfaces or wood. Many colonial American painters used panels of hardwood as their painting surface. Painters, or "limners," carried dry paint with them and mixed it with oil on the spot.

9

Science and Technology on the Land: Surveying and Cartography

Maps of the Americas made by Europeans and colonists progressed from crude outlines, based on dead reckoning and observation, to precise works reflecting the efforts of professional surveyors and cartographers. Mapping was part of the great endeavor of colonists and Europeans to know the strange lands of America. Mappers drew on Native American knowledge as well as their own observations and European cartographic techniques.

EARLY MAPS

European expansion in the fifteenth and sixteenth centuries was accompanied not only by a rising concern with accurate mapping, but also the difficulty of reconciling several accounts into a single map. Geographical knowledge was one of the goals of every journey of exploration and discovery, and cartographers accompanied explorers on their travels. The Casa de Contratación, founded in Seville in 1503 to oversee and regulate Spanish movements to the New World, emphasized accurate cartography and navigation. In 1512, the Royal Pattern, a continuously updated map was established. The Spanish could not maintain a monopoly on New World cartographic information, however, and maps circulated widely in sixteenth-century Europe. The first published map to include the word *America* was the German Martin Waldsemuller's *Cosmographica* (1507). New World maps were included in the first atlas, the Dutch bookseller Abraham Ortelius's *Theater of the World* (1570).

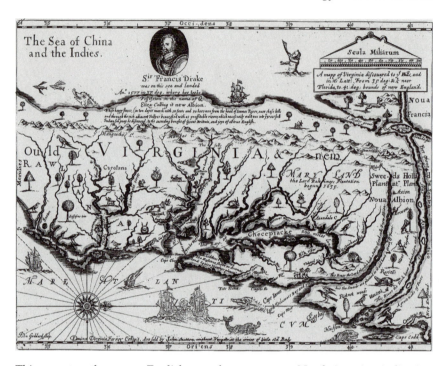

This seventeenth-century English map shows a narrow North America, indicating that overland access to the Pacific would be possible for settlers. Courtesy of the Library of Congress, Geography and Map Division.

Latecomers to the New World, the English were also latecomers to New World mapping. The first published map of the New World originally produced (as opposed to maps adapted from Continental ones) by an English cartographer was John White's map included in the 1590 edition of Thomas Harriot's *A Briefe and True Report of the New Found Land of Virginia*. Captain John Smith was another early English mapmaker. In many cases, English manuscript maps included more accurate geographical information than printed ones. Explorers and colonization companies often preferred to keep information as private as possible, rather than publishing it openly.

MAPS AND POLITICS

Maps served many functions in colonial society. They promoted exploration and colonization. All journeys of exploration and discovery included cartographers. The earliest English maps of the New World emphasize the easy access to the wealth of China and Japan through a wide—and yet to be actually discovered—Northwest Passage. Based more on wishful thinking than on observation, such maps were essentially fictional. Even maps with some pretensions to accuracy varied widely, both in what they conveyed and in what terrain features they emphasized. Military maps emphasized fortresses and the routes between them, whereas maps for trade emphasized natural resources and trade routes.

Maps expressed—and advanced—political claims. The French cartographer Guillame Delisle (1675–1726) published a technically excellent *Map of Louisiana and the Course of the Mississippi* (1718), which was particularly influential in its treatment of the Gulf of Mexico. The map also aggressively advanced the French position in North America, restricting the English holdings in the Southeast to the territory east of the Allegheny Mountains. French cartographers had the advantage over English of being more knowledgeable of the interior of North America. Herman Moll, a German or Dutch immigrant to England who had become a fierce British patriot, fired back in 1720 with *A New Map of the North Parts of America Claimed by France,* minimizing French claims and expanding British ones. Politically speaking, the most important map produced in the colonial era was that of Dr. John Mitchell. The first edition appeared in London in 1755, with the title *A Map of the British and French Dominions in North America.* Sponsored by the Lords Commissioners for Trade and Plantations, the Mitchell map precisely delineated the maximum extent of English claims, even to the Pacific. The fourth edition of the map, published in 1775 after the British conquest of Canada in the Seven Years War, was titled *A Map of the British Colonies in North America with the Roads, Distances, Limits and Extent of the Settlements.* This map was the cartographic basis of the territorial negotiations between Britain and America at the end of the Revolutionary War.

Maps were also used in political struggles within empires as well as between them. Poor understanding of local geography meant that grants of land made in London often had vaguely defined boundaries or overlapped with other grants. Colonies produced maps that supported their boundary claims against those of their neighbors, or advanced claims based on old maps. Maps also served economic arguments. New York officials, in communicating with the government in England, used deceptive maps that showed easy access from New York to the Iroquois country. They argued that this meant the British government should put more resources into the colony to support the fur trade with the Native Americans of the North. A map also helped represent ownership. Lord Baltimore, the proprietor of Maryland, rewarded the Prague-born Augustine Herman with a manor of 13,000 acres for his map *Virginia and Maryland as it is Planted and Inhabited this Present Year 1670* (1673). Hermann's fine map, which took many years to research and draw, set the standard for Chesapeake cartography well into the eighteenth century.

Cultural and economic differences influenced mapping styles. Dutch maps of upstate New York emphasized waterways and trade routes, reflecting the fact that early Dutch settlers in the region were mostly interested

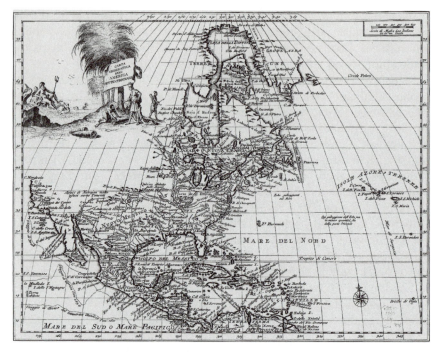

This map, drawn by Guillame Delisle and circulated widely in Europe, draws on
the knowledge gathered by French explorers and fur traders. This copy is from
an Italian atlas published in Venice in 1750. Courtesy of the Library of Congress,
Geography and Map Division.

in trading for furs with Native Americans. When the English took over
the territory, their maps emphasized delineating the ownership of land
suitable for agriculture and the relations of English and French fortresses.
Waterways were shown less as routes for trade than as boundaries.

SURVEYING

As more land in the Americas was conquered, settled, and known
by Europeans, there was a greater need for accurate, or at least mutu-
ally agreeable, boundary lines to demarcate individual properties. This
occurred at every level, from delineating the boundaries between colonies
or the claims of different European rulers, to determining the boundaries
of individual landholdings. Establishing boundaries, as well as laying out
towns, plotting the course of roads, dividing properties between heirs or
purchasers, and a host of other tasks was the work of surveyors. Surveying
had developed in Europe in the mid-sixteenth century as a mathematical
and astronomical discipline. Surveyors in America followed the procedures that had been developed in Europe, but were handicapped relative
to their European counterparts by the densely wooded nature of some

areas, which made taking a long view difficult if not impossible. European surveyors often used church spires, usually the highest point in a village or town, as a landmark; this was impossible in much of the Americas. The bulky theodolite, a standard tool in Europe for taking the azimuth, the position of a celestial object in the circle of the horizon, was less popular in America, to which the more portable circumferentor, or surveyor's compass, was better suited. The first basic text specifically adapted for American surveying, John Love's frequently reprinted *Geodaesia, or the Art of Surveying and Measuring of Land Made Easy* (1688), recommended against the theodolite based on Love's surveying experience in Jamaica and North Carolina.

Simple surveying, establishing property lines, was a common profession for landowners and sons of the landowning class, the most famous examples being the Virginia landowners and revolutionaries George Washington and Thomas Jefferson. Surveying could be a lucrative profession—in Virginia surveyors were allowed to charge 40 pounds of tobacco per 100 acres surveyed.

In addition to these private surveyors who were landowners themselves or working for landowners, individual colonies also appointed surveyors-general for government work and some counties did the same. An early example is Richard Norwood, employed by the Bermuda Company to survey its newly acquired islands in 1610. The scientist and historian Cadwallader Colden (1688–1776) was Surveyor-General of New York. In Virginia, the position of Surveyor-General was a perquisite of the College of William and Mary. Colonies also commissioned particular surveyors for specific missions. The great Virginia planter William Byrd was one of the commissioners of the official expedition of Virginia and North Carolina surveyors to establish the boundary between the two colonies in 1728. He described the miseries of surveying through the Great Dismal Swamp:

The Surveyors pursued their work with all Diligence, but found the Soil of the Dismal so Spongy that the Water ouzed up into every foot-step they took. To their Sorrow, too, they found the Reeds and Bryars more firmly interwoven than they did the day before. But the greatest grievance was from large Cypresses, which the Wind had blown down and heap'd upon one another. On the Limbs of most of them grew Sharp Snags, Pointing every way like so many Pikes, that requir'd much Pains and Caution to avoid.... Never was Rum, that cordial of Life, found more necessary than it was in this Dirty Place. (Byrd, *Histories,* 66)

The surveyor's tools included the magnetic compass and the chain. Chains were for laying on the ground to measure distances. The standard chain used in colonial British America was made of 100 iron links stretching a total of 22 yards. A constant problem for surveyors was the unreliability of chains. Because of the wear and distortions of the iron caused by climate, chains had to be remeasured before each use. Compasses were also imperfect instruments, because of the difference between magnetic north and true north.

SPANISH-AMERICAN CITY PLANNERS AND SURVEYORS

The pioneers and leaders in North American city planning for most of the colonial period were the Spanish. In 1573, King Philip II issued a decree known as the *Laws of the Indies* , which laid down very specific procedures for the building of Spanish towns, or *pueblos*, in the New World. Spanish towns were to be built in the rectangular grid pattern of streets that went back to the Romans. They were to be built around a central square or rectangular plaza. The corners of the plazas were to face the compass directions; the Spanish in the reign of Philip II continued to believe in the ancient idea that winds always blew in the compass directions. If the plaza and streets were oriented correctly, therefore, the streets would always be perpendicular to the wind rather than having winds blow straight down them. Although the exact directions contained in the *Laws of the Indies* were seldom carried out precisely in the conditions of the New World, most Spanish towns roughly followed this pattern.

Not all Spanish settlements along the northern frontier of its empire were towns. Some were missions and others were *presidios*, or forts controlled by the army. Although the town planning directives of the *Laws of the Indies* did not apply to these outposts, the presence of central authorities—the Catholic Church, the Franciscan Order, the Spanish army—meant that they too showed a relatively high degree of standardization. In the Spanish North American territories, where landowners played a much smaller social role compared to the church and the military, much surveying was done by missionaries such as the Italian Jesuit Eusebio Francisco Kino. Kino, who helped establish the first Spanish mission in California, traveled thousands of miles over the Southwest, even helping to establish a Spanish presence in the modern state of Arizona. His most notable geographic accomplishments were proving that Baja California, was an island rather than a peninsula, and drawing reliable maps of many southwestern areas being measured for the first time.

CITY PLANNING IN BRITISH AMERICA

The first permanent settlements in eastern North America were far different from the centrally planned Spanish-American communities. Early British-American and Dutch-American settlements were laid out haphazardly rather than following any previously established pattern or plan. The most notable examples were the cities of Boston and New York. By the late seventeenth century, British-American expectations had changed, and new cities were often laid out according to a plan incorporating a grid of straight streets meeting at right angles. The design of Philadelphia was particularly influential in this respect. Thomas Holme (1624–1695), Surveyor-General of Pennsylvania, planned and laid out the city in 1682. The straightness of the streets and the precision of the grid attracted wide admiration and were emulated by other planners of cities large and small. Only in New England did the old irregular pattern persist into the eighteenth century.

MAPPING AND SURVEYING IN THE LAST COLONIAL DECADES

The growing sophistication of American surveying helped improve cartography. The mid-eighteenth century saw an outburst of maps published by professional surveyors. Peter Jefferson and Joshua Fry's *Map of the Inhabited Parts of Virginia* (1754), commissioned by the colonial government, was frequently reprinted and one of the sources of Mitchell's map. Jefferson was a leading Virginia surveyor who also taught his son, Thomas Jefferson, the art of surveying, and Fry was a former professor of mathematics and natural philosophy at William and Mary. He had previously worked with Jefferson on the endless task of tracing the border between Virginia and North Carolina in 1747. The Welsh-born Lewis Evans was another significant surveyor-mapper, cartographer of *General Map of the Middle British Colonies in America* (1755).

The British acquisition of Florida following the Seven Years War led to a burst of surveying and mapmaking, at first more associated with the British government in London than with American cartographers. The German immigrant William Gerard de Brahm (c. 1717–1799), a surveyor and military engineer, had already produced important maps of the southeastern colonies, beginning with the frequently reprinted *Map of South Carolina and a Part of Georgia* in 1757. Appointed Surveyor-General for the new Southern Department, de Brahm and his assistant, the Dutchman Bernard Romans, surveyed the coasts of Florida in the 1760s and early 1770s. Romans established contacts with American scientists and mariners and combined natural history with cartography, publishing *Concise Natural History of East and West Florida* in 1775.

Despite the growing sophistication of American cartographers in the eighteenth century, however, printing maps was a different matter, requiring an ever-increasing amount of detail and precision. American printers were simply not up to the challenge of accurately representing the information gathered by the most advanced surveyors and cartographers. The best maps of America continued to be published in London or elsewhere in Europe to the end of the colonial period.

THE MASON–DIXON LINE

Many of the most expert surveyors and cartographers in the decades preceding the American Revolution were immigrants or visiting experts from Europe. The most famous, and technically the most sophisticated, boundary line drawn in colonial America was named after two Englishmen: the Mason–Dixon line establishing the boundary of Pennsylvania and Maryland. The boundary between the original royal grants to the Calverts of Maryland and the Penns of Pennsylvania had never been clear, leading to a boundary dispute that had lasted for many decades. American surveyors lacked the technical skill to resolve the issue, and English surveyors had the advantage of impartiality between the contenders. The astronomer Charles Mason (1730–1787) and the surveyor Jeremiah Dixon (d. 1779), along with their equipment, arrived in Philadelphia from England in November 1763. Before getting to the main business of tracing the Maryland–Pennsylvania boundary, the two Englishmen fixed the southern limit of Philadelphia and traced the boundary between Pennsylvania and Delaware. Finally they began their main task in 1765, accompanied by axemen clearing a corridor approximately 10 meters wide and employing a recently invented instrument, the zenith sector, used to observe the passage of stars crossing the meridian near the zenith, which the Mason–Dixon expedition introduced into American surveying. They also employed a very advanced field clock, lent to the expedition by the Astronomer Royal of Great Britain, Nevil Maskelyne. Mason, Dixon, and their companions faced bad weather, geographical barriers including the Susquehanna River and the Blue Ridge Mountains, and suspicion from local Native Americans. More than 233 miles long, the line was concluded on October 7, 1767. Mason and Dixon's effort not only established the boundary line, but their example and the techniques and instruments they introduced raised the level of American surveying.

FENCING—THE ZIGZAG FENCE

Once boundaries were established, or even before, putting fences around the land a person owned was important. There were practical reasons for this, such as protecting crops from animals. There were also cultural reasons—enclosing agricultural land was essential for a settler to claim it as his or her property, particularly for the English. A good example of how the material conditions of colonial life and the colonial economy shaped technology is the invention and spread of the zigzag fence in the English colonies. Early settlers built the kind of fences they had known about in Europe—vertical wooden posts set into the ground, with crossbeams nailed to them. (They made little use of hedges or stone fences at first.) The problems with these fences were the relatively large amount of labor involved and the scarcity of nails. The inventor of the zigzag fence, also known as the worm or snake fence, is unknown, but it was pioneered in the Chesapeake Bay region. Fence builders took advantage of two things America had in abundance—land and wood—and economized on others that were relatively scarce and expensive—labor and nails. Zigzag fences piled rails on top of each other in a zigzag formation held together by slanted stakes at the corners. The fences took up a lot of space and required a lot of wood, but they did not require nails, and they could be built quickly since no postholes needed to be dug. They could also be taken down quickly and moved if the need arose. Zigzag fences eventually became the most common type of wooden fence in the British colonies outside New England, which stubbornly stuck to post fences in an area where land was scarcer. The famous New England stone fence emerged late in the colonial period, partly as a response to deforestation.

Although the main functions of a fence were always the pragmatic ones of marking territory, holding livestock, or keeping out intruders, the rise of a colonial upper class given to displaying its superior level of taste and civilization in the eighteenth century led to the rise of decorative fences, combining practicality with attractive design.

10

Technology and War

The world of colonial America was a world of war. Both Europeans and Native Americans were familiar with organized violence long before their first encounters, and were willing, sometimes eager, to use force to assert their domination over the American land. The growing dominance of European colonists over Native American communities rested in large part on the colonists' superiority in war, which in turn rested on technological advantages ranging from the domestication of the horse to the use of iron weapons and gunpowder. Colonial attacks on Native Americans and Native American responses continued for several centuries, to the end of the colonial period. Conflicts between different communities of Europeans were also common from early in the colonial period, growing from violent encounters between small communities to colonial participation in the vast, worldwide imperial wars of the eighteenth century, culminating in the Seven Years War from 1754 to 1763 that destroyed French power in North America. Finally, the end of the colonial era was a bloody one, as the British colonies fought their way to freedom against Britain, and the Spanish colonies fought against Spain.

War presents unique technological challenges, pitting human ingenuity not only against the puzzles of nature but also against other people. American military technology was forged in the deadly rivalries of European and Native American societies. Although colonial armies and fighters shared in the military changes that swept the European world in the early modern period, they were also influenced by the American environment and their enemies. Whereas European war was developing in the direction of masses of infantry firing at each other, American war was more small-scale and individualistic. The presence of forests meant that formations were harder to hold while on the move and placed a premium on the ability to fire accurately from concealment. The kind of large-scale pitched battle in open country that was common in Europe was rare in America.

The contempt with which Europeans invaders and colonists viewed Native Americans legitimized ways of war that Europeans were reluctant to use against each other. The use of dogs to hunt and savage Natives, a practice the English adopted from the Spanish conquerors of South and Central America, began in the early seventeenth century and continued throughout the colonial period and even into the American Revolution. The dogs used to locate and attack Native Americans were English mastiffs, a large, strong breed of dog. Bloodhounds were also used for tracking. British colonists justified their use of dogs by asserting that the Native Americans were a particularly savage and inhumane foe. A more deadly example of the contempt in which whites held Native Americans was the contemplation, and occasionally the use, of biological warfare against Native American populations. During the great war waged by a Native American coalition against the British after the Seven Years War, British regulars distributed smallpox-infested blankets among Native Americans, a tactic endorsed by the British commander in America Jeffrey Amherst.

WEAPONS OF WAR

The foremost weapons used by the European invaders against the Native American population—and each other—were handheld missile weapons. The earliest invasions of North America, those of the early sixteenth century by the Spaniards in the Southwest and Southeast, relied on the crossbow. The crossbow's armor-piercing capacity had revolutionized European warfare in the Middle Ages, but it was slow and difficult to reload, and its power meant relatively little against unarmored Native Americans. Native bows, although they fired with less power than crossbows, could be fired at a much faster rate. The conquistador Álvar Cabeza de Vaca, whose party was devastated by Native American arrow fire, described the Natives as "the readiest people with their weapons of any I have seen in the world" (Cabeza de Vaca, *Chronicle of the Narvaez Expedition*, 68).

In the sixteenth century, the crossbow was forced out of war in both Europe and American by the gun, particularly the heavy military weapon called the "musket." However, the unique challenges presented by American warfare meant that American colonists were early adopters of many of the technological innovations of European gunmakers. In many cases, technical advances devised in Europe were commonly used in America before they were employed by European armies. Other European weapons and customs of war were abandoned in the New World.

The Spaniards, who in their early invasions of North American under Coronado and De Soto had worn armor to protect against the deadly archery of the Native Americans, eventually wilted under the heat and switched to heavy padded cloth, which they adopted from the Aztecs. By the eighteenth century, Spanish frontier soldiers were protecting themselves with a heavy leather coat down to the knees made from seven layers of buckskin, earning the nickname *soldados de cuero,* leather-jacket soldiers. Pole arms, long spears or pikes, integral to European battles, also proved useless against Native Americans and dropped out of use in the sixteenth century.

The dominant weapon in the conquest of the Americas was the long gun. Gunpowder, originally invented by the Chinese, had been used for weapons in Europe since the fourteenth century. Powder was a combination of saltpeter, sulphur, and charcoal. Simply grinding the three ingredients together, however, produced a powder that was hard to store, tended to form lumps, and left a residue in the gun. "Corned" powder, made by adding water to the mixture and forcing it through sieves under pressure, was more convenient.

Early modern guns were "muzzle-loaders." The gunner used a rod called a rammer or ramrod to put the bullet down into the gun where it could be fired. The modern breech-loading gun was only widely used after the colonial period.

Guns and replacement parts for guns were made by gunsmiths. Gunsmithing was recognized as a specialized trade, although many combined it with blacksmithing, brass work, or other metal crafts. Given the many different parts and materials that went into a gun, gunsmithing rivaled clockmaking as one of the most technically challenging branches of manufacturing in the colonial period. So complex was the process that relatively few gunsmiths made entire weapons. It was common for a gun to have different makers for the barrel, gunlock, and stock, or for American gunsmiths to work with imported locks and barrels.

The most important technological challenge presented by the gun in the sixteenth and seventeenth centuries was the firing mechanism. To explode, gunpowder had to be lit. The earliest type of gun used in the Americas, the matchlock, worked by the gunner actually applying an external source of fire, a slow match, to the powder. The match was usually composed of twisted strands of hemp or cotton, sometimes soaked in saltpeter or other flammable liquids to help it burn. This mechanism created many difficulties, from keeping the slow match lit and available to firing while keeping the gun steady. (The heaviest muskets, like the 20-pound Spanish muskets, required a wooden rest to hold them while being fired.) The slow match was also very vulnerable to rain or wet weather, further limiting the matchlock's effectiveness. The "wheelock," which worked by putting a fragment of iron pyrites against a spring-powered metal wheel to generate a spark, was developed in seventeenth-century Europe but was uncommon in the Americas. Matchlocks disappeared from the colonies around 1675, although European armies continued to use them into the early eighteenth century. The replacement for the matchlock in America was the flintlock, which worked by striking a piece of flint against steel. Since the flint and steel method works by igniting tiny particles of flint that the impact of the steel separates from the whole, one drawback of the flintlock was the necessity of frequently replacing the flint. Broken gun flints were not simply thrown away, however, as they were still usable as flints for lighting fires.

Loading, priming, and firing a flintlock was complicated. The Baron Frederick William von Steuben, who introduced the drill modeled on the Prussian army to George Washington's soldiers at Valley Forge, broke down the process by which a flintlock was prepared for firing into fifteen separate actions. One of the main purposes of drill was to accustom soldiers to performing these motions accurately and quickly, without much need for conscious thought.

In military encounters with Native Americans, colonists fired at individual enemies, not the ordered ranks of a conventional European army. This placed a premium on accurate shooting, and particularly, on accurate guns. (Of course, Native Americans also used accurate guns when possible and developed their own sharpshooters.) Hunting also required accuracy. Even the seventeenth-century Dutch colonists of Albany, far from the most militaristic of European settlers, valued accurate fire. The burghers opened the trading season from May to November, the *handelstijd*, with a traditional Dutch contest called "shooting the parrot." Shooters competed for prizes by taking aim at a wooden parrot set up on a stick. Accuracy, however, was technically limited by the dominance of the smoothbore musket.

Despite the superior accuracy and firing rate of the Native bow and arrow, it was not usually adopted by colonists. In range and penetrating power, guns exceeded bows. (Although a Spanish military engineer on a visit of inspection to New Mexico in 1766 complained that the Spanish colonists there were so short of ammunition they had reverted to bows and arrows and lances as their primary weapons.) Instead, the influence went the other way, as Native Americans adopted guns as their weapon of choice. Frequently repeated prohibitions on trading guns to Native Americans were mostly ignored by profit-hungry colonists. The Europeans even deliberately supplied shoddy, easily broken guns to the Natives, so they would be dependent on the Europeans for repairs. This whole development was ultimately disastrous for the Native Americans; although they quickly learned to be competent gunners, they could not manufacture guns, gunpowder, or bullets themselves. Because the Native Americans relied on trade or gifts from colonists, when their supplies were cut off, they lost military effectiveness. Ultimately guns, like many other European-derived manufactures adopted by Native Americans, drew them more tightly into the colonial economy.

GUNS IN THE EIGHTEENTH CENTURY

The eighteenth century was a relatively stable period in the development of guns, seeing no changes rivaling the importance of the shift from matchlock to flintlock. The flintlock musket remained the most common long gun in America to the Revolutionary War. Anglo-Americans were influenced by the eighteenth-century British military's move to standardize weapons. The famous Brown Bess musket, introduced in the early eighteenth century, was the first standardized musket in the British army. Many circulated in British America, which imported most of its guns from the mother country, and the Brown Bess was often imitated by colonial gunmakers. Like other guns, the Brown Bess muskets also had an afterlife in that their parts were incorporated into new guns.

One of the few technical innovations associated with eighteenth-century American gunmaking was the American rifle, also known as the Pennsylvania or Kentucky rifle. Like many technical advances in colonial America, the early American rifle drew on the skills and traditions of German immigrants. Germans had been making and using rifles for hunting and war for many years. The fundamental idea of the rifle—putting grooves inside the barrel of a gun to improve its accuracy—was already well known in Germany. German gunsmiths in Pennsylvania made the American rifle by modifying German rifles to have a longer barrel and improved balance. Much of the rifle differed little from the standard gun, the main change being the rifling of the barrel. The barrel was rifled after it was bored. A gunsmith used a special tool called a rifling bench, which pulled a cutting rod with a cutter attached to its end through the barrel, rotating it as it went. One after another, the gunsmith put grooves, usually seven, in the barrel.

In the hands of a skilled marksman, the American rifle was accurate at a range of 3 to 400 yards. The rifle was the weapon of the frontiersman rather than the soldier. It was principally used for hunting and for fighting Native Americans, where accuracy was at a premium. It was less effective in full-scale wars like the Seven Years War or the American Revolution because reloading it was such a difficult, time-consuming process. Both musket and rifle were single-shot weapons, which had to be reloaded every time they were fired. (There were a few repeating weapons in eighteenth-century America, but they were rare and expensive.) Rifle reloading, however, was even more difficult than musket reloading. Greased cloth was used around the bullet to ensure a tight fit, another practice originating in Germany, and both cloth and bullet had to be loaded into the muzzle. Eighteenth-century battle tactics, based on masses of infantrymen facing other masses, relied on rapidity of fire rather than accuracy, hence finding little use for the rifle. Another handicap of the rifle in war was that it did not take a bayonet, rendering riflemen defenseless against a charge once they had fired their weapons.

Another weapon that became popular in the eighteenth century was the blunderbuss, a short flintlock musket with a flared muzzle. The blunderbuss was loaded with multiple bullets, and its purpose was to cause devastation at short range, with little long-range effectiveness. Not a military weapon, it was particularly useful in urban situations, on shipboard, or for guards of coaches; in short, for anyone who expected to face a foe at close range.

AMMUNITION

Guns could be loaded either with individual bullets or with a mixture of smaller projectiles called small shot. The large bullet did more damage when it hit, while small shot, with a loss of velocity and range, covered a larger area and was more likely to hit something. The use of small shot was more common in America than in Europe. It compensated for the small size of colonial forces, and the wider volume of small shot was particularly advantageous in facing loose Native American units rather than closely packed European armies.

The most common material for shot was lead. North America produced relatively little lead, although the French had some lead mines along the Mississippi and in the Great Lakes region that supplied their forces in Canada and the Illinois region with shot. A lot of the ammunition used in American guns had been originally imported from Europe. However, lead-poor Americans eagerly recycled lead into new shot as well. Since lead has a relatively low melting point (about 327 degrees Centigrade) it was easier for nonspecialists to use than iron or copper, both of which melted at well over one thousand degrees. Many soldiers, hunters, and gun owners made their own shot.

A process for making shot introduced in the seventeenth century was called Rupert shot, named after the seventeenth-century general Prince Rupert of the Rhine, who promoted the process. To make Rupert shot, liquid lead was poured through a brass vessel with circular holes, held over water. The lead fell into the water in slightly elliptical form but made usable shot. In 1769, William Watts discovered that by dropping the molten lead from a great height, it was possible to produce perfectly round shot. This was known as drop shot. Molten lead was also cast in roughly spherical molds, either individually or in sets. The skill to do this was widely dispersed among the population.

The key innovation in ammunition during the eighteenth century was the introduction of the "cartridge," a combination of powder and bullet that greatly simplified the loading and firing of a gun. The Prussian drillmaster of the Revolutionary army, the Baron von Steuben, described the proper handling of a cartridge: "Bring your right hand short round to your pouch, slapping it hard, seize the cartridge, and bring it with a quick motion to your mouth, bite the top off down to the powder, covering it instantly with your thumb, and bring the hand as low as the chin, with the elbow down. Shake the powder into the pan, and covering the cartridge again, place the three last fingers behind the hammer, with the elbow up" (Steuben, *Baron von Steuben's Revolutionary War Drill Manual*, 18).

ARTILLERY AND CANNON

Of course, some guns were too large for an individual to carry and fire. Called artillery, these weapons were used on ships, on the battlefield, and in sieges. Siege artillery employed guns, although at the very beginning of North American colonization, the Spaniard Pedro de Castaneda suggested that catapults would be useful both in knocking down Native American settlements and in intimidating the people. Artillery did not merely serve a combat function. Shooting off guns became an integral part of colonial political and diplomatic culture.

The functional division in land artillery was between siege and garrison pieces, designed to attack and defend fortifications respectively, and smaller battlefield pieces, designed to inflict death and injury to enemy fighters. Artillery was made of iron or an alloy of copper and tin called gun metal or brass. Siege guns, and some large battlefield weapons, fired round shot, cast-iron balls between 3 inches and 4.25 inches in diameter. These weapons were classified by the weight of shot they fired, as three-pounders, six-pounders, etc. Lighter battlefield weapons, called howitzers, fired antipersonnel charges including shells, grapeshot, and canister shot. They were classified by the diameters of their bores. Both the British and the French tried to standardize calibers in the eighteenth century. The British were more successful, but standardization remained a distant goal rather than a practical reality.

Although round shot was unequaled at battering down fortifications, there was a variety of ammunition for battlefield use. Shells were hollow metal balls filled with gunpowder. A fuse going through a hole in the outer shell was lit when the gun was fired, and ideally the shell exploded in the midst of the enemy. Grape and canister were designed to shred human flesh. Grapeshot consisted of small metal balls around a metal rod attached to a wooden base, which held the charge, and wrapped in netting, holding it together. When grapeshot was fired, the missile disintegrated, and the small "grapes" filled the air. Canister, used at very short ranges, consisted of a group of small iron balls in a thin iron can with a wooden base. The can disintegrated in firing, leaving the balls to wreak havoc.

Gun charges from the seventeenth century on came in the form of cloth bags filled with powder, rather than gunners loading powder loose in battlefield conditions. After the bag was loaded, through the muzzle in large guns, priming wires were run through the vent to break up the cloth and free the powder. Some smaller guns used cartridges, ammunition packed along with the charge. Cartridges were also the norm with grape and canister shot.

Powder and ammunition was loaded in large guns with a rammer, a rod used to push it into the base of the gun. Smaller guns and howitzers could have the powder inserted directly into the base. Another common gunner's tool was a worm, a long rod with a twisted piece on the end resembling a corkscrew. Worms were used to remove fragments left in the barrel of a gun after firing or to unload a charged gun without firing. The powder was lit through the vent.

Firing a cannon was difficult, dangerous work requiring special training. Experienced gunners were some of the most technically trained soldiers in an army, as using a weapon to its maximum effectiveness involved mathematical calculation. Eighteenth-century gunners used an instrument called a gunner's quadrant to calculate the angle to set their guns and employed printed tables of angles and elevations. The first artillery company in British America was the Ancient and Honorable Artillery Company of Boston, founded in 1638, but throughout the colonial period, most skilled gunners, like the guns themselves, came from Europe. By the late eighteenth century, a large battlefield gun required a crew of 16 to move it into position, set the angle of the gun properly, load, and fire it.

FORTIFYING A NEW WORLD

The construction of fortresses to hold territory was an established part of European war in the early modern period. European powers applied this practice to their American colonial territories. The fortresses they built varied greatly in size, function, and materials. Fortresses could be constructed from wooden palisades—suitable for small outposts— earthenworks, bricks, stone, or a combination of materials. Some coastal forts in the South used "tabby," a concrete made from oyster shells. The most unusual fortification occurred during the uprising of Chief Pontiac in 1763, when a British unit attacked by Native Americans in western Pennsylvania used bags of flour to temporarily fortify their position—the "Flour-bag Fortress." Different kinds of material had different advantages and disadvantages. Forts with wooden palisades were easier and cheaper to build than stone or earthworks, and also easier for a retreating force to destroy to prevent it from falling into the hands of the enemy. However, because large guns could not be mounted on the wall, such forts could not be defended against artillery. Walls thick enough to mount guns on could be made of stone, which was very expensive, or of earthworks, great mounds of earth held up between wooden walls.

A basic distinction between fortresses was functional: What kind of attacker was the fort built to defend against? Some forts were built to withstand attacks by Native Americans, insurrectionary slaves, or small parties of whites, and some, particularly in the eighteenth century, were built to withstand whole armies of besiegers by land or water-equipped with artillery. (Forts near bodies of water that could support naval guns were especially vulnerable and were frequently made of stone.) The latter group were usually larger and made of more durable materials. Another distinction is what it was that fortresses were defending. Fortresses protected cities, trading posts, waterways, and passes. They protected ports from attack by sea, as Castle William stood guard over Boston. (One of the reasons that the Chesapeake Bay was a perpetual security headache for the British government was that its mouth was too wide for the guns of a fort to cover.) Lines of fortresses protected military communications, or defended frontiers from attacks by colonial or Native American enemies. The purposes of a fortress were not always purely defensive—they served as bases for armies or raiding parties, both European and Native. They were secure storehouses for trade goods or food. They also psychologically intimidated Native American or settler populations. Fort Albany, built by Sir Edmund Andros in 1676 after the English takeover of New York, stood on a height above the Dutch town of Albany, providing the resentful Dutch inhabitants with a constant reminder of English power.

Fortified places could hold only a few people, or a garrison of several hundred soldiers. Some larger fortifications resembled small cities, and many cities, particularly in Spanish and French North America, were themselves surrounded by walls. At the other extreme, even a private house could be fortified. Fortified houses appear as early as the Spanish settlement of Mexico. The classic examples of fortified private dwellings in British-American colonies occurred not in mainland North America but in the Caribbean islands, where slaveowning planters lived in constant apprehension of slave revolts. The largest single house in the seventeenth-century British colonies was Colbeck Castle in Jamaica, literally a castle laid out with attention to defense and gun emplacements. In seventeenth-century New England, more modest fortified dwellings served as designated rallying points in villages under assault from Native Americans—a strategy with a mixed record of success.

Another kind of fortification was temporary, put up for a specific encounter. An effective temporary fortification was the *abati*, made of trees. (The term is derived from the French words *arbes abbatus*, fallen trees.) The abati was a way of taking advantage of North America's wealth of trees, which were cut down and laid in front of the area to be defended, with branches sharpened and knit together so as to present a nearly impassible barrier for attacking infantry, who could be shot at while advancing slowly through the abati. The abati was used with great effectiveness by the French general Montcalm, defending Ticonderoga in the early phase of the Seven Years War. Wave after wave of British redcoats advanced against the fortification, only to be mowed down by French gunners. Joseph Plumb Martin, a member of the Sappers and Miners Corps in the Revolutionary army charged with digging trenches and attacking siege works, described the preparations for the American assault on the abati set up by the British forces at Yorktown in the last battle of the Revolutionary War: "The Sappers and Miners were furnished with axes and were to proceed in front and cut a passage for the troops through the abatis, which are composed of the tops of trees, the small branches cut off with a slanting stroke which renders them as sharp as spikes. These trees are then laid at a small distance from the trench or ditch, pointing outwards, and the butts fastened to the ground in such a manner that they cannot be removed by those on the outside of them. It is almost impossible to get through them. Through these we were to cut a passage before we or the other assailants could enter" (Martin, *Private Yankee Doodle*, 234–35).

FORTRESSES AND SOCIETY

Permanent fortification was expensive, having to compete with other projects for the necessary labor and materials. Other demands, like housing, often seemed more important in time of peace than fortification. The original fortress at Plymouth, a wooden palisade enclosing settlers' houses and a blockhouse, was later cannibalized for its wood, which was used for more houses. Shortly after the Dutch purchase of Manhattan island, the Dutch West India Company's ambitious plan for Fort New Amsterdam" at its southern tip had to be considerably cut back when the governor of the colony, Peter Minuit, diverted laborers and building materials to building houses for the colonists. The hastily built fortress had to be reconstructed in 1633, but many of the workers sent over from the Dutch Republic were drafted into the colony's military forces, and the work was finished by the company's slaves. Even then the expert Dutch builders and engineers had to sue the company for their wages. Nor did the expense of a fortress stop when building was completed. A fortress was useless unless garrisoned, and establishing a permanent fort meant a long-term commitment to adequately man it.

Expense was not the only reason colonists did not always welcome fortifications. They sometimes saw a fortress not merely as a protection from Native Americans or rival colonists, but as a way for the central government, whether of a colony or of the imperial power itself, to exert its power over local communities. Governor William Berkeley of Virginia's plan to build a chain of nine fortresses along the frontiers of Virginia aroused considerable opposition from frontiersmen, who feared that the government would prevent them from waging war on local Native Americans. The fortresses, which were never built, were one of the factors precipitating a violent uprising of frontiersmen, Bacon's Rebellion, in 1676. Pacifist Quakers opposed fortification as they did other warlike activities; even the construction of a redoubt to protect Philadelphia from privateers was preceded by a heated debate. (The Swedish traveler Peter Kalm, visiting Wilmington in 1748, observed that such was the fear of privateers that even the Quakers were helping fortify the town. He noticed that many

Quakers were too scrupulous to actually work on the defenses but aided financially and helped to prepare.)

NATIONAL STYLES IN FORTIFICATION

Native Americans had been fortifying themselves in both wood and stone long before the arrival of Europeans, and continued to do so. Simple walls or fences round a Native village mostly served the purpose of keeping out animals, but more elaborate fortifications against hostile attacks were not uncommon. Iroquois towns, surrounded by double or triple wooden palisades and other defenses, were referred to as castles by Europeans. The Narragansetts of Rhode Island built several forts. The elaborate wooden fort the Narragansetts built in the Great Swamp in 1675 was destroyed by the colonists who took heavy casualties in doing so. Another impressive Narragansett fort was the stone fort known as Queen's Fort. Both these fortresses show evidence that the Native Americans incorporated European ideas about fortification into their own military tradition.

English settlers came from a country where there were few worries about invading armies and large fortresses were relatively little used. Most British-American cities were originally unfortified or lightly fortified, which gave them greater geographic flexibility as opposed to being confined in heavy fortifications. Among the few exceptions were New York, which was originally Dutch, Charleston, and Savannah.

Continental Europeans, whose countries were routinely ravaged by invading armies, were by contrast used to building fortresses, and they built the most impressive strongholds in North America. The great stone fortress of Fort San Marcos at the Spanish town of St. Augustine was built from 1672 to 1687, on the same site of previous wooden forts, to protect Spanish Florida from English aggression and to serve as the base for Spanish troops. San Marcos, one of the few large stone fortresses in the Americas, was built of a local shellstone called coquina, mortared together with shell lime. It took the classic square shape of early modern Continental European fortresses, with bastions extending from the corners to enable gunners to attack besiegers at any point. The walls were 30 feet high and 12 feet thick in places. San Marcos, which held dozens of cannon and hundreds of soldiers, withstood attacks from the British generals James Moore in 1702 and James Oglethorpe in 1740, as well as sieges from pirates and Native Americans. Other Spanish towns in North America, surrounded by large numbers of potentially hostile Native Americans and socially and politically dominated by the army, were nearly always walled.

Although few fortresses could challenge the might of San Marcos, the greatest fortress builders in colonial North America were not the Spanish but the French. By the late seventeenth century, France led Europe in fortress building with the best engineers, the most careful planning, and the most advanced techniques. Whereas British forts were built somewhat

Fort San Marcos of Spanish Florida, the greatest fortress in colonial America. Courtesy of the Library of Congress.

haphazardly with little central direction until the eighteenth century, French forts followed lines south and west from the mouth of the St. Lawrence south and west through the Great Lakes and down the Mississippi, controlling strategic locations on the inland waterways and trails.

EIGHTEENTH-CENTURY FORTIFICATION

Fortification reached its peak in colonial America in the middle of the eighteenth century, as the French and British staked out their claims and prepared themselves for conflict over the interior. Following the Peace of Utrecht in 1712, the French built a new fortress, Louisbourg (named after their king Louis XIV), on Cape Breton Island at the mouth of the St. Lawrence. Incorporating the latest in European fortress design, Louisbourg hung as a perpetual threat over New England. The capture of the fortress by New England troops (aided by a small British fleet) in the War of the Austrian Succession (King George's War) was a celebrated achievement, partly due to French ineptitude in allowing the Americans to capture usable guns from the outlying Grand Battery. The British government's decision to hand the fortress back to France in return for concessions in India as part of the peace settlement provoked great resentment among colonists, although the British established a fortified base at Halifax in Nova Scotia to keep Louisbourg in check. This was a common pattern in this period, as new French fortresses inspired British responses, and vice versa. Immediately before the outbreak of the next and final war between Britain and France for control of the North American interior, the Seven Years War, the young Virginia planter and surveyor George Washington was put in charge of a project to build 21 small frontier fortresses for protection against the French and their Native American allies.

Typical of these new eighteenth-century French forts was Fort de Chartres, an isolated outpost on the Mississippi in the Illinois country. The impressive fortress featured 18-foot stone walls, about two feet thick, with a capacity to house a garrison of 400 men. The seat of French power in the Illinois country, it was never actually tested in war. Like most of the rest of the French fortification system, Fort de Chartres met its end as a result of French defeat in the Seven Years War. Louisbourg was also taken again in 1758 by British regular forces under the command of Jeffrey Amherst. This time the fortress was destroyed. The following year the French themselves destroyed the limestone Fort St. Frederic on the narrows of Lake Champlain rather than let it fall into English hands. Fort St. Frederic, a formidable structure with walls 18 feet wide, had been a base for numerous armies and raiding parties, French and Native, against New York and New England. Fort de Chartres, which survived the war unharmed, handed over to the British and eventually destroyed by them in 1772.

The colonies lacked the educational system to produce masters of fortification engineering. The British army had brought its own specialists to design and supervise the construction of its American fortresses. This colonial lack was felt keenly at the outset of the American Revolution, although American craftsmen made a partially successful effort to fortify the territory held by the rebels. In the end, it was necessary for the Continental army to employ European specialists, mostly French officers, for much of its engineering work.

11

Natural Knowledge in American Colonial Societies

European colonists in the Americas had inherited many intellectual traditions in understanding the natural world. They applied what they knew to the new conditions of the Americas.

NATURAL THEOLOGY

The Europeans who settled in the Americas were heirs to a long tradition of viewing nature in religious terms, as the handiwork of God. The English-educated Puritan minister and religious poet Edward Taylor used a series of metaphors drawn from industry to emphasize the greatness of God as an artificer and the magnificence of creation:

> Upon which base was fixt the Lath, wherin
> He turn'd this Globe, and riggalld it so trim?
> Who blew the bellows of his Furnace vast?
> Or held the mould wherein the world was Cast?
> Who laid its Corner Stone? Or whose command?
> Where stand the Pillars upon which it stands?
> Who Lac'de and Fillitted the earth so fine,
> With Rivers like green Ribbons Smaragdine?
> Who made the Sea's its Selvedge, and it locks
> Like a Quilt Ball within a Silver Box?
> Who spread its Canopy? Or Curtains Spun?
> Who in this Bowling Alley Bowl'd the Sun?
> Who made it always when it rises set,

To go at once both down, and up to get?
Who th'Curtain rods made for this Tapistry?
Who hung the twinckling Lanthorns in the Sky?
(Taylor, *The Poems of Edward Taylor*, 387)

Taylor exalted God's raw power, not really ascribing Him a level of skill beyond that of the skilled blacksmith at his furnace or the housewife adorning her cloth with ribbons. Others exalted God's wisdom and design as well as His power. Long before the settlement of the Americas, Christian theologians had divided theology into two branches, natural and revealed. Revealed theology was that known only because God had revealed it in the Bible, or, for Catholics, through the tradition of the Church. It included specifically Christian truths such as the Trinity and the divinity of Christ. Natural theology was based on the evidence of the universe, and, as such, could be understood by anyone, Christian or not. It covered such issues as the existence and watchful care of God and the existence of the human soul. Knowledge of the natural world was obviously relevant to natural theology. A classic example is the argument from design, which seizes on the complexity and functionality of the universe to argue that it must have been designed by an intelligent mind, rather than coming together through random chance. This intelligent and benevolent mind could only be God.

Natural theology was very popular in the seventeenth century, particularly among those who wanted to emphasize the areas of agreement, rather than disagreement, among different groups of Christians. Most natural philosophers with strong religious beliefs had a positive attitude toward natural theology, and often presented their work as a contribution to it. This was one of the justifications for doing science in the first place. England was the European country where the natural-theological tradition was strongest and most creative. Some of the greatest English scientists, such as the chemist Robert Boyle, wrote on natural theology. English natural-theological books, such as the seventeenth-century naturalist John Ray's *The Wisdom of God Manifested in the Works of Creation* (1691), appeared frequently in the libraries of American ministers.

American intellectuals who followed English intellectual developments, such as the leading Puritan ministers in Massachusetts, often also promoted natural theology. Natural theology was taught in the textbooks of Harvard College and diffused throughout New England in sermons and commentaries. The possibility of understanding the glory and purposes of God through His works was a spur to the study of nature—the warfare of science and religion had not been conceived of in the seventeenth century. The Copernican theory of the earth's motion around the sun, which had led the Catholic Church to condemn Galileo in 1633, was much less controversial in the Protestant world.

The connection of natural philosophy with natural science meant that the natural philosopher was also expected to be a wise man, rather than

Remembered today primarily as a persecutor of witches, Cotton Mather was one of the most scientifically aware men of early eighteenth-century America. He viewed science as testimony to the glory of God. Courtesy of the National Library of Medicine.

simply an expert like the modern scientist. Cotton Mather's sketch of John Winthrop Jr., the first American to be a Fellow of Britain's Royal Society, provides a view of Winthrop's wisdom colored by the author's own piety:

If one would therefore desire an exact picture of this worthy man, the description which the most solid and sober writers of the great philosophick work do give of those persons, who alone are qualified for the smiles of Heaven upon their enter-prizes, would have exactly fitted him. He was a studious, humble, patient, reserved and mortified person, and one in whom the love of God was fervent, the love of man sincere: and he had herewithal a certain extension of soul, which disposed him to a generous behavior to those who, by learning, breeding and virtue, deserve respects, though of a perswaysion and profession in religion very different from his own; which was that of a reformed Protestant, and a New-English Puritan. (Mather, *Magnalia Christi Americana*, 266)

GOD AND SATAN IN THE NATURAL ORDER

Although natural theologians most often emphasized God's design in the usual course of natural events, unusual events also had religious meaning. Prodigies—strange and aberrant events outside the usual order of nature, such as comets, monstrous births, apparitions of armies in the sky, or rains of blood—were often considered to be messages from God. In 1675, during the grim early days of King Philip's War, when a confederacy of Native American tribes was making successful attacks against the New England colonies, the Puritan magistrate Samuel Sewall expressed his foreboding in terms of the sky: "Morning proper fair, the wether exceeding benign, but (to me) metaphoric, dismal, dark and portentuous, some prodigie appearing in every corner of the skies" (Sewall, *Diary of Samuel Sewall*, 11). It wasn't only English Puritans who were likely to interpret prodigies as menaces; Jeremias van Rensselaer, a Dutch burgher of Albany, speculated as to the threats posed by comets in 1665, hoping that God would be merciful.

Among the most famous of all prodigies in seventeenth-century New England were the monstrous babies born to Anne Hutchinson and Mary Dyer. These women were the leaders of the Antinomian movement, which challenged the orthodoxy of the Puritan clergy. Hutchinson gave birth to a series of stillborn lumps and Dyer to what was described as a complex monster combining features of humans and beasts. The Puritan leader John Winthrop, in his pamphlet *A Short Story of the Rise, Raigne and Ruine of the Antinomians, Familists, and Libertines that Infected the Churches of New-England* (1645), implied that Dyer's monster was a sign of God's wrath against the heretical women and their "Monstrous Opinions" (Winthrop, A *Short Story*, 46).

But spectacular or hideous prodigies were not the only unusual natural events considered to bear a divine meaning. All kinds of strange happenings could be considered "special providences." The New England Puritan minister Increase Mather compiled a book on the topic, *An Essay for the Recording of Illustrious Providences*, published in Boston in 1684. Mather conceived of the book as only the beginning of a collective project, in which New England ministers would record the wonderful events that occurred in their locations and forward the accounts to Mather.

Of course, not all unusual events were caused by God. Some could be the work of his great enemy, the Devil and his hosts of demons. Christians in the early modern period believed that Satan and his devils intervened frequently in the natural world, whether directly or through their human agents, the witches. In his study of witchcraft, *The Wonders of the Invisible*

World, Cotton Mather discussed the Salem witch trials and how devils acted in the physical world in tormenting the possessed:

But of all the preternatural things which befell these people, there were none more unaccountable than those wherein the prestigious daemons would ever now and then cover the most corporeal things in the world with a fascinating mist of invisibility. As now; a person was cruelly assaulted by a specter, that, she said, run at her with a spindle, though no body else in the room could see either the spectre or the spindle: at last, in her agonies, giving a snatch at the spectre, she pulled the spindle away; and it was no sooner got into her hand, but the other folks then present beheld that it was indeed a real, proper iron spindle; which, when they locked up very safe, it was nevertheless by the daemons taken away to do further mischief. (Mather, *The Wonders of the Invisible World*, 162)

The practical uses of an alliance with Satan in day-to-day life from the perspective of a so-called witch can be seen in the case of an illiterate Mexican cowboy working in the Spanish borderlands, Luis de Ribera. Ribera was an immigrant from Spain, who claimed to have first learned witchcraft from a Native American, who taught him herbal magic, particularly for the purpose of attracting women. Ribera's initiator into demonic magic was an African slave, who Ribera claimed had a tattoo of Satan on his foot. The African sold Ribera a book of pictures of demons, in which Ribera wrote his name in blood drawn from his nose. Ribera claimed to have acquired this book in the land of the Chichimecs, a Native American tribe that many Mexican Catholics associated with demons and witchcraft. He used his new demonic powers in his job to control herd animals.

Ribera's witchcraft was revealed when a wagon train on the way to New Mexico with which he had signed on as a mule driver suffered a stampede. Others in the wagon train speculated that the loss was due to witchcraft, and Ribera broke down and confessed when the train reached its destination in Santa Fe. He was taken in irons to Mexico City, where he threw himself on the mercy of the Inquisition, claiming he now deeply regretted his youthful follies and was tormented by visions of Satan, telling him not to repent. Like most accused of Satanism in the Spanish colonies, he was far luckier than the condemned witches of Salem—the Inquisition let him off with a penance.

Another religious way of looking at prodigies was as signs that the end of the world was coming. Jews and Christians, ever since the biblical books of Daniel and Revelation, have always associated strange natural events with God's coming to overthrow the wicked and vindicate the righteous. Colonists in the New World were no exception, and indeed some, including Columbus, believed that the European discovery was itself a sign of the approaching end of time, which could only come when the Gospel had been preached to all nations. However, belief in a coming apocalypse was more identified with Protestants than with Catholics like Columbus.

THE BIBLE AND SCIENCE

Christian writers on science and religion considered the Bible to be a source of natural knowledge, although no one claimed that every statement in the Bible had to be interpreted literally. Natural knowledge was also pressed into service, not to challenge but to confirm the accuracy of the Bible. The fact that no one in colonial America, and very few in Europe, openly attacked Christianity did not mean that its advocates did not feel beleaguered by an alleged rising tide of atheism. Cotton Mather, who carried on the interest in science and religion held by his father and fellow minister Increase, received the news of the giant bones and teeth discovered at Claverack, New York, in 1705 with great excitement. Mather believed that this was fresh evidence confirming Biblical accounts of the giants existing before Noah's flood. He wrote in his first letter to the Royal Society, London's foremost scientific society, that "Concerning the Dayes before the Flood, the Glorious Historian has told us, There were Giants on the Earth in those dayes. Could any undoubted Ruines and Remaines of those Giants be found under the Earth, among the other Subterranean Curiousities in our Dayes, it would be an illustrious Confirmation of the Mosaic History, and an admirable obturation on the mouth of Atheism."

ARISTOTELIAN NATURAL PHILOSOPHY

Religion was not the only lens through which early modern investigators viewed the natural world. There was also a more secular tradition. The first colonists of the Americas, like the societies from which they came, lacked the concept of "science." Instead, the study of the natural world was usually put under the heading of "natural philosophy." Most European natural philosophers until the scientific revolution of the seventeenth century followed the philosophy of the ancient Greek Aristotle, as it had been modified again and again in the many centuries between Aristotle's time and the early modern period. Those parts of Aristotle's original philosophy that were incompatible with Christianity, such as the belief that the world was eternal, had been dropped. Although some did question it, Aristotle's philosophy dominated European universities and would continue to do so even when some became Protestant. Although few learned natural philosophers crossed the Atlantic, the creation of academic institutions would perpetuate the Aristotelian tradition.

Aristotelian natural philosophers usually saw natural things as compounds of substance and qualities such as color or heat. The material world itself was divided into four elements, earth, air, fire, and water, in various combinations. The universe, centered on the earth, was divided between the corruptible "sublunary sphere," containing all beneath the moon, and the perfect and unchanging heavens. This belief worked very well with the Christian contrast between earthly corruption and God's perfection. Aristotelian philosophers viewed natural things as endowed with purpose, the so-called Final Cause. Things fall, for example, because the earth is the proper place for them. Other things, like the stars, don't fall because the heavens are the proper place for them. Motions were divided into natural motions—expressions of a body's true nature—and violent—those imposed on a body from outside. The hurling of a rock, for example, combines natural motion—the rock's eventual falling to the ground—and violent motion—the rock's going in the direction it was thrown. A body's natural motion included things we would now call change and development as well as motion—Aristotle viewed the growth of a tree as a form of motion. Stars and planets moved in circles, because heavenly things were perfect, and Aristotle believed that the only motion suitable to perfection was circular motion.

MAGIC

A somewhat less-reputable tradition of interpreting the natural world than natural theology or Aristotelian philosophy was magic. In the sixteenth and seventeenth centuries, the line between science and technology on one side and magic on the other was not as clear as it later became. European magic was itself a complex phenomenon, the product of millennia of blending, including Greek, Mesopotamian, Chinese, Jewish, Egyptian, Arabic, and indigenous European elements. In the American colonies, Native American and African traditions were added to the mixture. Magic existed in highly elitist forms relying on the knowledge of learned languages such as Greek or Hebrew and in the common charms of the village witch or cunning man.

Much magic in the early modern period was based on ideas of correspondences between different things and qualities in different realms. The most famous correspondence was the microcosm-macrocosm analogy, whereby the human body and the universe were regarded as analogous; to take a crude example, the heart was the equivalent of the sun. Magic (like a lot of early modern science) did not draw rigid distinctions between that which is alive and that which is dead, and viewed various natural items as endowed with occult, or hidden, powers unexplainable in mechanical terms. Astrologers viewed the influences of the planets in this way. Magicians were often anti-Aristotelian, and opposed to the traditional natural philosophers of the universities.

The best-known and most intellectually developed branch of magic, astrology, was a complex discipline, taking several different forms. Natal horoscopes for people interpreted the position of stars at the time of the person's birth, but buildings, cities, and countries were also considered to have dates of founding that could be analyzed astrologically. High astrology correlated the movements of the stars with large-scale events on earth, such as plagues and wars. Astrologers took great interest in the relations of dramatic celestial events, such as comets and the great conjunctions of Saturn and Jupiter that occurred about every 20 years, with dramatic terrestrial ones. This type of astrology was particularly popular during times of crisis, such as the English Civil War of the seventeenth century. Questions about marriage, recovering stolen goods, and many other topics could be resolved through horary astrology, the bread-and-butter of consulting astrologers. Horary astrologers took a chart of the positions of the stars and planets for the moment when someone asked the astrologer a question. Interpretation of the figure revealed the answer. Astrological principles were conceived as covering a number of natural domains. Herbs, colors, and gems were all ruled by different planets. Herbals published for the use of physicians showed the different planets that ruled different herbs and how these matched up to the planets that governed various diseases.

ALCHEMY, SCIENCE, AND INDUSTRY

Another type of magic that had a wide influence in colonial America, particularly in the seventeenth century, was alchemy. Alchemy, at its most basic the art of refining and mixing various substances, had a long and complex history by the time of the colonization of America, involving Chinese, Greek, Jewish, and Arab influences on European thought. Like modern chemistry, alchemy involved furnaces, beakers, and tubes. The earliest chemical laboratories were for alchemical work and alchemists pioneered laboratory procedures such as distillation. Unlike modern chemistry, alchemy could also involve spells, prayers, incantations, and horoscopes taken at specific moments in the process. Some alchemists, following the magical idea of "correspondences" related different metals to different planets in the heavens. Alchemists also differed from modern chemists in viewing certain states of matter as more perfect than others, as gold represented the perfect state of metal. Alchemists could help this perfection emerge by purging impurities. Purging impurities was also one way of understanding the refinement of metals from ores, and it is unsurprising that alchemists were involved in some of the earliest American metallurgical industries.

There was an active alchemical community in early New England involved with the construction of New England's first ironworks at Braintree and Lynn in Massachusetts. The center of this group was the most active industrial and scientific promoter of the seventeenth-century colonies, John Winthrop Jr., and its most important innovator was the first original scientist born in a European New World community, the Harvard graduate George Starkey of Bermuda and Massachusetts. Like many other alchemists, Starkey was unable to support himself through his art and practiced as a physician; such was the lack of physicians in New England at that time that he was able to do so without a medical degree. Despite the presence of other chemists, New England was unable to support Starkey's experimental alchemy, and frustration with the difficulty of getting good laboratory equipment caused him to move to England in 1650.

Alchemy was not forgotten after the scientific revolution and non-magical chemistry reached American shores, but it moved farther down the social scale. The lure of getting rich quick appealed to many people, and alchemy seemed to offer one path. Alchemical con men continued to flourish. The counterfeiter and all-around rogue Stephen Burroughs, active in the decades following the American Revolution, described the operations of a fraudulent alchemist named Philips, who claimed to be able to turn copper into silver: "He, in the first place, weighed one half ounce of copper, and put it into a crucible, and then put the crucible into the fire; after it remained there a short period of time, he put in a paper, containing something wrapped in it, and immediately the matter in the crucible became turbid, and began to foam and boil with great violence, for about ten minutes, and then settled down into a clear beautiful metal, which, when poured off and cooled, was good silver, weighing one half an ounce. It stood the trial by aqua-fortis, and several ways, so that I had no doubt of its being good silver." After the experiment had been repeated by Philips and Burroughs with the same result, Philips crushed Burroughs's dreams of endless wealth by revealing the different ways he had introduced silver into the crucible, either with the powder, or with a coal he put over the crucible, or by the old trick of a silver core to a hollow iron stick he used to stir the molten copper. The molten copper was hot enough to melt the silver but not the iron (Burroughs, *Memoirs of Stephen Burroughs*, 60–62).

SCIENCE AND TECHNOLOGY IN COLONIAL SCHOOLING

As Europeans established permanent settlements in the New World, the institutions and practices of European intellectual life went with them. In early modern Europe, all but a few universities were teaching institutions rather than centers of scientific research. Institutions such as the University of Mexico City or Harvard College initially taught a mostly traditional Aristotelian curriculum in natural philosophy. The colonial universities in the seventeenth century adapted to new intellectual currents with some time lag relative to Europe.

Childhood education was pragmatically oriented, with little interest in theoretical science. In the seventeenth century, the only widely taught mathematical discipline, arithmetic, was taught almost entirely with an eye to business uses rather than science or technology. The development of the colonial economy in eighteenth-century British America led to the rise of independent teachers of applied and higher mathematics in the major cities. Night schools taught basic mathematics and technical subjects with a vocational slant to apprentices and tradesmen. Specialists taught geometry, trigonometry, and astronomy with an eye to the training of surveyors and navigators. The education they provided was aimed entirely at the male population.

The virtue of learning natural philosophy, however, was not solely based on its practical applications. To an increasing degree in this period, some knowledge of science was regarded as contributing to a person's all-around cultural polish. In 1749, Benjamin Franklin published a small treatise on education, *Proposals Relating to the Education of Youth in Pensilvania*. His argument for teaching natural science relied as much on the pleasure knowledge gave to both the knower and others as the profit:

With the History of Men, Times and Nations, should be read at proper Hours or Days, some of the best Histories of Nature, which would not only be delightful to Youth, and furnish them with Matter for their Letters, &c. as well as other History; but afterwards of great use to them, whether they are Merchants, Handicrafts, or Divines; enabling the first the better to understand many Commodities, Drugs, &c. the second to improve his Trade or Handicraft by new Mixtures, Materials, &c. and the last to adorn his Discourses by beautiful Comparisons, and strengthen them by new Proofs of Divine Providence. The Conversation of all will be improved by it, as Occasions frequently occur of making Natural Observations, which are instructive, agreeable and entertaining in almost all Companies (Franklin, *Writings*, 339–40).

ALMANACS, PERIODICALS, AND POPULAR SCIENCE

The preeminent printed source for natural knowledge produced in the British-American colonies was the annual almanac. Almanacs, already a well-established genre in England, were the most commonly printed kind of books other than religious works. Although they had many uses, the most basic was their function as calendars. When the great Virginia gentleman William Byrd mocked the ignorance of North Carolina colonists, he claimed that their letters had no dates because there were no almanacs in the province (Byrd, *William Byrd's Histories of the Dividing Line*, 27). Almanacs also included the dates of eclipses; the positions of the sun, moon, and planets; and the phases of the moon. They advised farmers on the proper times to plant and harvest their crops and even when to castrate their calves.

Cambridge, Massachusetts, was the earliest center of almanac printing in British America (the first almanac appeared in 1639, although no copies survive), and many were prepared by natural philosophers or ministers associated with Harvard University. Leading intellectual lights of late seventeenth-century New England such as the astronomer Thomas Brattle and the minister Cotton Mather prepared almanacs. This happened partly because America supported few professional astrologers, so other educated people filled the gap.

In the eighteenth century, almanacs were produced in many places outside New England; the first Anglo-American almanac outside Massachusetts was Philadelphia's *Kalendarium Pennsilvaniense 1686*. Eighteenth-century

almanacs were a more commercial proposition, less astronomically oriented, and often prepared by printers. They still included short scientific
articles among a plethora of other material, including lists of the distances
of various roads. This feature first appeared in the late seventeenth century and became standard.

The almanacs collected and transmitted a considerable body of weather
lore. It was commonly believed that the appearance of the moon was related
to weather conditions. Colonel Landon Carter of Virginia, a late eighteenth-
century tobacco planter, was a well-educated man and a member of both
the American Philosophical Society and the Virginian Society for the
Promotion of Usefull Knowledge, late colonial America's leading scientific
and technological societies. But he accepted traditional beliefs about the
moon's influence on weather: "We have at the appearance of every New
Moon constantly observed her Phasis, and she has been mostly with the
two horns tending to a Perpendicular to the Horison, which with us always
denoted a drye moon and the more perpendicular as she leaned to the
South a warm moon" (Carter, *The Diary of Colonel Landon Carter of Sabine
Hall*, 241). Much of this astrological lore was directly handed down from
Europe, but the new American crops such as corn acquired their own body
of lore as to propitious times to plant and harvest.

It wasn't just almanacs that spread scientific and technical knowledge in
print to ordinary people; in the eighteenth century, almanacs were rivaled
by the burgeoning newspaper press. Newspapers like Benjamin Franklin's
Pennsylvania Gazette disseminated accounts of natural historical oddities,
announced and described popular scientific lectures and demonstrations,
and sometimes included directions for new technical procedures. Colonel
Landon Carter of Virginia noted in his diary a recipe from a Philadelphia
newspaper for a wet-cure for meat: "Pack your meat close down in a tub
without rubbing Salt on it. Then 6 gallons of water and 6 quarts coarse salt,
1 1/2 brown sugar, 2 ounces SaltPetre. Put it in a pot over a fire. Skimming
it as the scum arises, and, when that is done rising, take the liquor off, Set
it to cool, then pour it on the packed meat so as to cover it as a pickle. This
cures 220 pounds of meat" (Carter, *The Diary of Colonel Landon Carter of
Sabine Hall*, 1069).

12

The Scientific Revolution in Colonial America

Western civilization in the late sixteenth and seventeenth centuries underwent a dramatic change in the way people thought about nature. This change is often referred to as the scientific revolution. New systems of thought arose in fundamental disciplines like astronomy, physics, chemistry, and natural history. Aristotelian natural philosophy, which had dominated Western science since the Middle Ages, was challenged and eventually overthrown by new philosophies. Great scientists like Galileo Galilei and Isaac Newton put forth new theories. New institutions such as scientific societies and scientific journals were founded, and science was an area of enormous cultural excitement. The center of these events was in Europe, far away from the struggling communities of European settlers in America, but colonial residents were aware of the scientific revolution, and in a modest way participated in the great transformation. Despite his disdain for England, Thomas Jefferson paid tribute to the importance of the scientific revolution (a term he did not use) when he commissioned portraits of the seventeenth-century English philosophers Francis Bacon, John Locke, and Isaac Newton "as I consider them the three greatest men that have ever lived, without any exception, and as having laid the foundation of those superstructures which have been raised in the physical and moral sciences, I would wish to form them in a knot on the same canvas, that they may not be confounded at all with the herd of other great men" (Jefferson, *Writings*, 939–40).

THE BEGINNINGS OF SCIENTIFIC RESEARCH IN THE AMERICAN COLONIES

Much of the earliest original science practiced in European colonies was done for the purpose of inventorying American resources for exploitation by colonial powers. Possible medical uses of New World plants were particularly interesting to European governments. The earliest leaders in colonial American natural history were the Spanish, the first great colonial power. The first major scientific expedition to America was carried out from 1571 to 1577 by a Spanish physician, Francisco Hernandez. Hernandez was already an experienced medical botanist when Philip II of Spain ordered him to go to Mexico to study its natural history with a view to medical uses. Hernandez traveled extensively in Mexico, gathering specimens, illustrations, and descriptions of plants and consulting with Native American healers on Mexican plants and their medicinal uses. Hernandez learned the language of the local Native Americans and translated some of his materials into it for their use. His return to Spain brought disappointment, as the bulk of his work remained unpublished and many of his manuscripts were destroyed in a fire in 1671. The writings of the early Spanish naturalists were not limited in their influence to Spanish writers. They were translated into other languages and served as the foundation for American natural history generally.

Early English science in the New World differed from that of the French and Spanish in not being state-sponsored. This was a consequence of the fact that the earliest English colonization efforts were carried on by private groups with government charters rather than directly by the government. Much of the earliest English science concerning America, Thomas Harriot's 1588 *A Briefe and True Report of the New Found Land of Virginia* being the earliest and most notable example, painted a rosy picture of the living conditions and economic possibilities of the new colonies. This "promotional" science was planned to attract immigrants to the new colonies being established and investors to the colonizing companies. Harriot and other early English scientific authors emphasized the bounty of the New World and the usefulness of American animals and plants. Discussions of American birds, for example, focused on which ones were edible rather than scientific identification and classification.

Promotional natural history did not end with the early period of colonization, although the people writing it were less likely to be European colonial promoters like Harriot and more likely to be persons and groups in the colonies themselves. The Virginia landowner and scientist William Byrd published *William Byrd's Natural History of Virginia* in 1737, not in America itself, or even in England, but in Bern, Switzerland, as part of a German-language volume called *New-Found Eden*. Byrd's emphasis on the fertility of American soil and the deliciousness of American wildlife was part of his effort to attract Swiss Protestant immigrants to Virginia.

COLONIAL NATURAL HISTORY AND EUROPEAN SCIENCE

Once the settled population was large and established enough so that simple survival was not everyone's foremost concern, it was able to support amateur natural investigators, and eventually, communities of them. However, even where scientific circles were established, they were peripheral to European science. In order to be noticed in Europe, colonial scientists had to take advantage of their peripheral position to do the kind of science that was impossible across the Atlantic. The principal form of science that could be done only in the colonies continued to be the natural history of America, and most colonial scientists who gained a European reputation were natural historians. Jesuit and other Catholic missionaries sent back natural information along with their reports to the European headquarters of their orders. The pages of the first English scientific journal, *Philosophical Transactions*, were full of communications from British Americans describing the unique plants, animals, minerals, and industries of the land, but few American contributions to scientific theory.

Another science of growing importance that Americans were geographically suited to make a unique contribution to was astronomy. The distance of America from Europe meant that Americans were able to observe many things in the sky that Europeans could not. The separation of America from Europe also meant that Americans were able to add valuable information on the position and timing of celestial phenomena such as eclipses and comets. Astronomy was a science whose empirical precision was rapidly growing in the seventeenth century, after the introduction of telescopes. American observers, while they lacked the latest, up-to-date observatories and instruments found in Europe, were able to add valuable data to astronomers' knowledge. One seventeenth-century American astronomer, Thomas Brattle of Harvard College, was praised by none other than Isaac Newton for his accurate telescopic observations of a comet.

Although natural history specimens and astronomical observations flowed from America to Europe, American scientists suffered from both intellectual isolation and the difficulty, if not impossibility, of obtaining high-quality scientific equipment. The most important original scientist the seventeenth-century English colonies produced, the physician and alchemist George Starkey of Bermuda and Harvard University, emigrated to England partly because of the impossibility of getting laboratory equipment suitable for serious research in New England.

THE QUESTION OF RACE

The category of race was not as important for Europeans thinking about human divisions before their discovery of the Americas as it became later. The rise of "scientific racism"—treating the differences between human groups as biologically determined—was inextricably entangled with the

European conquest of the Americas and the creation of societies based on the enslavement of Africans and their descendants. In the sixteenth century, the term *race* was not in common use, and when used to refer to a people, it could refer to the social class of the European elite rather than to a race in the modern sense. For most people, religion remained the most important way of categorizing the world's peoples. A roughly four-fold division of the world into Christians, Jews, Muslims, and "Idolaters"— a category including Native Americans—was common. A simpler division was twofold, between the so-called civil European elite and everyone else. The uncivil could include European peasants as well as non-Europeans, and comparisons between American Natives and the European lower classes were quite common. Another common way of categorizing differences was the climatic theory that the character of different societies was determined by their natural environments, a theory with classical roots. Thus the darker pigments of Africans and Americans were due to their exposure to the heat of the sun. (Some objected to this theory by pointing out that children retained their parents' coloration, no matter where they were born.) The dominant planet and astrological sign of a given area could also determine or influence the nature of its people.

The Spanish conquests in America provoked the most vigorous debate on the subject of race to occur in the sixteenth century and one of the last major intellectual debates to be conducted purely in Aristotelian terms. The central religious question—whether Native Americans had souls and were therefore both human and potentially Christian—was settled in the affirmative by a Papal Bull, *Sublimi Deus,* in 1537. This was a victory for the Catholic religious orders, who wanted to convert Native Americans to Christianity, over Spanish landlords, who wanted to be free to treat their Native American workers like domestic animals. Vigorous debate on whether Natives were barbarians in the Aristotelian sense, and therefore naturally slaves, continued in Spanish universities during the sixteenth century, where the justification of the Spanish conquests remained highly controversial. Both sides produced voluminous treatises, one side stigmatizing the differences between Native American and European society, the other arguing that since the Aztecs of Mexico and the Incas of Peru had lived in urbanized and political societies, they were not barbarous, merely idolaters in need of the Christian revelation. Champions of the non-barbarous interpretation, who located the Spanish right to rule in the need to bring Christianity to pagans, included the Dominican Bartolomeo de las Casas and the Jesuit Jose de Acosta, both of whom had direct experience of the New World. The greatest champion of the natural slave interpretation was the humanist Aristotelian Juan Gines de Sepulveda, who did not. The great debate between las Casas and Sepulveda staged at Valladolid in Spain in 1550 was inconclusive (the term *debate* is misleading, as the two never actually faced off), but the opponents of natural slavery won the argument in the Spanish intellectual world as a whole.

However, their influence on actual Spanish practice in the New World, which remained extremely harsh, was slight.

Partly because many Africans had already been enslaved when they fell into the hands of European Christians, the question of African slavery was not initially as intellectually important to Europeans and their American descendants as that of the status of Native Americans. In the seventeenth century, African slavery was often explained and legitimated in religious terms, as justified by Africans' non-Christian beliefs or by the Biblical curse on descendants of Ham.

THE ROYAL SOCIETY AND COLONIAL SCIENCE

What intensified English science in the Americas was the founding in 1660 of the Royal Society for the promotion of natural knowledge, a London-based organization with state sponsorship, but financial and organizational independence. The Boston minister Cotton Mather, himself a Fellow of the Royal Society, later described its origin and purpose:

For whereas, in pursuance of the methods begun by that immortally famous advancer of Learning, the most illustrious Lord Chancellour [Francis] Bacon, a select company of eminent persons, using to meet in the lodgings of Dr. [John] Wilkins of Wadham College in Oxford, had laid the foundation of a celebrated society, which by the year 1663, being incorporated with a royal charter, hath since been among the glories of England, yea, and of mankind; and their design was to make faithful records of all the works of nature or of art, which might come under their observation, and correct what had been false, restore what should be true, preserve what should be rare, and render the knowledge of the world, as well more perfect as more useful; and by multiplied experiments both of light and fruit, advance the empire of man over the whole visible creation. (Mather, *Magnalia Christi Americana*, 265)

As Mather points out, the society's initial goal was to gather and compile records of scientific and technological phenomena—the "works of nature and art." If it wanted information from the Americas, and it did, it needed the help of American residents. The first colonial admitted as a fellow of the society was a visitor to London, the Puritan statesman and promoter John Winthrop Jr. Winthrop practiced medicine and alchemy, promoted ironworks, and brought the first telescope to New England. During the period from 1660 to 1783, dozens of men with colonial connections ranging from substantial to slight would be admitted as fellows, and hundreds of letters from the colonies were published in the society's journal *Philosophical Transactions*. Colonial fellows benefited from not having to pay admission fees or dues until 1753, when the society's financial needs led them to abolish the exemption. Difficulties in communication could still lead to problems, however, as when Mather was wrongly accused of passing himself off as a fellow because his name did not appear on printed lists of fellows.

The leaders of the Royal Society in England viewed colonial fellows more as sources of knowledge and American natural history items and artifacts than as original thinkers. Colonial residents not only had access to the plants, animals, and minerals of America but they also were particularly valued for their ability to explain those technical processes peculiar to the colonies. The first paper read to the Royal Society by a colonial was Winthrop's explication of the way that Americans made pitch. However, the society's leaders knew that they could not simply rely on having colonial men as well informed as Winthrop in London. Information would also have to be gathered systematically. The Royal Society sent lists of queries with persons journeying to the colonies in hopes of gathering information about colonial technology and natural history. In doing so, the society hoped to combine scientific curiosity with strengthening the economy of the British Empire and identifying colonial resources for exploitation. The Royal Society promoted visits to America by scientists to gather information. One of the most productive of the early correspondents of the Royal Society in America was a Church of England minister named John Clayton, who spent two years in Virginia at a church in Jamestown.

In French Louisiana, the French Royal Academy of Sciences, founded in 1667, played a role like that of the Royal Society in the British colonies. However, the Royal Academy was organized on a far more tightly controlled and limited basis than the loose and informal Royal Society. Unlike the Royal Society, the Royal Academy arranged its members in a hierarchy and paid the scientific elite. No French colonial residents were admitted to the highly prized and competitive position of full membership in the Royal Academy. The military and trade-dominated French colonies also produced fewer persons interested in scientific research, although some physicians and Catholic priests investigated nature. Another Paris-based French scientific organization interested in Louisiana was the Royal Botanical Garden, which along with the government encouraged projects for acclimating potentially profitable exotic crops, such as coffee. However, Louisiana never attracted as much interest from French scientists as did New France and the French Caribbean colonies. Spain, which by the seventeenth century had become a backward country scientifically, lacked effective scientific societies and made little effort to investigate the resources of its colonies between the expedition of Francisco Hernandez in the sixteenth century and the Royal Botanical Expedition to Mexico during the late eighteenth century.

ANGLO-AMERICAN COLONIAL SCIENTISTS IN THE EIGHTEENTH-CENTURY

Colonial scientists in the eighteenth-century English colonies were a heterogeneous lot, but two groups prominently represented in the northern colonies were physicians and ministers. Physicians as a group had more education in the sciences than any other profession. Ministers like Cotton Mather, a Fellow of the Royal Society, had a high general level of education, and in many cases, extensive libraries. The old tradition of the minister as medical practitioner dealing with the physical complaints of his parishioners when a physician was unavailable also led many to study science. Ministers were also moved to study nature as a way of understanding God. Natural theology was not marginalized in the early eighteenth century, but instead received a new lease on life from the popularity of Isaac Newton's philosophy and the example of pious scientists like Robert Boyle. Mather's scientific masterwork *The Christian Philosopher* (1721) was one of many works using the properties of the created world to exalt the glory and providence of God.

New England's clerical and medical intellectual culture made scientists there more likely to be connected to a university than elsewhere. Although natural philosophy had been part of the university curriculum since the Middle Ages, study intensified in the eighteenth-century colonies with the founding of chairs specifically devoted to scientific subjects. The most prestigious of these was the Hollis Chair of Natural Philosophy at Harvard. The chair was founded by the generosity of an English merchant, Thomas Hollis, a religious dissenter sympathetic to Harvard's Puritanism. (Hollis had previously endowed a chair of divinity at Harvard.) The first holder of the chair was Isaac Greenwood, a complex character who despite numerous character flaws—he eventually lost the chair for drunkenness—did much to promote natural science in New England. Greenwood also wrote the first math textbook by an American, *Arithmetick Vulgar and Decimal.*

The middle colonies, particularly Pennsylvania, were increasingly active in the sciences in the early eighteenth century. As the adopted Philadelphian Benjamin Franklin would later assert, Philadelphia's central geographical position made it potentially the ideal location for the central institutions of American science. The Philadelphians, led by Franklin, were great institution builders, establishing the University of Pennsylvania, the Pennsylvania Hospital, and eventually America's first successful scientific society, the American Philosophical Society.

The colonies south of the Chesapeake Bay were different. Although ministers and physicians were also mainstays of the scientific community in the southern colonies, they were joined by wealthy landowners and planters such as William Byrd, Landon Carter, and Thomas Jefferson. Given the basis of their prosperity, these investigators were particularly interested in agricultural improvement. Virginian natural philosophers were more isolated from each other than New Englanders or Philadelphians, however, given the colony's lack of a significant urban center. The closest thing to an intellectual center in Virginia was the College of William and Mary. South Carolina, on the other hand, had an urban center in Charleston that had a small scientific community, but by and large, South Carolinians were less interested in the sciences than their fellow colonists in the North.

Exceptions included the Charleston physician Alexander Garden and the planter and agricultural improver Eliza Lucas Pinckney.

Garden was one example of the new and invigorating element that came to eighteenth-century science in British America from Scotland. Scots, like many other non-English people, had been excluded from free immigration to the earliest English colonies even though the two countries had shared a common ruler since 1603. An event nearly as important as the founding of the Royal Society for advancing scientific knowledge in England's American colonies was the Act of Union of 1707. This Parliamentary act brought England and Scotland together into a single country, the Kingdom of Great Britain. The English, now British, colonies were thrown open to Scottish immigration. Scotland produced many educated emigrants, as its fine system of schools and universities produced more scientifically and medically knowledgeable men than the country had jobs for. Scottish merchants, Scottish colonial officials, Scottish Presbyterian and Episcopal ministers, and above all, Scottish physicians like Garden flooded into America in the following decades, and many became leaders of colonial science.

INVESTIGATING AND COLLECTING—COLONIAL NATURAL HISTORY

Natural history continued to be the quintessential colonial science. The immediate fieldwork of natural history could only be carried out on the spot, either by colonial residents or by visitors from Europe. Colonial residents joined networks of correspondence and exchange but usually as subordinates. European scientists were particularly interested in animals and plants unique to the New World, some of whom touched off scientific controversies. Two of the most puzzling American creatures for European and colonial scientists were the rattlesnake and the opossum, neither of which had close relatives in Europe. It was widely believed that rattlesnakes had a power of so-called fascination that charmed their prey into helplessness. The late eighteenth-century American naturalist William Bartram described the rattlesnake's powers of fascination:

They are supposed to have the power of fascination in an eminent degree, so as to inthral their prey. It is generally believed that they charm birds, rabbits, squirrels and other animals, and by stedfastly looking at them possess them with infatuation: be the cause what it may, the miserable creatures undoubtedly strive by every possible means to escape, but alas! their endeavours are in vain, they at last lose the powers of resistance, and flutter or move slowly, but reluctantly, towards the waiting jaws of their devourers, and creep into their mouths, or lie down and suffer themselves to be taken or swallowed. (Bartram, *Travels and Other Writings*, 224)

The opossum was the first marsupial animal that Europeans had ever encountered (contact with Australia's marsupial fauna would not begin until the late eighteenth century). Marsupials rear their young, which emerge as fetuslike creatures, in a pouch rather than in a womb in the fashion of most mammals. Investigators were puzzled by the way American opossums reproduced, and scientists argued whether or not the animal's pouch should be considered a womb. The mystery and legend that surrounded the opossum can be seen in the Virginia landowner and Fellow of the Royal Society William Byrd's *Natural History*, published in 1737. Byrd's descriptions of most Virginia animals was level-headed and designed to attract potential emigrants, emphasizing the creature's practical uses. The description of the opossum, by contrast, is soaked in legend and focuses on the animal's utter bizarreness:

This animal is found nowhere else in the whole world except in America; it is a phenomenon among all animals living on land. Its shape and color are similar to a badger. The male's genital member sticks out in the back, because of which they turn backs to each other at the time of copulation. The female bears her young in the teats, or breasts, at which they grow. At first they are no larger than a pea, and cling fast to them before they seem even to be alive. This animal has another stomach; in addition to the natural one, in which it carries its young—after they fall away from the breasts—until they can help themselves. Meanwhile they run in and out of it as they desire, until they have become large. If a cat has nine lives, as one commonly says, then this animal has certainly nineteen, for if all the bones in its body are broken, so that it lies there as if dead, still it recovers again in a short time, and very soon gets well again. (*William Byrd's Natural History of Virginia*, 85–86)

Europeans who collected plants, animals, and minerals naturally wished to add American specimens to their collections. The great British collectors like James Petiver or Sir Hans Sloane, the founder of the British Museum (who had come to Jamaica as physician to the governor and written a book on its natural history), established networks of contacts in the Americas from whom to receive specimens for their collections. The London Quaker merchant Peter Collinson (1694–1768) was a correspondent of the leading mid-eighteenth-century colonial scientists, and served as their agent in London. John Bartram of Philadelphia parlayed his connections with Sloane and other English collectors into a leading position in American botany, despite his lack of formal training.

Plant exchanges could work the other way as well. Some wealthy or scientifically inclined Americans wished to acquire exotic plants for their own gardens. Having a garden attached to a house became particularly important as a mark of gentlemanly status in the eighteenth century. Exotic plants in a garden functioned both as marks of the owner's wealth and as conversation pieces, providing the pretext for elegant discussions. The desire to knowledgeably discuss garden plants led many colonial men and women to study botany, even if not at a very deep level. The largest gardens employed gardeners, whether free or enslaved, and they had considerable practical knowledge of both domestic and exotic plants.

THE NEW PHILOSOPHY AND THE OLD WISDOM

As more advanced science spread among the educated, it came into conflict with established ideas about nature and its workings. The struggle did not end quickly and took place on many levels. Traditional Aristotelian natural philosophy had lost the struggle by the early eighteenth century, but popular ideas about weather and magic persisted for many decades longer, well past the end of the colonial era, and in many cases, to the present day, as we are reminded every February 2, on Groundhog Day. Nor were traditional ideas held only by the uneducated masses. The eighteenth-century Virginia planter Landon Carter, an early member of the American Philosophical Society, recognized the difference between traditional weather wisdom and natural philosophy while not rejecting either.

The Phasis of this moon on her first appearance after her change was a very small matter leaning on her back. I take notice of this as a common observation that the more she leans on her back the weather is generally the better. Astronomy perhaps may condemn this, because those appearances are only occasioned by her situation as to the earth, so that the first illuminated part will place her appearance either more or less on her back; and therefore does not probably affect the weather; However observation has the right to determine in a point although Philosophy can't be reconciled to it, especially where things though extremely probable are nevertheless free from absolute certainty. (Carter, *The Diary of Colonel Landon Carter of Sabine Hall*, 285)

FROM PROVIDENTIAL TO NATURAL EXPLANATIONS

One of the most important struggles for the colonists was between explanations of natural events by God's direct providential interventions and explanations based on the workings of natural law. By the early eighteenth century, wonderful, prodigious events such as aurora borealises and earthquakes were less often claimed to carry messages from God than they had been in the previous centuries. The Puritan ministers of New England had always been among the foremost to proclaim divine messages in everyday events, but even the pious and learned Cotton Mather hesitated more and more to call specific events prodigies and to use them to prognosticate the future. His pamphlet on the New England aurora borealis of 1719, *A Voice from Heaven*, despite its title, did not affirm that the aurora was the direct work of God or the angels, an affirmation that in the seventeenth century would have gone without saying.

If even ministers did not always assert the divine significance of strange events, among laypeople, the idea that prodigies and wonders could be heralds of the apocalypse was taken less and less seriously. Eliza Lucas, a well-educated young South Carolina woman, did not display much concern over the possibility that a recent comet heralded the end of the world, even though she claimed that the revered Isaac Newton had endorsed the idea. In a letter to a friend she wrote: "But I can't conclude yet till I have told you I see the Comett Sir I. Newton foretold should appear in 1741 and which in his oppinion is that that will destroy the world. How long it may be traveling down to us he does not say; but I think it does not concern us much as our own time of action is over at our death, the exact time of which is uncertain" (Pinckney, *The Letterbook of Eliza Lucas,* 29).

The fact that people were less quick to describe wonderful events as divine signs did not mean that they viewed scientific explanation as a modern secularist might. Natural explanations could be compatible with ultimate divine causation. Divine causation could persist, even though expressed in a very different vocabulary. Enlightenment rationalists talking about nature did not always sound very different from Christian ministers talking about God. Thomas Jefferson, arguing that the fossil mammoth bones found in America meant that mammoths had to be still around somewhere, claimed: "Such is the oeconomy of Nature, that no instance can be produced of her having permitted any one race of her animals to become extinct; of her having formed any link in her great work so weak as to be broken" (Jefferson, *Writings,* 176).

13

The Age of Benjamin Franklin

In the middle of the eighteenth century, the American colonies exhibited their first great original scientist: the electrical theorist, inventor of bifocals, and all-around technological marvel Benjamin Franklin. Although Franklin advanced on the basis of his individual scientific genius and undoubted talent for self-promotion, he was also part of a cultural transformation as leaders in the Anglo-American colonies attempted to foster technological and scientific development to put themselves on a par with the countries of Europe. The inexhaustibly creative and inventive Philadelphian was foremost among a host of scientists, "improvers," and passionate amateurs of natural philosophy in the mid-eighteenth-century British colonies.

The colonies were no longer struggling agricultural outposts intellectually dominated by planters and ministers, but a diversified economy with urban centers and an active middle class who could, and sometimes did, read the latest books and journals of the European Enlightenment. In America itself, many periodicals and other publications devoted space to scientific news, in addition to the increasing volume of European publications in circulation. The scientific amateur could see exhibitions or buy equipment for research or entertainment and could come together with others in formal and informal societies and clubs.

Technology as well as science was being transformed. By the early eighteenth century, the growing wealth, population, and sophistication of the colonies meant that technology had become more ambitious and

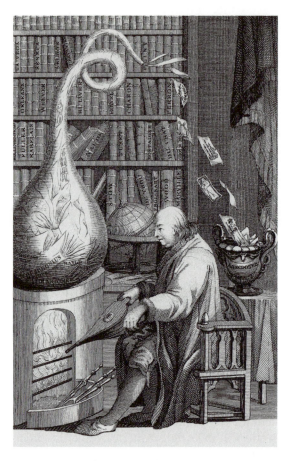

Not everyone admired Franklin. This satire suggests that Franklin "melted down" works by European writers into his own works. Courtesy of the Edgar Fahs Smith Collection, University of Pennsylvania Library.

complex. A growing class of technological specialists included surveyors, navigators, clockmakers, almanac-writers, and the builders of scientific instruments. Private schools and teachers catered to men who wanted to learn some technical mathematics, and the subject even began to creep into the university curriculum. Colonial governments and ruling elites were now able to plan and carry out large engineering projects, such as the 1,600-foot-long wharf built at Boston from 1710 to 1713 and the later Newport wharf, more than 2,000 feet long. Merchant interests pressed for further infrastructure improvements, including the improvement of harbors, dredging of channels, and building of roads.

AMERICAN SCIENTISTS IN THE EIGHTEENTH CENTURY

From around the middle of the eighteenth century, colonial residents began to be independent voices in Western science. The botanists John Clayton of Virginia (not the same John Clayton as the seventeenth-century minister) and Dr. Alexander Garden of Charleston were respected correspondents and colleagues of European botanists, not persons principally valued for their collecting ability as was John Bartram. Europe's greatest classifier, the Swede Carolus Linnaeus, gave his blessing to naming the cape jasmine after Garden. The flower is now known as the gardenia.

Colonial scientists also made their presence felt in new fields outside of natural history. One reason for Benjamin Franklin's fame was that he was the first colonial scientist, born and resident in a colony, to make an important original contribution to experimental physics. This led to his acceptance as a peer by Europe's leading scientists. Franklin was fortunate to be working in electrical studies, a relatively young field where there was not a great deal of previous literature or mathematized theory to master. (Franklin's mathematics was somewhat rough-and-ready, not at all comparable to that of Continental European physicists. This was less because of colonial mathematical backwardness than British mathematical backwardness.) The disadvantage of colonial isolation for people who were more interested in theoretical and mathematical physics can be seen in the work of Franklin's New York contemporary, the surveyor, politician, and scientific polymath Cadwallader Colden (1688–1776). Colden's ambitious *An Explication of the First Causes of Action in Matter; and the Cause of Gravitation* (1745) showed little awareness of the work that European scientists had done in mechanics and physics since Isaac Newton. His ignorance led to harsh reviews when his book was read in Europe.

As the status of colonial scientists rose in the eighteenth century, colonial scientific communities began to emphasize their separateness from Europe. Studying local natural history helped colonials establish a separate identity, as did scientific disputes with Europeans. Particularly important for New World natural historians was defending the honor of the Western Hemisphere from European scientists like the great French naturalist the Comte de Buffon and Cornelius de Pauw, who claimed it was "inferior" to the Eastern Hemisphere. Buffon pointed to cases where New World animals were smaller than those of the Old World, as pumas were smaller than lions, to argue that the New World's climate and humidity produced generally inferior fauna. This argument was also given a racist twist, as Native Americans were considered inferior to Old World peoples, Europeans in particular. Some went even further and asserted that Europeans themselves would inevitably degenerate when transplanted to the Americas. These claims aroused the regional pride of New World scientists. The scientist and patriot Thomas Jefferson (1743–1826) defended New World beasts from the aspersions of Buffon and others in *Notes on Virginia* (1785), demonstrating that American animals compared favorably in size to their European and Asian counterparts. Resentments between colonial and European scientists and the desire to build an independent scientific culture could easily lead to support for political independence. Both Franklin and Jefferson combined support for American independence with contributions to an independent American science.

POPULAR SCIENTIFIC CULTURE

Even among those barred by poverty, race, or gender (universities and scientific societies were restricted to men, and nearly always white men) from participation in organized science, a popular scientific culture began to emerge, with public lectures and demonstrations and the publication of books on science. Many of the lecturers, like Franklin's friend, the Reverend Ebenezer Kinnersley, were showmen as well as educators. Kinnersley turned to electrical lectures when his church condemned him for attacking another minister from the pulpit, so he was already experienced at addressing groups of people. Lectures did more than promote the latest theories and help create popular interest in science; they also provided entertainment. Franklin helped promote Kinnersley's course of lectures on electricity offered in Philadelphia in 1751, which featured such tricks as the electrified woman, the charge from whose lips would purportedly discourage anyone from kissing her, "Electrified Money, which scarce any Body will take when offer'd to them," and "Spirits kindled by Fire darting from a Lady's Eyes (without a Metaphor)" (Franklin, *Writings*, 355–57). Kinnersley also offered to kill animals instantaneously with electricity, provided a member of the audience provided the animals.

The most spectacular development in mid-eighteenth-century electrical science and showmanship was a European import, the Leiden Jar, or as Kinnersley's announcement referred to it, "Mr. Musschenbroek's wonderful Bottle." The jar was the first electrical condenser and had been accidentally invented by the Leiden-based Dutch physicist Pieter van Musschenbroek (1692–1761) early in 1746. No theory of electricity was able to explain the jar, but its main effect in the minds of most people was not to raise questions as to the fundamental nature of electricity but to hand out the most severe electrical shocks available. The jar captured people's imaginations the way no piece of experimental apparatus had since the excitement over air pumps, which for the first time allowed people to create vacuums, in the late seventeenth century. Some loved to tell exaggerated stories of the damage the shocks caused.

Less spectacular but more practical scientific implements than the Leiden Jar became more widely owned in the eighteenth century, often by people who viewed them not as professional aides but as educational toys. Esther Edwards Burr, daughter of the New England theologian Jonathan Edwards and mother of the politician Aaron Burr, wrote to her

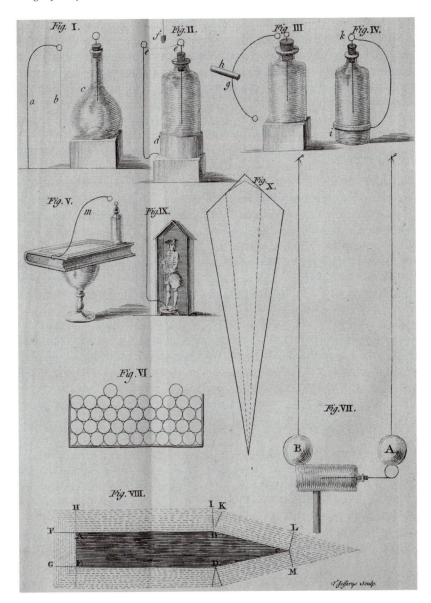

This illustration from Franklin's electrical treatise shows Leiden Jars as well as other electrical equipment. Courtesy of the Annenberg Rare Book & Manuscript Library, University of Pennsylvania.

friend Sarah Prince: "We have a very fine Microscope, and Telescope. Indeed we have Two Microscopes—and we make great discoveries 'tho not yet any new ones that I know of. The Microscope Magnifies a Lous to be 8 foot long upon the wall—The Telescope is very short not above 14 inches but we can see to read small print as small as in our common Bibles

across the streat, which is about 7 Rod, and we can see Jupiters moons—
I want you here prodigeously to see and wonder with us" (Burr, *The
Journal of Esther Edwards Burr*, 123). The dispersion of scientific instruments
like thermometers and barometers also led some scientific enthusiasts to
make systematic measurements of the weather, kept in weather diaries.

Knowledge of new scientific and technological developments, particularly in the field of agriculture, spread by means of the rapidly expanding periodical press. America lacked the purely scientific publications
found in Europe, but general-interest American newspapers and journals
covered scientific topics. European journals also circulated, including
Americans in the scientific "republic of letters." Benjamin Franklin's
introduction to electrical studies is a classic example of how scientific
information circulated in and between Europe and America. His interest
was first piqued in 1743, when he saw a lecturer and demonstration by a
traveling Scottish electrical showman, Dr. Archibald Spencer. His interest
was further aroused in 1745, when he read an article in a London-based
periodical, the *Gentleman's Magazine*. The journal had been sent to the
Library Company of Philadelphia by the tireless London promoter of
American science, the Quaker merchant Peter Collinson. The *Gentleman's
Magazine* article itself was a translation of a piece in a French-language
journal based in the Dutch Republic, *Bibliotheque Raïsonée*. The author of
the article was the great Swiss scientist Albrecht von Haller, who was
reporting on the work of three German electricians, Georg Matthias Bose,
Christian August Hausen, and Johann Heinrich Winkler.

EARLY PALEONTOLOGY IN AMERICA: BIG BONE LICK

One important development in eighteenth-century science was an
increased interest in fossils. There had been a prolonged debate in scientific
circles in the seventeenth century as to whether or not fossils were actually relics of animals that lived perhaps hundreds or thousands of years
ago (of course, no one then was thinking in terms of our present geologi-
cal time scale of millions or billions of years), or whether they were sports
or jokes of nature. By the eighteenth century, the idea that fossils had once
been part of real animals had won—whether or not scientists thought the
animals had drowned in Noah's flood! Natural historians analyzed fossils
to determine which animals they had come from and whether or not they
were known as living in the contemporary world.

One of the most exciting scientific events in eighteenth-century America
was the discovery of a rich fossil bed at Big Bone Lick in the Ohio country.
Big Bone Lick was first encountered by Europeans when a French military
party ran across it in 1739, but the news and the fossils themselves quickly
came into British America. The fossils were of Pleistocene mammals,
including a mastodon, and their sheer size greatly impressed those who
saw or even just heard about them. Christopher Gist, the explorer of the

Ohio, described a conversation with Robert Smith, one of the first English traders to see Big Bone Lick: "He assured me that the Rib Bones of the largest of these beests were eleven feet long and the skull bone six feet wide, and the other bones in proportion; and that there were several teeth there, some of which he called horns, and they said they were upwards of five feet long, and as much as a man could carry" (Gist, *The Journal of Christopher Gist, 1750–1751*, 12). Gist brought back a tooth weighing four pounds for his employers in the Ohio Company.

The Big Bone Lick fossils attracted interest far beyond America. In 1767, George Croghan of Philadelphia sent teeth to Franklin and others in London, where they were interpreted as evidence that elephants had once roamed America. The enquiry into the teeth, however, also showed the advantages that European inquirers possessed over American ones. Peter Collinson, the London correspondent of many American scientists, took some of the American fossil teeth to a warehouse "where there were teeth of all sorts and sizes for sale." By comparing the fossils to elephant teeth, he determined that the tusks were the same as those of the elephant, but that the biting and grinding teeth were different, leading him to conclude that the fossils belonged to "another species of elephant, not yet known" (*Philosophical Transactions* [1767]: 458). American scientists would not have had so many elephant tusks and teeth available to make the comparison.

THE PEAK OF COLONIAL AMERICAN PRACTICAL SCIENCE: BENJAMIN FRANKLIN'S LIGHTNING ROD

Most of the scientific advances made in the eighteenth-century colonies had few practical consequences. The most dramatic exception, and the most famous technological breakthrough to stem from colonial America, was Benjamin Franklin's lightning rod. From the beginning of his electrical studies, Franklin hoped to find practical uses for electricity beyond mere entertainment and the posing of philosophical puzzles. For example, Franklin was interested in the possibility of using electricity to slaughter chickens and turkeys, claiming that this was not only more humane but resulted in a more tender bird.

Although many before Franklin had suggested that lightning was electrical in nature, Franklin was the first to demonstrate it experimentally. Lightning was not merely an interesting phenomenon to study; it was also a scourge to many residents of the colonies, where lightning storms were more common then they were in Europe. Franklin suggested that his lightning studies pointed to a way (other than prayer) for people to defend themselves against the heavenly scourge. He believed that sharp objects caused the electrical fluid to dissipate rather than concentrating in the form of a lightning bolt: "The clouds have often more of this fluid in proportion than the earth; in which case as soon as they come near enough (that is, within striking distance) or meet with a conductor, the fluid quits them and strikes into the earth" (Franklin, *The Ingenious Dr. Franklin*, 58). Franklin's suggestion for lightning rods in *Experiments and Observations on Electricity* laid great stress on their pointedness.

Franklin's friend and fellow electrical researcher, the Reverend Ebenezer Kinnersley, helped spread the gospel of lightning rods in his lecture tours of the colonies in 1751, using miniature buildings and electrical charges to show how they protected from lightning damage and fire. Other leading colonial scientists, including the Harvard professor John Winthrop, a direct descendant of the great Winthrop Puritan statesmen of the seventeenth century, endorsed the new devices. Lightning rods quickly spread as protectors of large structures, despite the misgivings of some religious people who saw them as an impious attempt to thwart the will of God. (Despite the fact that church towers, often the highest structures in an area, were frequent targets of lightning strikes, many were reluctant to protect them from future instances of God's displeasure.) Looking back about 20 years after the introduction of the lightning rod, Franklin took pride in its success in America.

Pointed conductors to secure buildings from lightning have now been in use nearly 20 years in America, and are there become so common, that numbers of them appear on private houses in every street of the principal towns, besides those on churches, public buildings, magazines of powder, and gentlemen's seats in the country. Thunder storms are much more frequent there than in Europe, and hitherto there has been no instance of a house so guarded being damaged by lightning; for wherever it has broke over any of them the point has always received it, & the conductor has conveyed it safely into the earth, of which we have now 5 authentick instances. (Franklin, *The Ingenious Dr. Franklin*, 62)

Franklin's fellow member of the American Philosophical Society, the Virginia planter Landon Carter, was less enthusiastic about the new "points." In 1773, after lightning struck his house and injured several of his household, he wrote: "The invention of points, only imagines an attractive atmosphere which perhaps this instance will shew to be mere imagination or that power of attraction is to be overruled acording [sic] to the quantity of fire Collected; for I have points on the western corner chimney, and yet they never discharged any of this lightning" (Carter, *The Diary of Colonel Landon Carter of Sabine Hall*, 751).

From a technical viewpoint, the termination of the rod was the great problem, as Franklin and his followers, who were defenders of pointed rods, clashed with the English electrician Benjamin Wilson (1721–1788), a champion of short, rounded rods. Wilson argued that long, pointed rods might attract electricity that otherwise would pass harmlessly overhead. Wilson and Franklin butted heads on a committee of the Royal Society established in 1772 to decide how the British gunpowder magazines at Purfleet should be protected from lightning. Franklin triumphed, but when the Purfleet magazines, equipped with pointed rods, were damaged by lightning in 1777, the pointed rods were replaced by rounded ones. By that time Franklin, in Paris promoting the American Revolution, had lost interest in the dispute, and openly hoped that George III would have no lightning rods at all! The lightning rod became a standard example of the actual, practical benefits of science during the late Enlightenment, and, on his death, Franklin was eulogized as the man who had snatched the scepter from tyrants and the lightning from the heavens.

THE CREATION OF SCIENTIFIC INSTITUTIONS IN THE BRITISH COLONIES

Science acquired an institutional form in the eighteenth century. It became more prominent in the university curriculum. Like British universities, Anglo-American colonial universities adopted a Newtonian curriculum in the physical sciences in the eighteenth century. A key moment was the founding of the Hollis Professorship in Natural Philosophy and Mathematics at Harvard in 1727. Its first two incumbents, Isaac Greenwood and the astronomer John Winthrop, did much to spread advanced physics, astronomy, and mathematics in New England. At Yale, Thomas Clap, president of the university from 1745 to 1766, also promoted modern science in the curriculum.

The universities of colonial America, however, were not the most dynamic centers of science in the eighteenth century. In this, America resembled most European countries, including the leading scientific cultures of England and France. Universities (with a few exceptions such as the Scottish universities) were not among the most important institutional forces in eighteenth-century science. Instead, scientific societies like Britain's Royal Society, which emerged in seventeenth-century Europe, were the leading institutions. Although some Americans belonged to the Royal Society and other European groups, America sorely lacked its own institutions, as colonial scientists like Franklin were keenly aware. The Puritan minister Increase Mather's attempt to found a philosophical society in Boston in the 1680s had come to nothing. Not until the twilight of the colonial era, many decades after the founding of the Royal Society and France's Royal Academy of Sciences, did colonial America produce and support its own ongoing scientific societies.

Science was far from the only activity that based itself on societies in the eighteenth century. It was a great age of so-called sociability, of the spontaneous formation of all kinds of clubs and organizations. The first successful scientific society founded in British America was the American Philosophical Society, founded in Philadelphia in 1768. A similar phenomenon took place in French colonies. The sugar colony of Saint Domingue on the island of Hispaniola had a private group with some public support, the Circle of Philadelphes founded in 1784. It eventually received a royal charter.

Purely scientific groups were only one variety of sociable science. Many of the library companies formed in the mid-eighteenth century also had scientific interests, the most famous being Franklin's Library Company of Philadelphia, founded in 1731. Franklin's company and many of its successors and imitators included not only scientific books in their collections, but also scientific equipment. Medical societies, which sprang up all over in the mid-eighteenth century (in 1766 alone, medical societies were formed in Philadelphia, New Jersey, and Litchfield, Connecticut), also attracted persons with general scientific interests, a combination particularly common among America's many Scottish and Scottish-educated medical doctors. Informal groups of persons interested in science existed in many colonial cities.

Another aspect of sociability that contributed to the spread of science was the rise of a new movement sweeping the eighteenth-century British colonies, the Freemasons. Franklin himself was a proud member. The eighteenth century in Europe and America saw the rise of this secret society, a development intertwined with the progress of science. The leader of the Masonic movement in early eighteenth-century London, the base from which it spread over the Continent and to the Americas, was the Newtonian experimentalist and minister John Desaguliers. Many of the early leaders of the Grand Lodge of London, the group with which most American Masons were affiliated, were also Fellows of the Royal Society, Britain's leading scientific organization. Much of the mythology and rhetoric of early Masonry was congenial to Newtonian natural philosophy, as it emphasized a "great architect" who had created the universe in a mathematical fashion. Freemasons also spoke of society as bound together by the "attraction" of its individual members as gravity bound together the Newtonian universe.

Sociability was not the only wellspring of scientific organization. Another powerful motivation for the foundation of colonial scientific institutions was economic development. The French founded a network of botanical gardens in their island colonies of Mauritius, Reunion, Saint Domingue, and Guadeloupe hoping to acclimate economically productive crops, as coffee was acclimated in the French Caribbean colonies. France was building on a long tradition of active botanical investigation of the New World dating back to Samuel Champlain's sending American plants to Paris in the early seventeenth century. French colonial gardens often employed botanists trained at the Royal Botanical Garden in Paris, who reported back to it. Britain lagged behind France botanically, only setting up a centralized system after the American Revolution with the founding of Kew Gardens. The Spanish also turned to a more aggressive approach to the resources of their empire in the late eighteenth century, sending the Royal Botanical Expedition to Mexico in 1787. The leading scientific center of Spain's American empire was Mexico City, which received a Royal Botanical Garden in 1788 and a Royal Mining College in 1792.

THE AMERICAN PHILOSOPHICAL SOCIETY

The American Philosophical Society for the Promotion of Useful Knowledge, America's first successful scientific society, was formed in Philadelphia in 1768 by a merger of two other groups, although Franklin had been promoting the idea since 1743. Franklin's original broadside had called for "One Society be formed of Virtuosi or Ingenious Men residing in the several Colonies, to be called *The American Philosophical Society*, who are to maintain a constant Correspondence." Franklin pointed out that Philadelphia, the central city of the colonies, was best suited for the new society's headquarters and offered his own services as secretary. This first American Philosophical Society was short-lived, meeting only from 1743 to 1746. Besides Franklin, its leading members included the inventor of the octant Thomas Godfrey, and the plant collector John Bartram. The group revived in 1767 still using the name American Philosophical Society, but now dominated by Pennsylvania members of the Church of England. On December 20, 1768, this American Philosophical Society merged with a similar Philadelphia-based group, the Quaker-dominated American Society for Promoting and Propagating Useful Knowledge. At the time of the merger, the American Society had just absorbed yet another group, the Philadelphia Medical Society founded in 1766. The new society's official name was a compromise, "American Philosophical Society for the Promotion of Usefull Knowledge."

The new society's organization was modeled on Britain's Royal Society, with a large, unpaid, and theoretically equal membership and a small body of elected officers. Like its British prototype and the vast majority of European scientific societies, the new society restricted its membership to men. Women researchers like the South Carolina agriculturalist Eliza Lucas Pinckney were certainly as intellectually qualified as all but a tiny minority of men who were members, but the participation of women was not even considered.

Franklin's unquestioned stature as America's leading scientist made him the obvious choice to be elected president at the new society's first meeting on January 2, 1769. Since he was in England at the time, he was elected President *in absentia*. He held the office until his death, dominating the society's image outside America—Europeans called it "Franklin's Society." The society made a determined effort to recruit scientists from elsewhere in the colonies as corresponding members, focusing on the middle and southern colonies rather than New England. It also had corresponding members in Europe. The new society was supposed to be supported by admission fees and annual dues, both of 10 shillings, but these often went unpaid, particularly as attendance and interest in the society waned after the excitement of its founding. In addition to Franklin, leading colonial scientists among the society's members included the elderly naturalist John Bartram, who was inactive, and the young astronomer David Rittenhouse, a future leader of American science after the Revolution. The society's unofficial leader was the Philadelphia surgeon Thomas Bond, an unsung hero of colonial American science. Elected vice-president of the society in 1769, he served until his death in 1784. In Franklin's absence, Bond presided over meetings and handled the society's correspondence even through the difficult period of the American Revolution.

The society's first major project was the collection of astronomical observations of the transit of Venus. The transit is a time when Venus, as viewed from earth, crosses the disk of the sun. Getting exact measurements of the time Venus first appeared to touch the solar disk and the time it took to cross the sun's face from as many places as possible were extremely important to astronomers. The idea of using transits to measure the solar parallax, the angular size of the earth as seen from the sun, and thus arriving at the distance of earth and sun by observing and timing Venus from different parts of the earth had been put forth by the English astronomer and all-around scientist Edmond Halley in 1716 and had been the object of anticipation for decades.

Transits of Venus occur in pairs, about eight years apart. Then they do not recur for more than a century. (Transits of Mercury were much more common but less suited for drawing conclusions about astronomical distances. The transits of Mercury in 1723 and 1753 did provide practice for the transits of Venus, as well as helping maintain interest in the subject.) There had been a transit in 1761, so the 1769 transit would be the last one anyone alive at the time would ever see. These transits, the first since the technology was devised that enabled astronomers to predict and observe them, had been keenly anticipated for years. They called forth a massive coordinated effort from Europe's scientific societies, which sent expeditions to many parts of the globe, including North America, as well as encouraging local observers. Sadly, the most tragic episode of the entire worldwide set of observations was the death from disease of all but one of the party sent from France to observe the transit from Baja California. The transits provided an ideal opportunity for the new society to prove its worth. The society applied for and received a grant from the Pennsylvania legislature for this purpose, and coordinated and collected more than 20 observations of astronomers throughout the British colonies in North America, although not all American observers worked through the society. David Rittenhouse even built a field clock to observe the transit, the most advanced clock seen in America since the Mason–Dixon expedition. The data gathered were printed in volume one of the society's *Transactions*, published in 1771. Copies were sent to several other scientific societies, and Franklin distributed them in Europe, where they made a favorable impression.

Much of the society's activity was devoted to the rather less glamorous tasks of economic development and improving American technology; in other words: "Useful Knowledge." Of the six original standing committees, two were devoted to technological improvement—the committee on mechanics and architecture, and the committee on husbandry and American improvements. The society received a grant from the Pennsylvania Assembly of 1,000 pounds, matched by another 1,000 pounds raised by subscription, to start a silkworm industry in Pennsylvania—the latest of the many fruitless efforts to develop a colonial silk industry. The society also received 200 pounds from local merchants to examine possible routes for a canal from the Delaware River to the Chesapeake Bay. The canal was not built until several decades later, and at the time, Benjamin Franklin, among others, urged the promoters to get expert engineers from Europe. The group also requested that clays be submitted to it to determine the best deposits for different kinds of ceramics, offered premiums for rags for papermaking, and supported one of the few American glassmakers attempting to make a superior product, Henry William Stiegel. Stiegel founded a glassworks at Manheim, Pennsylvania, in 1768, planning to manufacture the highest-quality glass, flint glass with the society's official approval. One important advantage of flint-glass was its superior optical qualities, which the society as America's leading scientific organization was in a position to certify. Stiegel was also among the earliest manufacturers of glass inkwells; previously inkwells had been ceramic and usually imported from England. Unfortunately, the society's efforts were in vain—high labor costs and foreign competition forced Stiegel to close his glassworks in 1774.

The second American scientific society founded in the eighteenth century, the Virginia Society for the Promotion of Usefull Knowledge founded in 1773, was even more oriented to practical, technological improvements than was the American Philosophical Society. John Hobday, the inventor of a threshing machine, was awarded a gold medal shortly after the society's foundation. The irascible planter Landon Carter, a member of both societies, complained that Virginians were insufficiently interested in science, specifically in his own discoveries on the weavel fly. After his paper on the fly had appeared in the *Transactions of the American Philosophical Society,* Carter complained that "here I publish my discoveries on the Weavel fly, and it was hardly so much noticed, as to encourage but here and there a sensible gentleman to attempt to experience its good effects." He consoled himself by recalling that Thomas Bond, showing the ability to massage egos that made him so successful a scientific administrator, had told Carter that "so great is the veneration that Europe has for me, as to Pronounce me the greatest Natural Philosopher of this age, and from my writings they are convinced of my almost Universal Knowledge" (Carter, *The Diary of Colonel Landon Carter of Sabine Hall,* 880). The Virginia Society was quickly swept away in the turmoil of the American Revolution. The next major learned society in America was actually founded during the Revolution, the Boston Academy of Arts and Sciences. The founding of the academy in 1780 was a patriotic act, encouraged by New England Revolutionary leaders, including John Adams.

THE GROWTH OF "SCIENTIFIC RACISM"

The eighteenth century saw the growth of "scientific racism," the belief that racial inequalities were rooted in the biological nature of different human races. Racist scientists in the period also shifted much of their interest from the differences of European-descended, or "white" peoples, from Native Americans to the differences of whites and African-descended peoples, "blacks." This movement marked both European and American science, but people coming from European colonies where black slavery was the basis of the economy were particularly likely to invoke black inferiority to justify slavery, an institution coming under increasing attack in the late colonial period. Although defenders of racial slavery continued to make claims about its Biblical justification, they were also likely to refute abolitionists and assert the goodness and naturalness of slavery by invoking so-called scientific data about racial hierarchies. The Jamaican Edward Long's *The History of Jamaica* (1774) described blacks as a separate species similar to apes. The slaveowner Thomas Jefferson's *Notes on Virginia* linked blacks to apes by claiming that the alleged preference of blacks for white sexual partners was paralleled by the male "Oranootan's" (probably referring to the chimpanzee) alleged preference for black women over females of his own species. All of Jefferson's numerous claims about black inferiority were presented as based on empirical observation, not the analysis of Biblical or classical texts, and couched in the language of eighteenth-century science:

They have less hair on the face and body. They secrete less by the kidnies, and more by the glands of the skin, which gives them a very strong and disagreeable odor. This greater degree transpiration renders them more tolerant of heat, and less so of cold, than the whites. Perhaps too a difference of structure in the pulmonary apparatus, which a late ingenious experimentalist has discovered to be the principal regulator of animal heat, may have disabled them from extricating, in the act of inspiration, so much of that fluid from the outer air, or obliged them in expiration, to part with more of it. (Jefferson, *Writings*, 265)

Not all American scientists agreed with Jefferson. After visiting a school for black children in Philadelphia, Benjamin Franklin wrote to a friend: "Their Apprehension seems as quick, their memory as strong, and their Docility in every Respect equal to that of white Children. You will wonder perhaps that I should ever doubt it, and I will not undertake to justify all my Prejudices, nor to account for them" (Franklin, *Writings*, 800). Franklin later became one of the first American abolitionists. But Jefferson's racist position would become orthodoxy in the nineteenth-century American South, not to mention very influential in the North as well.

ENCOURAGING TECHNOLOGICAL DEVELOPMENT

The industrial growth of the British colonies in the eighteenth century was apparent to colonists and European observers alike. Iron underwent remarkable growth, as did textiles. As the economy became more diversified, regional specializations in manufacturing began to emerge. Germantown, Pennsylvania, was known for Germantown stockings, of which many thousands of pairs were made annually. Philadelphia ruled American buttonmaking. Lynn, Massachusetts, was a center of shoemaking.

Not all promotion of colonial technology was the work of colonists themselves. Some persons in the mother country shared an interest in introducing technological advances to America. The founding in 1754 of the Society of Arts, a London group devoted to improving technology and agriculture by offering prizes for innovations gave American technology a boost similar to that given American science by the founding of the Royal Society in the seventeenth century. American members of the Society of Arts included leading scientists like Franklin and Charleston's physician-botanist Alexander Garden. Franklin and other colonial American scientists shared with the Society of Arts a belief in the fundamentally utilitarian orientation of science, although Franklin eventually came to detest the society's prizes and competitions, believing they distorted the American economy for the benefit of Britain.

Many efforts at technological improvement were applied to agriculture, still the mainstay of the colonial economy. A Connecticut clergyman and physician, the Reverend Jared Eliot (1685–1763), had noticed how poorly cultivated some Connecticut lands were when visiting some of his patients and parishioners. Eliot sought to remedy this situation by introducing some of the improvements in agricultural technology associated with the English writer Jethro Tull (1674–1741) to America and showing how they could be adapted to different American conditions. Eliot's series of six essays, *Essays on Field-Husbandry in New England* (1749–1757) advocated the use of a drill-plough, a machine for evenly planting seeds along rows rather than scattering them by hand. Eliot's son-in-law Benjamin Gale (1715–1790), a member of the Society of Arts and the American Philosophical Society, won a medal from the Society of Arts for an improved drill-plough in 1770, then he got into a lawsuit with his co-inventor, wheelwright Benoni Hylliard, the following year. However, use of the drill-plough did not catch on until the early nineteenth century. Eliot also published a book on extracting iron from black sand for which he won a medal from the Society of Arts at a time when Britain wanted to increase colonial iron production.

BRITISH-AMERICAN TECHNOLOGY AND THE
MOTHER COUNTRY

The governments of imperial powers were in a difficult position in evaluating colonial manufactures. Naturally, the imperial governments wanted their colonies to be strong and prosperous, if possible economically self-supporting. However, the growth of colonial manufactures could also threaten industries in the home country itself, and home country businesspeople were in a far better position to lobby their governments than were their colonial rivals. Because Britain had by far the most economically developed American colonies, this was far more an issue for the British government than for those of Spain and France. British concern with American technological development varied in different economic sectors. The general pattern was for the British to encourage manufactures of materials that could then be finished in Britain or which Britain was unsuited to manufacture itself. Thus pig and bar iron were encouraged but not steel. Hoping to exploit America's abundance of wood, the British Parliament encouraged production of potash (potassium carbonate), an alkaline chemical made from wood ash with a variety of commercial uses. American settlers had been making potash for their own use since the earliest settlements; it was used in soapmaking, glassmaking, and the preparation of saltpeter for gunpowder. The British Parliament, facing a shortage, lifted the tariff against colonial potash in 1751, and this was followed by a boom in the first American chemical industry. By 1770 the colonies, whose easy access to wood made them ideal for potash making, were exporting 2,000 tons of potash to Britain, about two-thirds of British consumption.

Americans in the years immediately preceding the American Revolution took little notice of the technological advances made in Britain, then in the early stages of the industrial revolution. Nor did the British encourage the colonies to establish competitive industries. There were only three steam engines in the colonies, and these were of the older and less efficient Newcomen type rather than the improved designs of James Watt and other eighteenth-century innovators. Christopher Colles (1738–1816), an Irish immigrant, tried to promote steam engines and gave lecture courses at the American Philosophical Society in Philadelphia on hydraulics and pneumatics in 1772, but he had little success. (Colles went to New York in 1774, where he promoted a plan to pipe water into the city through hollow logs. The plan garnered some support but was cut short by the American Revolution.) Americans were interested in emulating the canal-building movement transforming the internal communications of Great Britain, but talk again greatly exceeded action. In addition to the Chesapeake-Delaware canal, there were plans to build a canal connecting Beaufort and the Neuse River in North Carolina and one connecting the James and York Rivers in Virginia. Despite these and several other canal plans, no substantial transport canals were built before the American Revolution.

TECHNOLOGY AND AMERICAN NATIONALISM

Development of American technology acquired a political edge in the period following the end of the Seven Years War in 1763, as Americans believed that domestic manufactures would lessen the colonies' economic subjugation to Great Britain. Patriotic activists hoped to foster American economic (but not necessarily political) independence and make profits at the same time by founding new industries. The New York Society of Arts, founded in 1763 by businessmen from the city's Patriot faction and modeled after the London Society of Arts, was less concerned with technological innovation in general than with the specific goal of fostering an independent linen industry in the city. As the divisions between the North American British colonies and their mother country widened, Americans began to consider what they might substitute for those products they imported from Britain or from the British Caribbean. Action to replace British imports took place on the household level as well as the industrial one. In New England, spinning parties sought to revive the tradition of New England homespun, and provide Americans with home textiles to replace British imports. Southern women also increased their production of homespun as a patriotic act, doing it in their own households, as there was no southern equivalent of the spinning parties. Landon Carter, Virginia tobacco planter and ardent patriot, experimented with the juice of cornstalks, hoping to find a substitute for the molasses colonists imported from the sugar islands of the Caribbean and distilled into rum. New industries, such as porcelain manufacture—the Philadelphia firm of Bonnin and Morris was the first American company to make porcelain, a very demanding product—sought to attract customers and investors by appealing to American patriotism.

TECHNOLOGY AND THE AMERICAN REVOLUTION

War has always been a spur to technological innovation, and the war of the American Revolution was no exception. A young Yale student, David Bushnell (1740–1826), invented and built a one-man submarine for use against the British. It was an effective submarine but an ineffective weapon. Less dramatic but more influential was the Rhode Island metalworker Jeremiah Wilkinson's development of a process for making nails out of cold iron rather than forging them. Other technical issues revealed the limitations of the colonies. One technological problem that was never completely solved during the war was that of gunpowder. Despite the efforts of some of America's sharpest minds, including the chemist and physician Benjamin Rush, the Continental army remained dependent on imported gunpowder. Another area in which colonial forces were desperately lacking was artillery. Throughout the war, the American army relied on captured British guns or guns donated by their French allies, and although a few foundries did make guns in America, they copied British designs. The Continental army also had to import technical military engineering knowledge from France. There was less shame in this, as France led Europe in the training of military engineers with its famous school at Mezieres. When the Continental Congress commissioned a Corps of Engineers in 1777, it was at first led by four French officers, and it remained dominated by foreigners throughout the war.

War posed many technical problems besides purely military ones. One of the urgent necessities for the Revolutionary government was to find a way to replace the salt that before the war the colonies had imported from Britain. The British were aware of this crisis and destroyed colonial saltworks when they could. The Continental Congress responded in 1776 by establishing a bounty on salt to encourage potential manufacturers. Some large saltworks were established near the sea, using windmills to pump seawater to evaporation pans. This new industry fulfilled much of wartime America's salt needs, but the salt it produced was too expensive to be the foundation of a viable postwar industry.

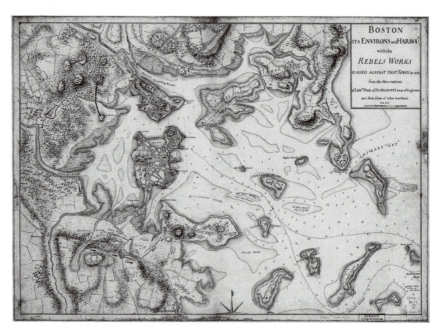

A map of the harbor and defenses of Boston, made by British engineers early in the Revolution. Courtesy of the Library of Congress, Geography and Map Division.

The momentum of American science was weakened by the concentration on the practical needs of the war. The American Philosophical Society did not meet from 1776 to 1779. But some science continued, and despite the bitterness of the conflict between Britain and her colonies, its internationalism was not destroyed. In 1779, Benjamin Franklin, the colonies' ambassador to France, followed the French example by directing captains of American ships not to molest the British scientific and geographical expedition led by Captain James Cook. Franklin lacked authority for this order, but it turned out to be unnecessary. Unknown to Franklin, or indeed anyone else in Europe and America, Cook had already been killed by Native Hawaiians after mapping much of the far northwestern seacoast of North America. In a more mundane example of the complexities

David Rittenhouse, shown here with a telescope, became President of the American Philosophical Society and a scientific leader in the independent United States. Courtesy of the Edgar Fahs Smith Collection, University of Pennsylvania.

of international science during the Revolution, Thomas Jefferson complained bitterly about the destruction of his meteorological equipment by British supporters, then ordered replacements—from England!

THE TRIUMPH OF THE ENLIGHTENMENT—THOMAS JEFFERSON CONSIDERS THE FLOOD

The European-descended male elite that led the Continental government, its armed forces, and its scientific establishment became the leaders of the new nation. They were also leaders of the American Enlightenment. In the new nation, science was advancing to the top of the intellectual world, in many ways replacing religion. Although the Boston minister Cotton Mather at the beginning of the eighteenth century had comfortably viewed the latest fossil discoveries as proving that the Bible's account of the flood was true, as the end of the century approached, the planter, statesman, and scientist of the new nation, Thomas Jefferson of Virginia, with even greater equanimity, dismissed the theory that fossil seashells found on the tops of mountains had been deposited there by the "universal deluge":

Near the eastern foot of the North mountain are immense bodies of *Schist*, containing impressions of shells in a variety of forms. have received petrified shells of very different kinds from the first sources of the Kentucky, which bear no resemblance to any I have ever seen on the tide-waters. It is said that shells are found in the Andes, in South-America, fifteen thousand feet above the level of the ocean. This is considered by many, both of the learned and unlearned, as a proof of an universal deluge. To the many considerations opposing this opinion, the following may be added. The atmosphere, and all its contents, whether of water, air, or other matters, gravitate to the earth; that is to say, they have weight. Experience tells us, that the weight of all these together never exceeds that of a column of mercury of 31 inches height, which is equal to one of rain-water of 35 feet high. If the whole contents of the atmosphere then were water, instead of what they are, it would cover the globe but 35 feet deep; but as these waters, as they fell, would run into the seas, the superficial measure of which is to that of the dry parts of the globe as two to one, the seas would be raised only 52 1/2 feet above their present level, and of course would overflow the lands to that height only. In Virginia this would be a very small proportion even of the champaign country, the banks of our tide-waters being frequently, if not generally, of a greater height. Deluges beyond this extent then, as for instance, to the North mountain or to Kentucky, seem out of the laws of nature. But within it they may have taken place to a greater or less degree, in proportion to the combination of natural causes which may be supposed to have produced them. History renders probable some instances of a partial deluge in the country lying round the Mediterranean sea. (Jefferson, *Writings,* 154)

Bibliography

PRIMARY SOURCES

Acrelius, Isaac. *A History of New Sweden*. Translated from the Swedish by William B. Reynolds. 1874. Facsimile reprint, Ann Arbor, Mich.: University Microfilms, 1966.

American Husbandry. Edited by Harry J. Carman. New York: Columbia University Press, 1939.

Bartram, William. *Travels and Other Writings*. New York: Library of America, 1996.

Brereton, John. *A Briefe and True Relation of the Discoverie of the North Part of Virginia*. 1602. Facsimile reprint published as *Discoverie of the North Part of Virginia*, Ann Arbor, Mich.: University Microfilms, 1966.

Burr, Esther Edwards. *The Journal of Esther Edwards Burr, 1754–1757*. Edited by Carol F. Karlsen and Laurie Crumpacker. New Haven and London: Yale University Press, 1984.

Burroughs, Stephen. *Memoirs of Stephen Burroughs*. With a preface by Robert Frost and a foreword by Philip F. Gura. Boston: Northeastern University Press, 1988.

Byrd, William. *William Byrd's Histories of the Dividing Line betwixt Virginia and North Carolina*. New York: Dover, 1967.

———. *William Byrd's Natural History of Virginia or the Newly Discovered Eden*. Edited and translated from a German version by Richmond Croom Beatty and William J. Mulloy. Richmond, Va.: Dietz Press, 1940.

Cabeza de Vaca, Álvar Núñez. *Chronicle of the Narvaez Expedition*. Translated by Fanny Bandelier, revised and augmented by Harold Augenbraum. New York: Penguin Books, 2002.

Carter, Landon. *The Diary of Colonel Landon Carter of Sabine Hall, 1752–1778*. Edited with an introduction by Jack P. Greene. Charlottesville: University Press of Virginia for the Virginia Historical Society, 1965.

Castaneda, Pedro de, et al. *The Journey of Coronado*. Translated and edited by George Parker Winship. 1904. Reprint, New York: Dover Publications, 1990.

Crèvecoeur, J. Hector St. John de. *Letters from an American Farmer and Sketches of Eighteenth-Century America*. Edited with an introduction by Albert E. Stone. New York: Penguin Books, 1981. Dankers, Jaspar, and Peter Sluyter. *Journal of a Voyage to New York and a Tour in Several of the American Colonies in 1679–80*. Translated and edited by Henry C. Murphy. Reprint, n.p.: Readex Microprint, 1966.

Franklin, Benjamin. *The Ingenious Dr. Franklin: Selected Scientific Letters of Benjamin Franklin*. Edited by Nathan G. Goodman. Philadelphia: University of Pennsylvania Press, 1931.

———. *Writings*. New York: Library of America, 1987.

Gist, Christopher. *The Journal of Christopher Gist, 1750–1751*. Edited by Lewis Summers. 1929. Electronic version by Donald Chesnut, 2000. http://www.users.mis.net/~chesnut/pages/gistjournal.pdf

Horry, Harriot Pinckney. *A Colonial Plantation Cookbook: The Receipt Book of Harriot Pinckney Horry, 1770*. Edited with an introduction by Richard J. Hooker. Columbia: University of South Carolina Press, 1984.

Jefferson, Thomas. *Writings*. New York: Library of America, 1984.

Kalm, Peter. *Peter Kalm's Travels in North America: The English Version of 1770*. Revised from the original Swedish and edited by Adolph B. Benson. New York: Dover Publications, 1966.

Lawson, John. *A New Voyage to Carolina*. Edited with an introduction and notes by Hugh Talmage Lefler. Chapel Hill: University of North Carolina Press, 1967.

Martha Washington's Booke of Cookery and Booke of Sweetmeats: being a Family Manuscript, Curiously Copied by an Unknown Hand Sometime in the Seventeenth Century, which was in her Keeping from 1749, the time of her Marriage to Daniel Custis, to 1799, at which time she gave it to Eleanor Parke Custis, her granddaughter, on the occasion of her Marriage to Lawrence Lewis. Transcribed by Karen Hess, with historical notes and copious annotations. New York: Columbia University Press, 1995.

Martin, Joseph Plumb. *Private Yankee Doodle: Being a Narrative of Some of the Adventures, Dangers and Sufferings of a Revolutionary Soldier*. Originally published as *A Narrative of Some of the Adventures, Dangers and Sufferings of a Revolutionary Soldier, Interspersed with Anecdotes of Incidents that Occurred Within His Own Observation*. 1830. Reprint, edited by George F. Scheer. Eastern Acorn Press, 1991.

Mather, Cotton. *Magnalia Christi Americana, Books I and II*. Edited by Kenneth B. Murdock with the assistance of Elizabeth W. Miller. Cambridge and London: Belknap Press of Harvard University Press, 1977.

———. *The Wonders of the Invisible World*. London: John Russell Smith, 1862.

Petit, Mathurin le. "Letter from Father le Petit, missionary, to Father d'Avaugour, Procurator of the Missions in North America." In *The Jesuit Relations and Allied Documents: Travels and Explorations of the Jesuit Missionaries in*

New France 1610–1791, vol. 68, edited by Reuben Gold Thwaites, 120–223. New York: Pageant Book Company, 1959.

Philosophical Transactions of the Royal Society of London.

Pinckney, Eliza Lucas. *The Letterbook of Eliza Lucas Pinckney.* Edited, with a new introduction by Elisa Pinckney, with the editorial assistance of Marvin R. Zahniser. Columbia: University of South Carolina Press, 1997.

Sewall, Samuel. *Diary of Samuel Sewall 1674–1729.* Collections of the Massachusetts Historical Society, 5th ser., vol. 5. Boston: Massachusetts Historical Society, 1878.

Simmons, Amelia. *American Cookery: or, the Art of Dressing Viands, Fish, Poultry and Vegetables, And the Best Modes of Making Puff-Pastes, Pies, Tarts, Puddings, Custards, and Preserves, and All Kinds of Cakes from the Imperial Plumb to Plain Cake. Adapted to this Country, and all Grades of Life.* 1794. 2d ed. Facsimile reprint, with an introduction by Karen Hess, Bedford, Mass.: Applewood Books, 1996.

Steuben, Frederick Wilhelm, Baron von. *Baron von Steuben's Revolutionary War Drill Manual: A Facsimile Reprint of the 1794 Edition.* New York: Dover Publications, 1985.

Taylor, Edward. *The Poems of Edward Taylor.* Edited by Donald E. Stanford. New Haven and London: Yale University Press, 1960.

Winthrop, John. *A Short Story of the Rise, Raigne and Ruine of the Antinomians, Familists, and Libertines that Infected the Churches of New-England.* London, 1645.

SECONDARY SOURCES

Allan, D.G.C., and John L. Abbot, eds. *The Virtuoso Tribe of Arts and Sciences: Studies in the Eighteenth Century Work and Membership of the London Society of Arts.* Athens and London: University of Georgia Press, 1992.

Anderson, Fred. *Crucible of War: The Seven Years' War and the Fate of Empire in British North America, 1754–1766.* New York: Vintage Books, 2001.

Axtell, James. *After Columbus: Essays in the Ethnohistory of Colonial North America.* New York and Oxford: Oxford University Press, 1988.

Beall, Otho T., Jr. "Cotton Mather's Early 'Curiosa Americana' and the Boston Philosophical Society of 1683." *William and Mary Quarterly*, 3d ser., no. 18 (1961): 360–72.

Bedini, Silvio. *Early American Scientific Instruments and Their Makers.* Rancho Cordova, Calif.: Landmark Enterprises, 1986.

———. *Jefferson and Science.* [Charlottesville, Va.]: Monticello Foundation, 2002.

———. *Thinkers and Tinkers: Early American Men of Science.* New York: Charles Scribner's Sons, 1975.

———. *With Compass and Chain: Early American Surveyors and Their Instruments.* Frederick, Md.: Professional Surveyors Publishing Company, 2001.

Bell, Whitfield J. *Patriot-Improvers: Biographical Sketches of Members of the American Philosophical Society.* 2 vols. Philadelphia: American Philosophical Society, 1997–1999.

Bidwell, Percy W., and John I. Falconer. *History of Agriculture in the Northern United States 1620–1860.* Washington, D.C.: Carneige Institution, 1925. Reprint, Clifton, N.J.: Augustus M. Kelley, 1973.

Bookbinding in America, 1680–1910. From the Collection of Frederick E. Maser. Bryn Mawr, Pa.: Bryn Mawr College Library, 1983.

Bridenbaugh, Carl. *Cities in Revolt: Urban Life in America, 1743–1776*. New York: Knopf, 1955.

———. *Cities in the Wilderness: The First Century of Urban Life in America, 1625–1742*. 2d ed. New York: Knopf, 1955.

———. *The Colonial Craftsman*. Reprint. Chicago: University of Chicago Press, 1961.

Burns, William E. *An Age of Wonders: Prodigies, Politics and Providence in England, 1657–1727*. Manchester, Engl. and New York: Manchester University Press, 2002.

Bushman, Richard L. *The Refinement of America: Persons, Houses, Cities*. New York: Knopf, 1992.

Butler, Jon. "Magic, Astrology, and the Early American Religious Heritage, 1600–1760." *American Historical Review* 84, no. 2 (1979): 317–46.

Campbell, Mary Baine. *Wonder and Science: Imagining Worlds in Early Modern Europe*. Ithaca, N.Y.: Cornell University Press, 1999.

Carlson, R. F., et al. *North American Apples: Varieties, Rootstocks, Outlook*. East Lansing, Mich.: Michigan State University Press, 1970.

Carney, Judith A. *Black Rice: The African Origins of Rice Cultivation in the Americas*. Cambridge: Harvard University Press, 2001.

Carson, Jane. *Colonial Virginia Cookery*. Williamsburg, Va.: Colonial Williamsburg, 1968.

Chet, Guy. *Conquering the American Wilderness: The Triumph of European Warfare in the Colonial Northeast*. Amherst and Boston: University of Massachusetts Press, 2003.

Cohen, David Steven. *The Dutch-American Farm*. New York and London: New York University Press, 1992.

Cohen, Patricia Cline. *A Calculating People: The Spread of Numeracy in Early America*. Chicago: University of Chicago Press, 1982.

Cumming, William P. *The Southeast in Early Maps: With an Annotated Check List of Printed and Manuscript Maps of Southeastern North America during the Colonial Period*. Chapel Hill: University of North Carolina Press, 1958.

Cutting, Charles L. *Fish Saving: A History of Fish Processing from Ancient to Modern Times*. London: Leonard Hill, 1955.

Daniels, Christine. "'WANTED: A Blacksmith Who Understands Plantation Work:' Artisans in Maryland 1700–1810." *William and Mary Quarterly*, 3d ser., no. 50 (1993): 743–67.

Davis, Richard Beale. *Intellectual Life in the Colonial South 1585–1763*. 3 vols. Knoxville: University of Tennessee Press, 1978.

Deetz, James. *In Small Things Forgotten: The Archaeology of Early American Life*. New York: Doubleday, 1977.

Dow, George Francis. *Whale Ships and Whaling: A Pictorial History of Whaling during Three Centuries with an Account of the Whale Fishery in Colonial New England*. 1925. Reprint, New York: Argosy Antiquarian, 1967.

Dunmire, William W. *Gardens of New Spain: How Mediterranean Plants and Foods Changed America*. Austin: University of Texas Press, 2004.

Earle, Alice Morse. *Home Life in Colonial Days*. 1898. Reprint, Stockbridge, Mass.: Berkshire Traveller Press, 1974.

Gill, Harold. *The Gunsmith in Colonial Virginia*. Williamsburg, Va.: Colonial Williamsburg Foundation, 1974.

Giraud, Marcel. *A History of French Louisiana Volume Two: Years of Transition, 1715–1717.* Translated by Brian Pearce. Baton Rouge and London: Louisiana State University Press, 1993.

Goldenberg, Joseph A. *Shipbuilding in Colonial America.* Charlottesville: University Press of Virginia for the Mariners Museum, Newport News, 1976.

Grant, Bruce. *American Forts: Yesterday and Today.* New York: Dutton, 1965.

Grasso, Christopher. "The Experimental Philosophy of Farming: Jared Eliot and the Cultivation of Connecticut." *William and Mary Quarterly*, 3d ser., no. 50 (1993): 502–28.

Hannaford, Ivan. *Race: The History of an Idea in the West.* Washington, D.C.: Woodrow Wilson Center Press, 1996.

Hardeman, Nicholas P. *Shucks, Shocks and Hominy Blocks: Corn as a Way of Life in Pioneer America.* Baton Rouge and London: Louisiana State University Press, 1981.

Hawke, David Freeman. *Everyday Life in Early America.* New York: Harper and Row, 1988.

Haynes, Williams. *American Chemical Industry: Background and Beginnings.* Toronto: D. Van Nostrand Company, 1954.

Heilbron, J. L., *Electricity in the 17th and 18th Centuries: A Study in Early Modern Physics.* Mineola, N.Y.: Dover Publications, 1999.

Hess, Karen. *The Carolina Rice Kitchen: The African Connection.* Columbia: University of South Carolina Press, 1992.

Hindle, Brooke. *The Pursuit of Science in Revolutionary America.* Chapel Hill: University of North Carolina Press for the Institute of Early American History and Culture, Williamsburg, Virginia, 1956.

———, ed. *America's Wooden Age: Aspects of Its Early Technology.* Tarrytown, N.Y.: Sleepy Hollow Restorations, 1975.

Hodges, Graham Russell. *New York City Cartmen, 1667–1850.* New York: New York University Press, 1986.

Holmes, Oliver Wendell, and Peter T. Rohrbach. *Stagecoach East: Stagecoach Days in the East from the Colonial Period to the Civil War.* Washington, D.C.: Smithsonian Institution Press, 1983.

Hood, Adrienne D. "The Material World of Cloth: Production and Use in Eighteenth-Century Rural Pennsylvania." *William and Mary Quarterly*, 3d ser., no. 53 (1996): 43–66.

Hood, Graham. *Bonnin and Morris of Philadelphia: The First American Porcelain Factory, 1770–1772.* Chapel Hill: University of North Carolina Press for the Institute of Early American History and Culture, Williamsburg, Virginia, 1972.

Hughes, Sarah S. *Surveyors and Statesmen: Land Measuring in Colonial Virginia.* Richmond: Virginia Surveyors Foundation, 1979.

Hume, Ivor Noel. *A Guide to the Artifacts of Colonial America.* 2d ed. Philadelphia: University of Pennsylvania Press, n.d.

Hunter, Dard. *Papermaking: The History and Technique of an Ancient Craft.* 2d ed., rev. and enl. New York: Alfred A. Knopf, 1947.

Kauffman, Henry J. *American Axes: A Survey of Their Development and Their Makers.* Brattleboro, Vt.: Stephen Green Press, 1972.

Kebabian, Paul B., and William C. Lipke, eds. *Tools and Technologies: America's Wooden Age.* Burlington: University of Vermont for the Robert Hull Fleming Museum, 1979.

Kennedy, Roger G. *Architecture: Men, Women and Money in America, 1600–1860.* New York: Random House, 1985.

Kurlansky, Mark. *Salt: A World History.* New York: Penguin Books, 2003.

Landsman, Ned C. *From Colonials to Provincials: American Thought and Culture 1680–1760.* New York: Twayne Publishers, 1997.

Lemay, J. A. Leo. *Ebenezer Kinnersley: Franklin's Friend.* Philadelphia: University of Pennsylvania Press, 1964.

Levin, David. "Giants in the Earth: Science and the Occult in Cotton Mather's Letters to the Royal Society." *William and Mary Quarterly,* 3d ser., no. 45 (1988): 751–70.

Little, Elizabeth A. *The Indian Contribution to Along-Shore Whaling at Nantucket.* Nantucket Algonquian Studies, no. 8. Nantucket, Mass.: Nantucket Historical Association, 1981.

MacMillan, Ken. "Sovereignty 'More Plainly Described': Early English Maps of North America." *Journal of British Studies* 42, no. 4 (2003): 413–47.

Malone, Patrick. *The Skulking Way of War: Technology and Tactics among the New England Indians.* Lanham, Md.: Madison Books, 1991.

Marcus, Alan I., and Howard P. Segal. *Technology in America: A Brief History.* 2d ed. Fort Worth, Tex.: Harcourt Brace, 1999.

Mastromarino, Mark A. "Teaching Old Dogs New Tricks: The English Mastiff and the Anglo-American Experience." *The Historian* 49, no. 1 (1986): 10–25.

McAfee, Michael J. *Artillery of the American Revolution 1775–1783.* Washington, D.C.: American Defense Preparedness Association, 1974.

McCusker, John J., and Russell R. Menard. *The Economy of British America, 1607–1789.* Chapel Hill: University of North Carolina Press for the Institute of Early American History and Culture, Williamsburg, Virginia, 1985.

McGaw, Judith A., ed. *Early American Technology: Making and Doing Things from the Colonial Era to 1850.* Chapel Hill: University of North Carolina Press for the Institute of Early American History and Culture, Williamsburg, Virginia, 1994.

McNamara, Kevin R. "The Feathered Scribe: The Discourses of American Ornithology before 1800." *William and Mary Quarterly,* 3d ed., no. 47 (1990): 210–34.

Merwick, Donna. *Possessing Albany, 1630–1710: The Dutch and English Experiences.* Cambridge: Cambridge University Press, 1990.

Middleton, Arthur Pierce. *Tobacco Coast: A Maritime History of Chesapeake Bay in the Colonial Era.* Newport News, Va.: Mariners Museum, 1953.

Moran, Lynn L. *Craft Industries at Fort Michilimackinac, 1715–1781.* Archeological Completion Report Series, no. 15. Mackinac Island, Mich.: Mackinac State Historic Parks, 1994.

Morgan, Philip D. *Slave Counterpoint: Black Culture in the Eighteenth-Century Chesapeake and Low Country.* Chapel Hill and London: University of North Carolina Press for the Omohundro Institute of Early American History and Culture, 1998.

Mulholland, James A. *A History of Metals in Colonial America.* University, Ala.: University of Alabama Press, 1981.

Nickell, Joe. *Pen, Ink and Evidence: A Study of Writing and Writing Materials for the Penman, Collector, and Document Detective.* Lexington: University Press of Kentucky, 1990.

Pagden, Anthony. *The Fall of Natural Man: The American Indian and the Origins of Comparative Ethnology.* Cambridge: Cambridge University Press, 1982.

Peskin, Lawrence. *Manufacturing Revolution: The Intellectual Origins of Early American Industry.* Baltimore: Johns Hopkins University Press, 2003.

Peterson, Harold L. *Arms and Armor in Colonial America 1526–1783.* Harrisburg, Pa.: The Stackpole Company, 1956.

Petroski, Henry. *The Pencil: A History of Design and Circumstance.* New York: Knopf, 1990.

Plante, Ellen M. *The American Kitchen 1700 to the Present: From Hearth to Highrise.* New York: Facts on File, 1995.

Pope, Peter E. *Fish into Wine: The Newfoundland Plantation in the Seventeenth Century.* Chapel Hill and London: University of North Carolina Press for the Omohundro Institute of Early American History and Culture, 2004.

Reps, John W. *Cities of the American West: A History of Frontier Urban Planning.* Princeton, N.J.: Princeton University Press, 1979.

Robbins, Michael W. *The Principio Company: Iron-Making in Colonial Maryland 1720–1781.* New York and London: Garland, 1986.

Rumsey, Peter Lockwood. *Acts of God and the People, 1620–1730.* Ann Arbor, Mich.: University Microfilms, 1986.

Ruttman, Darrett B. *Husbandmen of Plymouth: Farms and Villages in the Old Colony, 1620–1692.* Boston: Beacon Press for Plimoth Plantation, 1967.

Schodek, Daniel L. *Landmarks in American Civil Engineering.* Cambridge: MIT Press, 1987.

Schutte, Anne Jacobson. "Such Monstrous Births: A Neglected Aspect of the Antinomian Controversy." *Renaissance Quarterly* 38, no. 1 (1985): 85–106.

Shumway, George, Edward Durrell, and Howard C. Frey. *Conestoga Wagon 1750–1850: Freight Carrier for 100 Years of America's Westward Expansion.* York, Pa.: Early American Industries, Inc., and George Shumway, 1964.

Simmons, Marc. *Witchcraft in the Southwest: Spanish and Indian Supernaturalism on the Rio Grande.* Lincoln: University of Nebraska Press, 1974.

Slaughter, Thomas P. *The Natures of John and William Bartram.* New York: Alfred A. Knopf, 1996.

Sloane, Eric. *A Museum of Early American Tools.* New York: Ballantine Books, 1973.

———. *A Reverence for Wood.* New York: Ballantine Books, 1973.

Sokol, B. J. "The Problem of Assessing Thomas Harriot's *A briefe and true report* of his Discoveries in North America." *Annals of Science* 51, no. 1 (1994): 1–16.

Spruill, Julia Cherry. *Women's Life and Work in the Southern Colonies.* 1938. Reprint, with a new introduction by Anne Firor Scott, New York: Norton, 1972.

Stearns, Raymond Phineas. *Science in the British Colonies of America.* Urbana: University of Illinois Press, 1970.

Stowell, Marion Barber. *Early American Almanacs: The Colonial Weekday Bible.* New York: Burt Franklin, 1977.

Tunis, Edwin. *Colonial Craftsmen and the Beginnings of American Industry.* Baltimore and London: The Johns Hopkins University Press, 1999.

Ulrich, Laura Thatcher. *The Age of Homespun: Objects and Stories in the Creation of an American Myth.* New York: Alfred A. Knopf, 2001.

United States Department of the Interior. *Explorers and Settlers: Historic Places Commemorating the Early Exploration and Settlement of the United States.*

National Survey of Historic Sites and Buildings, no. 5. Washington, D.C.: National Park Service, 1968.

Vickers, Daniel. "Those Dammed Shad: Would the River Fisheries of New England Have Survived in the Absence of Industrialization?" *William and Mary Quarterly*, 3d ser., no. 54 (2004): 685–712.

Walsh, Lorena S. "Slave Life, Slave Society, and Tobacco Production in the Tidewater Chesapeake, 1620–1820." In *Cultivation and Culture: Labor and the Shaping of Slave Life in the Americas*, edited by Ira Berlin and Philip D. Morgan, 170–99. Charlottesville and London: University Press of Virginia, 1993.

Weber, David J. *The Spanish Frontier in North America*. New Haven and London: Yale University Press, 1992.

Weiss, Harry B., and Grace M. Weiss. *Early Tanning and Currying in New Jersey*. Trenton: New Jersey Agricultural Society, 1959.

Welsh, Peter C. *Tanning in the United States to 1850: A Brief History*. U.S. National Museum Bulletin, no. 94. Washington, D.C.: Museum of History and Technology, Smithsonian Institution, 1964.

Winship, Michael P. *Seers of God: Puritan Providentialism in the Restoration and Early Enlightenment*. Baltimore: Johns Hopkins University Press, 1996.

Wolfe, Stephanie Grauman. *As Various as Their Land: The Everyday Lives of Eighteenth-Century Americans*. New York: HarperCollins, 1993.

York, Neil Longley. *Mechanical Metamorphosis: Technological Change in Revolutionary America*. Westport, Conn.: Greenwood Press, 1985.

USEFUL WEB SITES

American Memory: Map Collections 1500–2004 http://memory.loc.gov/ammem/gmdhtml/gmdhome.html This Library of Congress site contains many maps from the colonial era.

American Shores: Maps of the Middle Atlantic Region to 1850 http://www.nypl.org/research/midatlantic/intro_middle.html This New York Public Library site includes many maps from the colonial era.

Benjamin Franklin—A Documentary History. http://www.english.udel.edu/lemay/franklin/ J. A. Leo Lemay's site, hosted by the University of Delaware, includes a detailed chronology of Franklin's life with many references to original documents.

Classics of American Colonial History: http://www.dinsdoc.com/colonial-1.htm Dinsmore Documentation maintains a growing site that puts many older, hard-to-find works of colonial history now in the public domain on the Web.

Colonial Williamsburg http://www.history.org/ This site contains discussion of individual trades practiced in eighteenth-century Williamsburg.

Columbus and the Age of Discovery http://muweb.millersville.edu/~columbus/ This is Millersville University's site on Columbus and the early days of European discovery, conquest, and settlement in the Americas.

Cultural Readings: Colonization and Print in the Americas http://www.library.upenn.edu/exhibits/rbm/kislak/index/cultural.html This site, maintained by the University of Pennsylvania, is a catalog of an exhibition on print in the early colonization of North and South America.

A Digital Archive of American Architecture. http://www.bc.edu/bc_org/avp/cas/fnart/fa267/contents.html The Boston College Department of Fine Arts maintains this site, which includes coverage of the seventeenth and eighteenth centuries.

Dutch Barn Preservation Society http://www.threerivershms.com/dbps.htm The Web page of a society devoted to studying Dutch-American barns in New York and New Jersey, many dating to the colonial era.

Flowerdew Hundred http://www.flowerdew.org/ The University of Virginia maintains this archeological Web site, devoted to the area of one of the earliest Virginia land grants. It contains a searchable database of many images of artifacts from the colonial period.

George Washington's Mount Vernon Estate and Gardens http://www.mountvernon.org/ The Mount Vernon Ladies' Association maintains this site, which includes much archeological information on Washington's large, economically diverse plantation.

Hargrett Rare Map Collection http://www.libs.uga.edu/darchive/hargrett/maps/maps.html The University of Georgia maintains this site, with maps from the colonial and Revolutionary period focusing on Georgia and its region.

Jamestown Historic Briefs http://www.nps.gov/colo/Jthanout/JTBriefs.html This site, maintained by the National Park Service, includes brief descriptions of early industrial processes.

Maps of the Pimeria: Early Cartography of the Southwest http://dizzy.library.arizona.edu/branches/spc/set/pimeria/index8.html The University of Arizona Library has put up many of its early maps of the Arizona region in the Spanish colonial period.

Plymouth Archaeological Rediscovery Project http://plymoutharch.tripod.com/ This site is devoted to the archeology of Plymouth colony and the surrounding area.

The Thomas Jefferson Papers at the Library of Congress http://memory.loc.gov/ammem/mtjhtml/mtjhome.html This site contains many items of scientific or technological interest.

University of South Alabama Archeology http://www.southalabama.edu/archaeology/index.htm This site includes much material on archeological digs relevant to the colonial period, with a particular emphasis on the Mobile area and the French colonies in North America.

Virtual Jamestown http://www.virtualjamestown.org/ This site, maintained by the Virginia Center for Digital History, includes many elements relevant to science and technology in seventeenth-century Virginia, including maps and firsthand accounts of the first permanent English settlement in the New World. It also includes an excellent database of more online resources.

Virtual Museum of New France http://www.civilization.ca/vmnf/vmnfe.asp This site, maintained by Canada's Museum of Civilization, includes images of many artifacts and maps from the French settlements in North America.

Voyageurs National Park—The Environment and the Fur Trade Experience—1730–1870. http://www.nps.gov/voya/futr/contents.htm This site, maintained by the National Park Service, discusses many aspects of the colonial fur trade, including trade goods and transportation, in the Rainy Lake region.

Index

Abati, 115–16
Acequias, 3
Acrelius, Israel, 10, 33; *History of New Sweden*, 33–34, quoted, 10, 13, 22–23, 34
Act of Union, 140
Adams, John, 157
Adobe, 66
Albany, New York, 74, 110, 115
Alchemy, 128–29
Almanacs, 90, 129–30
Ambergris, 50
American Beech, 20
American Husbandry, quoted, 2–3, 24
American Philosophical Society, 82, 91, 139, 142, 153, 155–57, 160; during American Revolution, 163
American Revoluton, 161–64
American Society for Promoting and Propagating Useful Knowledge, 155
Amherst, Jeffrey, 108, 119
Ammuntion, 112–13
Andros, Edmund, 85, 115
Apple ale, 23
Apple wood, 21

Apples, 22; Newtown Pippins, 22
Aristotelian philosophy, 126–27
Arizona, 5, 23
Artillery, 113
Association of Spermaceti Candlers, 49–50
Astrology, 127–28
Axes, 18–19
Azteks, 136

Bacon, 53
Bacon, Francis, 133
Bacon's Rebellion, 116
Baleen, 49
Baltimore, 85
Barley, 1, 8
Barrels, 39
Bartram, John, 141, 155
Bartram, William, quoted, 25, 46, 140
Barwick, Thomas, 43
Bating, 30
Bay Path, 83
Bayberry bush, 75
Bear fat, 53, 55
Beaver, 31–32
Beekeeping, 57

Berkeley, William, 69, 116
Berlin, Connecticut, 37
Bermuda Company, 101
Bern, Switzerland, 134
Bethlehem, Pennsylvania, 76
Bibliotheque Raisone, 150
Big Bone Lick, 150–51
Birch bark, 21, 79–80
Black Oak, 20, 30
Blacksmiths, 34–35
Blast furnace, 32–33
Bloomery, 32
Blunderbuss, 112
Boehner, John, 76
Bond, Thomas, 156, 157
Bonnin and Morris, 161
Bookbinding, 91–92
Bose, Georg Mathias, 150
Boston, 43–44, 70, 76, 77, 84, 102; fuel
    crisis, 73; stagecoach lines, 85–86;
    wharf, 146
Boston Academy of Arts and Sciences,
    157
Boyle, Robert, 122, 139
Bradford, William, 91
Brahm, William Gerard de, 103;
    *Map of South Carolina and a Part of
    Georgia*, 103
Braintree, Massachusetts, 28, 128
Brass, 36
Brattle, Thomas, 130, 135
Brereton, John, 17; *A Briefe and True
    Relation of the Discoverie of the North
    Part of Virginia*, quoted, 17–18
Brick, 66, 69–70
Bronze, 36
"Brown Bess," 111
Buckwheat, 8
Buell, Abel, 90, 94
Burlington, New Jersey, 28
Burr, Esther Edwards, 148; *Journal*,
    quoted, 149–50
Burroughs, Stephen, quoted, 128
Bushnell, David, 161
Byrd, William, 16, 101, 139; *Histories
    of the Dividing Line*, quoted, 101; on
    the ignorance of North Carolinians,
    130; *Natural History of Virginia*, 134;
    quoted, 23, 141

Cabeza de Vaca, Alvaro, quoted,
    42, 108; *Chronicle of the Narvaez
    Expedition*, quoted, 42
Cabot, John, 45
Calabashes, 39
California, 66
Cambridge, Massachusetts, 90, 130
Canals, 82–83
Cannon. *See* Artillery
Canoe, 20, 79–81
Cape Charles, 28
Cape Cod, 45
Carpenters Company of Philadelphia,
    71; Library, 71
Carter, Landon, 5, 13, 131, 139, 152,
    157; *Diary* quoted, 5, 13, 73, 131,
    142, 152, 157
Cartridges, 112–13
Casa de Contratación, 41, 97
Castaneda, Pedro de, 113
Castle William, 115
Cedar, 20, 39, 68
Ceramics, 39
Chain, surveyor's, 101
Chaise, 85
Charcoal, 21
Charleston, 35, 70, 82, 117, 139
Charlestown, Massachusetts, 43
Cherrywood, 21
Chester County, Pennsylvania, 60
Chichimecs, 125
Chiles, 10
Christensen, Hans Christopher,
    76
Cider, 22–23, 55, 59
Circle of Philadelphes, 153
Clap, Thomas, 153
Clapboards, 67
Claverack, New York, 126
Clayton, John (1694–1773), 147
Clayton, John, the Reverend, 138
Clock jack, 57
Coaches, 85–86
Cobblers, 31
Cod, 45, 46–47
Cod-liver oil, 46
Colbeck Castle, 115
Colden, Cadwallader, 101, 147; *An
    Explication of the First Causes of*

Action in Matter; and the Cause of Gravitation, 147

College of Philadelphia, 139

College of William and Mary, 101, 139

Colles, Christopher, 87, 160; *Survey of the Roads of the United States of America*, 87

Collinson, Peter, 141, 150, 151

Colombo, Cristoforo,"Christopher Columbus," 125

Colve, Anthony, 85

Compass, 41, 101–2

Conestoga wagon, 86

Conestoga Wagon Inn, 86

Connecticut, 43

Continental Congress, 162

Cook, James, 163

Coopers, 39

Copper, 36, 68, 125

Coppersmiths, 36

Cordwainers, 31

Corn, 1, 2, 6–8, 55–56

Cornbread, 8

Corncobs, 7

Corn whiskey, 8

Corps of Engineers, 162

Cotton, 15

Coxe, Daniel, 28

Cradle scythe, 9

Croghan, George, 151

Crossbows, 108

Cucumbers, 54

Currying, 30

Cuttyhunk Island. *See* Elizabeth's Island

Cypress, 20

Dagyr, John Adam, 31

Danckaerts, Jaspar, 67; *Journal of a Voyage to New York*, quoted, 67, 83

Deerskins, 30

Delisle, Guillame, 99; *Map of Louisiana*, 99

Desaguliers, John, 154

Dixon, Jeremiah, 104

Doolittle, Isaac, 90

Drogue, 48

Dudley, Paul, 21

Durham boat, 81–82

Dyeing. *See* Indigo

Dyer, Mary, 124

East Anglia, 66

Eliot, Jared, 159; *Essays upon Field Husbandry in New England*, 159

Eliot, John, 91

Elizabeth's Island, 17

English mastiffs, 108

"English wigwams," 66

Engraving, 94

Evans, Lewis, 103; *General Map of the Middle British Colonies in America*, 103

Felt, 31–32

Fences, 104–5

Fir, 68

Flail, 9

Flax, 15–16, 60

Flemish scythe. *See* Sith

Flintlocks, 110

Florida, 46, 66, 103

"Flour-bag Fortress," 114

Footwear, 31

Fort Albany, 115

Fort de Chartres, 119

Fort Duquesne, 86

Fort LeBouef, 81

Fort New Amsterdam, 116

Fort St. Frederic, 119

Fort San Marcos, 117–18

Fortresses, 114–19

Franklin, Benjamin, 22, 145, 147, 151–53, 163; and American Philosophical Society, 155; on canals, 82–83; on corn, quoted, 56; and electricity, 150; Freemason, 154; on Kinnersley, quoted, 148; on lightning rods, quoted, 152; Pennsylvania Fire Place, 73–74; *Pennsylvania Gazette*, 131; on printing, quoted, 89; *Proposals Relating to the Education of Youth in Pennsylvania*, quoted, 130; on race, quoted, 158; on roofing materials, 68; and Society of Arts, 159; on the virtue of spinning, quoted, 62; wins Copley medal, on wood supply, quoted, 73

Franklin, Josiah, 59
Freemasonry, 154
French and Indian War. *See* Seven
    Years War
Froe, 19, 39
Fry, Joshua, 103
Fur, 31–32

Gale, Benjamin, 159
Garden, Alexander, 139, 147, 159
Gardenia, 147
Gentleman's Magazine, 150
George III, 153
Georgia, 11
Georgian Architecture, 70–72
Germantown, Pennsylvania, 90, 91,
    93, 159
Gist, Christopher, 150–51; *Journal,*
    quoted, 151
Glass and Glassmaking, 28
Gluten, 9
Godfrey, Thomas, 155
Gosnold, Bartholomew, 17, 45
Gourds, 39
Grapes, 23–24
Great Dismal Swamp, 16, 101
Greenwood, Isaac, 139, 153;
    Arithmetick Vulgar and Decimal, 139
Gristmill, 9, 38
Grits, 8
Guadeloupe, 154
Gunpowder, 109
Guns, 108–12
Gypsum, 2

Halifax, Nova Scotia, 118
Haller, Albrecht von, 150
Halley, Edmond, 156
Harriot, Thomas, 93, 134; *A Brief and*
    True Report of the New Found land of
    Virgina, 98, 134
Harrison, Peter, 72
Harvard College, 122, 129, 135
Hat Act, 32
Hatmaking, 31–32
Hausen, Christian August, 150
Hellebore, 7
Hemlock, 30

Hemp, 16
Herman, Augustine, 99; *Virginia*
    and Maryland as it is Planted and
    Inhabited this Present Year 1670, 99
Hernandez, Francisco, 134
Hetchel, 15
Hickory, 20
Hispaniola, 79
Hobday, John, 9, 157
Hobnails, 31
Hoe-cake, 57
"Hog and Hominy," 8
Hollis Chair of Mathematics and
    Natural Philosophy, 139, 153
Hollis, Thomas, 139
Holme, Thomas, 103
Hominy, 8
Hominy Block, 8
Honey, 57–58
Hornos, 57
Horry, Harriot Pinckney, 15, 53, 54;
    Colonial Plantation Cookbook, quoted,
    15, 53–54, 54–55
Housewifery manuals, 51–52
Hull, John, 35
Hussey, Christopher, 48
Hutchinson, Anne, 124
Hylliard, Benoni, 159

Incas, 136
Indigo, 1, 14–15
Ink, 92–93
Ireland, 60
Iron, 5, 18, 27, 28, 32–34
Iron Act, 34
Iroquois, 81

Jamestown, 12, 69
Jefferson, Peter, 103
Jefferson, Thomas, 101, 139, 148,
    164; as early "scientific racist,"
    158–59; and Monticello, 72; *Notes on*
    Virginia, 147–48, 158; quoted, 49, 87,
    133, 143, 158, 164
Jeffery, John, 43
Jerky, 54

Kalendarium Pensilvaniense, 130

Kalm, Peter, 70, 116–17; *Peter Kalm's Travels in North America*, quoted 23, 47, 74, 75, 80–81
Kennebec, 43
Killingworth, Connecticut, 90
King George's War. *See* War of the Austrian Succession
King Philip's War, 124
Kinnersley, Ebenezer, 148, 152
Kino, Eusebio Francisco, 102
Knight, Sarah Kemble, 81

Lallemant, Jerome, 29
Lancaster, Pennsylvania, 86
Las Casas, Bartolomeo de, 136
Laws of the Indies, 102
Lawson, John, *New Voyage to Carolina*, quoted, 2, 81
Lead, 90, 93, 112
Leather, 29–30
Leiden Jar, 148
Library Company of Philadelphia, 150, 153
Lightning Rods, 151–53
Linen, 161. *See also* Flax
Linnaeus, Carl, 147
Litchfield, Connecticut, 153
Locke, John, 133
Locust wood, 20
Log cabins, 67
London, 141
Long, Edward, 158
Louisbourg, 118, 119
Louisiana, 23, 29, 138
Love, John, *Geodaesia*, 101
Lucas, Eliza (Pinckney), 1, 14, 139, 142–43, 155
Lye, 55, 59–60
Lynn, Massachusetts, 28, 31, 128, 159

Mahogany, 21
Malcolm, Noel, 70
Manheim, Pennsylvania, 157
Map of the Inhabited Parts of Virginia, 103
Maple, 20
Maple Sugar/Syrup, 21–22, 57–58

Martha Washington's Booke of Cookery, quoted, 54
Martin, Joseph Plumb, 115, quoted, 56, 116
Maryland, 99
Maskelyne, Nevil, 104
Mason, Charles, 104
Mason-Dixon Line, 103–4
Massachusetts, 19, 27, 35
Matchlocks, 109–10
Mather, Cotton, 130, 139, 164; *Christian Philosopher*, 139; on fossil bones, quoted, 126; *Magnalia Christi Americana*, quoted, on John Winthrop Jr., 123–24, on the Royal Society, 137; *Voice from Heaven*, 142; *Wonders of the Invisible World*, 124–25, quoted, 125
Mather, Increase, 153; *Essay for the Recording of Illustrious Providences*, 124
Mathook, 9
Mauritius, 154
Mexico, 134
Mexico City, 90, 125, 154
Micmac Pipe, 14
Mills, 38. *See also* Gristmill; Sawmills
Minuit, Peter, 116
Mitchell, John, 99; *Map of the British and French Dominions in North America*, 99
Mobile, Alabama, 25
Molasses, 57
Moll, Herman, 99; *New Map of the North Parts of America Claimed by France*, 99
Moore, James, 117
Morro, El, 94
Mortar and Pestle, 11
Muskets. *See* Guns
Musschenbroek, Pieter van, 148

Nantucket, 48
Narragansetts, 117
Native Americans, 29, 38, 39, 48, 79, 104, 110, 136; and Hernandez expedition, 134; and writing, 93–94
Natural Theology, 121–24

Naval Stores, 44
Needlework, 62–63
New Amsterdam. *See* New York City
New Brunswick, New Jersey, 70
New England Company, 28, 43
New-Found Eden, 134
New Haven, Connecticut, 90
New Jersey, 20, 85, 154
New London, Connecticut, 43
New Mexico, 5, 23, 30, 66, 94, 110, 125
New Netherland, 19
New Orleans, 70
New York, 22, 29, 99, 102
New York City, 47, 69, 73, 77, 84, 117,
    160; stagecoach lines, 85–86
New York Society of Arts, 161
Newport, Rhode Island, 85, 146
Newton, Isaac, 133, 135, 143
Nicot, Jean, 12
"Niddy-Noddys," 61
Norman, John, 72
North Carolina, 44, 81, 101
Northwest Passage, 98
Norwood, Richard, 101

Oats, 8
Oglethorpe, James, 117
Onate, Juan de, 94
Onondaga, 29
Opossums, 140–41
Ortelius, Abraham, *Theater of the
    World*, 97
Ovens, 57
Oysters, 47

Painting, 95
Paper, 91
Parliament, English and British, 14,
    160
Parlor, 68
Pattison, Edward, 37
Peaches, 23, 54–55; Peach brandy, 55
Pearlash, 25
Pencils, 93
Penn, William, 43
Pennsylvania, 67, 85, 90, 139
Pens, 92
Petiver, James, 141
Pewter, 36

Philadelphia, 35, 65, 76, 77, 85, 102–3,
    154; brick construction in, 69; and
    Conestoga wagons, 86; as scientific
    center, 139, 153; as shipbuilding
    center, 43–44
Philadelphia Medical Society, 155
Philip II, King of Spain, 102, 134
Philosophical Transactions, 135, 137
Pig Iron, 33
Pine Tree Shillings, 35
Pine-knots, 20
Pit saw, 19
Pitch, 20, 24–25
Plows, 5, 8
Plymouth Colony, 43, 116
Pontiac, 114
Poplar, 20
Portsmouth, Massachusetts, 43, 86
Potash, 25, 39, 169
Potato, 10
Pounding Mills, 11
Printing press, 89–91

Quebec, 58
Queen's Fort, 117
Quern, 9

Race, 135–37, 158–59
Ratcliff, John, 91
Rattlesnakes, 140
Ray, John, 122; *Wisdom of God
    Manifested in the Works of Creation*,
    122
Red Oak, 20, 30, 39
Rensselaer, Jeremias van, 124
Reunion, 154
Revere, Paul, 35, 94
Rhoads, Samuel, 82
Rhode Island, 67
Ribera, Luis de, 125
Rice, 1, 10–12, 58; Carolina Gold, 12, 58
Rifle, 111
Rittenhouse, David, 156
Rittenhouse, William, 91
Roads, 83–85
Rockweed, 2
Rolfe, John, 13
Romans, Bernard, 103; *Concise Natural
    History of East and West Florida*, 103

Rowley, Massachusetts, 28
Royal Academy of Sciences, 138
Royal Botanical Garden (Mexico City), 154
Royal Botanical Garden (Paris), 138, 154
Royal Mining College, 154
Royal Navy, 20
Royal Society, 21, 24, 137–38; and lightning rods, 152
Rum, 57, 59
Rupert shot, 112
Rush, Benjamin, 161
Russia, 16, 24
Rye, 8

St. Augustine, 117
St. John de Crèvecouer, Hector, 49; *Letters from an American Farmer*, quoted, 49, 57–58
St. Pierre and Miquelon, 47
Salem, Massachusetts, 28, 43
Salisbury, Massachusetts, 43
Salt, 28–29, 53, 162
Saltbox house, 68
Saltworks, 28–29
Santa Fe, 125
Santo Domingo/Sainte Domingue, 153, 154
Sassafrass, 21
Saump Mill. *See* Hominy Block
Savannah, 117
Sawmills, 19–20, 38
Scotland, 140
Scots-Irish, 8
Seining, 45
Sepulveda, Juan Gines de, 136
Sergeant, Peter, 70
Seven Years War, 107, 119
Seville, 97
Sewall, Samuel, 44; *Diary*, quoted, 44, 124
Shay. *See* Chaise
Shipbuilding, 42–44
Shucking Peg, 7
Sickle, 9
Silk, 28
Silversmiths, 35
Simmons, Amelia, 52; *American Cookery*, 52, quoted 55

Simsbury, Connecticut, 36
Sith, 9
Sloane, Hans, 141
Smith, Eliza, 52; *Compleat Housewife*, 52
Smith, John, 98
Smith, Robert, 151
Smoke jack, 57
Smoking meat, 53
Snowshoes, 83
Snuff, 14
Soap and soapmaking, 59–60
Society of Arts (London), 159
Soldados de Cuero, 109
Sons of Liberty, 62
South Carolina, 5, 81, 139; African housing styles in, 69; rice culture, 10–12, 58
Spencer, Archibald, 150
Spermaceti, 49, 76
Spinning, 60–62
Spinning wheels, 61–62
Squanto, 5
Squash, 1
Starkey, George, 128, 135
Steel, 34
Steuben, Frederick William von, 110, quoted, 112–13
Stiegel, Henry William, 157
"stone-ender," 67–68
Sublimi Deus, 136
Sumac, 30
Surveying, 100–104
Swan, Abraham, 71; *British Architect*, 71
Sweden, 24
Sweet Potato, 10
Swingling, 15

Tallow, 59–60, 74
Tannin, 21, 30
Tanning and Tanneries, 29–30
Tar, 20, 24–25
Tawing, 30
Taylor, Edward, 61; quoted, 61, 121–22
Teredo Navalis, 82
Thatch, 68; palmetto-leaf thatch, 68
Thompson, Benjamin, 73
Ticonderoga, 115

Tin, 36
Tinkling cones, 36
Tinsmithing, 37
Tobacco, 1, 12–14, 82; Spanish
    tobacco, 12
Tortillas, 8, 55
Touro Synagogue, 72
Transits of Venus, 156
Tree-nails, 20, 66
Turpentine, 20, 24
Turtles, 46

Valladolid, 136
Vargas, Diego de, 94
Vermont, 22
Virgil, 1
Virginia, 12, 27, 29, 65, 69, 101, 116;
    ferry law, 85
Virginia Company, 18, 27–28, 43

Waldsemuller, Martin, *Cosmographica*,
    97
War of the Austrian Succession, 118
War of the League of Augsburg, 43
War of the Spanish Succession, 43
Washington, George, 69, 76, 81, 91,
    101, 119; and Mount Vernon, 72;
    shifts from tobacco to wheat farm-
    ing, 10
Water supplies, 76
Watt, William, 112
Weaving, 60–61
Whale oil, 76
Whaling, 47–50

Wheat, 1, 8–10, 82
Wheelocks, 109–10
Wheelwrights, 35
White, John, 98
White Ash, 20
White Oak, 20, 30, 39
White Pine, 20, 68
Whitesmiths, 35
Whitpaine, Richard, 70
Wilkinson, Jeremiah, 161
Williamsburg, Virginia, 70
Willow, 20
Wilmington, Delaware, 116
Wilson, Benjamin, 152
Winemaking, 23
Winkler, Johann Heinrich, 150
Winnowing Fans, 11
Winthrop, John, 43, 124, 153; *A Short
    History of the Rise, Raigne and Ruine
    of the Antinomians, Familists and
    Libertines that Infected the Churches of
    New-England*, 124
Winthrop, John (the astronomer),
    152
Winthrop, John Jr., 24, 28, 128, 137;
    Cotton Mather on, 123–24
Wool, 60–61

Yale College, 153
Yorktown, 115
Yucatan, 29

Zigzag fence. *See* Fences
Zinc, 36

About the Author

WILLIAM E. BURNS has taught at the University of Pennsylvania, the University of Maryland, and Mary Washington College. His earlier books include *An Age of Wonders: Prodigies in Later Stuart Politics and Culture* (2002) and *Witch Hunts in Europe and America: An Encyclopedia* (Greenwood, 2003).

The Greenwood Press "Science and Technology in Everyday Life" Series

Science and Technology in Nineteenth-Century America
Todd Timmons